Macmillan/McGraw-Hill Edition

McGRAW-HILL READING

McGraw-Hill
School Division
New York   Farmington

Contributors

The Princeton Review, Time Magazine

The Princeton Review is not
affiliated with Princeton
University or ETS.

McGraw-Hill School Division

A Division of The **McGraw·Hill** Companies

McGraw-Hill School Division
Two Penn Plaza
New York, New York 10121

Printed in the United States of America

ISBN 0-02-184746-0/K, U.6

2 3 4 5 6 7 8 9   043/073   04 03 02 01 00 99

McGraw-Hill
School Division

New York   Farmington

McGraw-Hill Reading
Authors
Make the Difference...

Dr. James Flood

Ms. Angela Shelf Medearis

Dr. Jan E. Hasbrouck

Dr. Scott Paris

Dr. James V. Hoffman

Dr. Steven Stahl

Dr. Diane Lapp

Dr. Josefina Villamil Tinajero

Dr. Karen D. Wood

Contributing
Authors

Dr. Barbara Coulter

Ms. Frankie Dungan

Dr. Joseph B. Rubin

Dr. Carl B. Smith

Dr. Shirley Wright

iv

Part 1
START TOGETHER

Focus on Reading and Skills

All students start with the SAME:
- Read Aloud
- Pretaught Skills
  Phonics
  Comprehension
- Build Background
- Selection Vocabulary

...Never hold a child back. Never leave a child behind.

Part 2
MEET INDIVIDUAL NEEDS

Read the Literature

Core Selection

Pupil Selection

Leveled Books

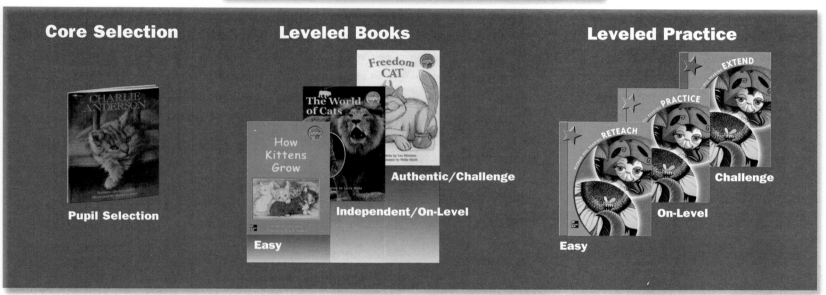

Authentic/Challenge

Independent/On-Level

Easy

Leveled Practice

Challenge

On-Level

Easy

Examples Taken From Grade 2

Part 3
FINISH TOGETHER

Build Skills

All students finish with the SAME:
- Phonics
- Comprehension
- Vocabulary
- Study Skills
- Assessment

McGraw-Hill Reading
Applying the Research

Phonological Awareness

Phonological awareness is the ability to hear the sounds in spoken language. It includes the ability to separate spoken words into discrete sounds as well as the ability to blend sounds together to make words. A child with good phonological awareness can identify rhyming words, hear the separate syllables in a word, separate the first sound in a word (onset) from the rest of the word (rime), and blend sounds together to make words.

Recent research findings have strongly concluded that children with good phonological awareness skills are more likely to learn to read well. These skills can be improved through systematic, explicit instruction involving auditory practice. McGraw-Hill Reading develops these key skills by providing an explicit Phonological Awareness lesson in every selection at grades K-2. Motivating activities such as blending, segmenting, and rhyming help to develop children's awareness of the sounds in our language.

Guided Instruction/ Guided Reading

Research on reading shows that guided instruction enables students to develop as independent, strategic readers. The *reciprocal-teaching model* of Anne-Marie Palincsar encourages teachers to model strategic-thinking, questioning, clarifying, and problem-solving strategies for students as students read together with the teacher. In McGraw-Hill Reading, guided instruction for all Pupil Edition selections incorporates the Palincsar model by providing interactive questioning prompts. The *guided-reading model* of Gay Su Pinnell is also incorporated into the McGraw-Hill Reading program. Through the guided-reading lessons provided for the leveled books offered with the program, teachers can work with small groups of students of different ability levels, closely observing them as they read and providing support specific to their needs.

By adapting instruction to include successful models of teaching and the appropriate materials to deliver instruction, McGraw-Hill Reading enables teachers to offer the appropriate type of instruction for all students in the classroom.

Phonics

Our language system uses an alphabetic code to communicate meaning from writing. Phonics involves learning the phonemes or sounds that letters make and the symbols or letters that represent those sounds. Children learn to blend the sounds of letters to decode unknown or unfamiliar words. The goal of good phonics instruction is to enable students to read words accurately and automatically.

Research has clearly identified the critical role of phonics in the ability of readers to read fluently and with good understanding, as well as to write and spell. Effective phonics instruction requires carefully sequenced lessons that teach the sounds of letters and how to use these sounds to read words. The McGraw-Hill program provides daily explicit and systematic phonics instruction to teach the letter sounds and blending. There are three explicit Phonics and Decoding lessons for every selection. Daily Phonics Routines are provided for quick reinforcement, in addition to activities in the Phonics Workbook and technology components. This combination of direct skills instruction and applied practice leads to reading success.

Curriculum Connections

As in the child's real-world environment, boundaries between disciplines must be dissolved. Recent research emphasizes the need to make connections between and across subject areas. McGraw-Hill Reading is committed to this approach. Each reading selection offers activities that tie in with social studies, language arts, geography, science, mathematics, art, music, health, and physical education. The program threads numerous research and inquiry activities that encourage the child to use the library and the Internet to seek out information. Reading and language skills are applied to a variety of genres, balancing fiction and nonfiction.

Integrated Language Arts

Success in developing communication skills is greatly enhanced by integrating the language arts in connected and purposeful ways. This allows students to understand the need for proper writing, grammar, and spelling. McGraw-Hill Reading sets the stage for meaningful learning. Each week a full writing-process lesson is provided. This lesson is supported by a 5-day spelling plan, emphasizing spelling patterns and spelling rules, and a 5-day grammar plan, focusing on proper grammar, mechanics, and usage.

Meeting Individual Needs

Every classroom is a microcosm of a world composed of diverse individuals with unique needs and abilities. Research points out that such needs must be addressed with frequent intensive opportunities to learn with engaging materials. McGraw-Hill Reading makes reading a successful experience for every child by providing a rich collection of leveled books for easy, independent, and challenging reading. Leveled practice is provided in Reteach, Practice, and Extend skills books. To address various learning styles and language needs, the program offers alternative teaching strategies, prevention/intervention techniques, language support activities, and ESL teaching suggestions.

Assessment

Frequent assessment in the classroom makes it easier for teachers to identify problems and to find remedies for them. McGraw-Hill Reading makes assessment an important component of instruction. Formal and informal opportunities are a part of each lesson. Minilessons, prevention/intervention strategies, and informal checklists, as well as student self-assessments, provide many informal assessment opportunities. Formal assessments, such as weekly selection tests and criterion-referenced unit tests, help to monitor students' knowledge of important skills and concepts. McGraw-Hill Reading also addresses how to adapt instruction based on student performance with resources such as the Alternate Teaching Strategies. Weekly lessons on test preparation, including test preparation practice books, help students to transfer skills to new contexts and to become better test takers.

McGraw-Hill School
TECHNOLOGY

*inter*NET **CONNECTION** For information on research that supports this program, visit **www.mhschool.com/reading**

McGraw-Hill Reading

Theme Chart

MULTI-AGE Classroom

Using the same global themes at each grade level facilitates the use of materials in multi-age classrooms.

GRADE LEVEL	**Experience** Experiences can tell us about ourselves and our world.	**Connections** Making connections develops new understandings.
Kindergarten	**My World** We learn a lot from all the things we see and do at home and in school.	**All Kinds of Friends** When we work and play together, we learn more about ourselves.
Subtheme 1	At Home	Working Together
Subtheme 2	School Days	Playing Together
1	**Day by Day** Each day brings new experiences.	**Together Is Better** We like to share ideas and experiences with others.
2	**What's New?** With each day, we learn something new.	**Just Between Us** Family and friends help us see the world in new ways.
3	**Great Adventures** Life is made up of big and small experiences.	**Nature Links** Nature can give us new ideas.
4	**Reflections** Stories let us share the experiences of others.	**Something in Common** Sharing ideas can lead to meaningful cooperation.
5	**Time of My Life** We sometimes find memorable experiences in unexpected places.	**Building Bridges** Knowing what we have in common helps us appreciate our differences.
6	**Pathways** Reflecting on life's experiences can lead to new understandings.	**A Common Thread** A look beneath the surface may uncover hidden connections.

Themes: Kindergarten – Grade 6

Six Units IN EVERY GRADE

Expression	Inquiry	Problem Solving	Making Decisions
There are many styles and forms for expressing ourselves.	By exploring and asking questions, we make discoveries.	Analyzing information can help us solve problems.	Using what we know helps us evaluate situations.
Time to Shine We can use our ideas and our imagination to do many wonderful things.	**I Wonder** We can make discoveries about the wonders of nature in our own backyard.	**Let's Work It Out** Working as part of a team can help me find a way to solve problems.	**Choices** We can make many good choices and decisions every day.
Great Ideas	**In My Backyard**	**Try and Try Again**	**Good Choices**
Let's Pretend	**Wonders of Nature**	**Teamwork**	**Let's Decide**
Stories to Tell Each one of us has a different story to tell.	**Let's Find Out!** Looking for answers is an adventure.	**Think About It!** It takes time to solve problems.	**Many Paths** Each decision opens the door to a new path.
Express Yourself We share our ideas in many ways.	**Look Around** There are surprises all around us.	**Figure It Out** We can solve problems by working together.	**Starting Now** Unexpected events can lead to new decisions.
Be Creative! We can all express ourselves in creative, wonderful ways.	**Tell Me More** Looking and listening closely will help us find out the facts.	**Think It Through** Solutions come in many shapes and sizes.	**Turning Points** We make new judgments based on our experiences.
Our Voices We can each use our talents to communicate ideas.	**Just Curious** We can find answers in surprising places.	**Make a Plan** Often we have to think carefully about a problem in order to solve it.	**Sorting It Out** We make decisions that can lead to new ideas and discoveries.
Imagine That The way we express our thoughts and feelings can take different forms.	**Investigate!** We never know where the search for answers might lead us.	**Bright Ideas** Some problems require unusual approaches.	**Crossroads** Decisions cause changes that can enrich our lives.
With Flying Colors Creative people help us see the world from different perspectives.	**Seek and Discover** To make new discoveries, we must observe and explore.	**Brainstorms** We can meet any challenge with determination and ingenuity.	**All Things Considered** Encountering new places and people can help us make decisions.

Choices

We can make many good choices and decisions every day.

"Tommy" a poem by *Gwendolyn Brooks*

Subtheme: Good Choices

SKILLS			
Phonics	**Comprehension**	**Vocabulary**	**Beginning Reading Concepts**
• **Introduce** Initial /h/h • **Review** Initial /h/h; /b/b; Blending with Short *a, e, i, o, u*	• **Introduce** Cause and Effect • **Review** Cause and Effect	• **Introduce** High-Frequency Words: *with* • **Review** *with, go, the, me, and*	• **Review** Shapes: Circle, Triangle

Hop with a Hog

SKILLS			
Phonics	**Comprehension**	**Vocabulary**	**Beginning Reading Concepts**
• **Introduce** Initial /w/w • **Review** /w/w, /h/h; Blending with Short *a, e, i, o, u*	• **Introduce** Make Inferences • **Review** Make Inferences	• **Introduce** High-Frequency Words: *was* • **Review** *was, with, I, he, she*	• **Review** Shapes: Square, Rectangle

We Win!

The Vet Van

SKILLS			
Phonics	**Comprehension**	**Vocabulary**	**Beginning Reading Concepts**
• **Introduce** Initial /v/v • **Introduce** Final /x/x • **Review** /v/v, /x/x; Blending with Short *a, e, i, o, u*	• **Review** Cause and Effect	• **Introduce** High-Frequency Words: *not* • **Review** *not, was, is, do, we, are, with*	• **Review** Categories

Jen and Yip

SKILLS			
Phonics	**Comprehension**	**Vocabulary**	**Beginning Reading Concepts**
• **Introduce** Initial /qu/qu • **Introduce** Initial /j/j • **Introduce** Initial /y/y and /z/z • **Review** Blending with Short *a, e, i, o, u*	• **Review** Make Inferences	• **Introduce** High-Frequency Words: *of* • **Review** *of, not, that, my*	• **Review** Categories

Zack and Jan

SKILLS			
Phonics	**Comprehension**	**Vocabulary**	**Beginning Reading Concepts**
• **Review** Blending with Short *a, e, i, o, u*	• **Review** Cause and Effect • **Review** Make Inferences	• **Review** *with, was, not, of*	• **Review** Shapes and Categories

Unit Planner

Hop with a Hog

We Win!

	WEEK 1 — Hop with a Hog	WEEK 2 — We Win!
📖 **Leveled Books**	Patterned Book: *Hen Had Her Ham*	Patterned Book: *Hello, Winter!*
☑ **Tested Skills**	☑ **Phonics and Decoding** Initial /h/h, 306W–306, 308C–308, 310C–310 Initial and Final /b/b, 310C–310 Blending with Short *a, e, i, o, u*, 312C–312, 316C–316 ☑ **Comprehension** Cause and Effect, 309C–309, 315A–315 ☑ **Vocabulary** High-Frequency Word: *with*, 311C–311 *with, go, the, me, and*, 317C–317 ☑ **Beginning Reading Concepts** Shapes: Circle, Triangle, 307C–307	☑ **Phonics and Decoding** Initial /w/w, 318I–318, 320C–320, 322C–322, Initial /h/h, 322C–322 Blending with Short *a, e, i, o, u*, 324C–324, 328C–328 ☑ **Comprehension** Make Inferences, 321C–321, 327A–327 ☑ **Vocabulary** High-Frequency Word: *was*, 323C–323 *was, with, I, he, she*, 329C–329 ☑ **Beginning Reading Concepts** Shapes: Square, Rectangle, 319C–319
Language Arts	✏ **Writing:** Letter Formation, 306W–306 Interactive Writing, 318A–318B	✏ **Writing:** Letter Formation, 318I–318 Interactive Writing, 330A–330B

CENTER Activities

Curriculum Connections		WEEK 1	WEEK 2
	Social Studies	Language Arts: What Letter Am I? 307B	Art: My Own Earth, 321B
	Mathematics	Art: Earth Posters, 309B	Math: Batter Up! 325/326D
	Science	Math: Where Does It Go? 311A	Art: Winter Wonderland, 329B
	Music	Music: Drawing Music, 313/314D	
	Art	Science: Pyramid Of Food, 317B	
	Drama		
	Language Arts		

 CULTURAL PERSPECTIVES

Quilts, 319B
Sculptures, 323A

The Vet Van

Jen and Yip

Zack and Jan

Patterned Book: *That's Not Violet!*

Patterned Book: *Six Yellow Ducks*

Self-Selected Reading of Patterned Books

Self-Selected Reading

☑ **Phonics and Decoding**
Initial /v/v, 330I–330, 334C–334
Final /x/x, 332C–332, 334C–334
Blending with Short *a, e, i, o, u*, 336C–336, 340C–340

☑ **Comprehension**
Cause and Effect, 333C–333, 339A–339

☑ **Vocabulary**
High-Frequency Word: *not*, 335C–335
not, was, is, so, we, are, with, 341C–341

☑ **Beginning Reading Concepts**
Categories, 331C–331

☑ **Phonics and Decoding**
Initial /qu/*qu*, 342I–342
Initial /j/j, 344C–344
Initial /y/y, /z/z, 346C–346
Blending with Short *a, e, i, o, u*, 348C–348, 352C–352

☑ **Comprehension**
Make Inferences, 345C–345, 351A–351

☑ **Vocabulary**
High-Frequency Word: *of*, 347C–347
of, not, that, my, 353C–353

☑ **Beginning Reading Concepts**
Categories, 343C–343

☑ **Phonics and Decoding**
Blending with Short *a, e, i, o, u*, 354I–354, 356C–356, 358C–358, 360C–360, 364C–364

☑ **Comprehension**
Cause and Effect, 357C–357
Make Inferences, 363A–363

☑ **Vocabulary**
High-Frequency Words: *with, was, not, of*, 359C–359, 365C–365

☑ **Beginning Reading Concepts**
Shapes: Circle, Triangle, Square, Rectangle; and Categories, 355C–355

☑ **Assess Skills**

Phonics and Decoding
Initial /h/h, /v/v, /qu/*qu*, /j/j, /y/y, /z/z
Final /b/b, /x/x
Blending with Short *a, e, i, o, u*

Comprehension
Cause and Effect
Make Inferences

Vocabulary
High-Frequency Words: *with, was, not, of, go, the, me, and, I, he, she, is, do, we, that, my*

Beginning Reading Concepts
Shapes: Circle, Triangle, Square, Rectangle
Categories

☑ **Unit 6 Assessment**

☑ **Standardized Test Preparation**

Writing: Letter Formation, 330I–330, 332C–332
Interactive Writing, 342A–342B

Writing: Letter Formation, 342I–342, 344C–344, 346C–346
Interactive Writing, 354A–354B

Writing: Interactive Writing, 366A–366B

Art: Color Creations, 333B

Social Studies: When I Grow Up, 337/338D

Art: Degrees of Color, 341B

Language Arts: Before and After, 343B

Science: Animal Colors, 345B

Drama: 347A

Math: Zig-Zag Math, 349/350D

Math: 353B

Language Arts: Number the Letter, 355B

Music: Earth Songs, 357B

Art: Animal Sculptures, 359A

Social Studies: Desert Life, 361/362D

Language arts: Earth Poems, 365B

Stamps, 331B
Homes, 335A

Unit Resources

LITERATURE

DECODABLE STORIES These four-color stories in the Pupil Edition consist of words containing the phonetic elements that have been taught, as well as the high-frequency words. The stories reinforce the comprehension and concepts of print skills.

LEVELED BOOKS These engaging stories include the high-frequency words and words with the phonetic elements that are being taught. They reinforce the comprehension skills and correlate to the unit themes.

Patterned
- *Hen Had Her Ham*
- *Hello, Winter!*
- *That's Not Violet!*
- *Six Yellow Ducks*

ABC BIG BOOK Children build alphabetic knowledge and letter identification as they enjoy a shared reading of this story that correlates to the theme.
- *The Big Box: An ABC Book*

LITERATURE BIG BOOKS Shared readings of the highest-quality literature reinforce comprehension skills and introduce children to a variety of genres.
- *The Earth and I*
- *White Rabbit's Color Book*

READ ALOUDS Traditional folk tales, fables, fairy tales, and stories from around the world can be shared with children as they develop their oral comprehension skills and learn about other cultures.
- *Annie's Pet*
- *Mae Jemison*
- *The Three Little Pigs*
- *The Little Red Hen*

STUDENT LISTENING LIBRARY
Recordings of the Big Books, Patterned Books, and Unit Opener and Closer Poetry.

SKILLS

PUPIL EDITION Colorful practice pages help you to assess children's progress as they learn and review each skill, including phonics, high-frequency words, readiness, comprehension, and letter formation.

PRACTICE BOOK Practice pages in alternative formats provide additional reinforcement of each skill as well as extra handwriting practice.

BIG BOOK OF PHONICS RHYMES AND POEMS Traditional and contemporary poems emphasize phonics and rhyme and allow children to develop oral comprehension skills.

BIG BOOK OF REAL-LIFE READING This lively big book introduces children to the resources of the library/media center in this unit. The context for the teaching is the Read Aloud selection children have just heard.

WORD BUILDING BOOK
Letter and word cards to utilize phonics and build children's vocabulary. Includes high-frequency word cards.

LANGUAGE SUPPORT BOOK
Parallel teaching and practice activities for children needing language support.

McGraw-Hill School
TECHNOLOGY

Phonics CD-ROM Provides interactive lessons for additional phonics support.

interNET CONNECTION Extend lessons through Research and Inquiry Ideas.

Visit www.mhschool.com

Resources for Meeting Individual Needs

	EASY	ON-LEVEL	CHALLENGE	LANGUAGE SUPPORT
UNIT 6				

Hop with a Hog

- **EASY**

  Hop with a Hog
  Teaching Strategies 306, 307, 308, 309, 310, 311, 312, 315, 316, 317
  Alternate Teaching Strategy T24–T27
  ✏ **Writing** 318B
  💿 Phonics **CD-ROM**

- **ON-LEVEL**

  Hop with a Hog
  Teaching Strategies 306–312, 315–317
  Alternate Teaching Strategy T24–T27
  ✏ **Writing** 318B
  📖 **Patterned Book** *Hen Had Her Ham*
  💿 Phonics **CD-ROM**

- **CHALLENGE**

  📖 **Patterned Book** *Hen Had Her Ham*
  Teaching Strategies 306, 307, 308, 309, 310, 311, 312, 315, 316, 317
  ✏ **Writing** 318B
  💿 Phonics **CD-ROM**

- **LANGUAGE SUPPORT**

  Teaching Strategies 306, 307, 308, 309, 310, 311, 312, 315, 316, 317
  Alternate Teaching Strategy T24–T27
  ✏ **Writing** 318B
  💿 Phonics **CD-ROM**

We Win!

- **EASY**

  We Win!
  Teaching Strategies 318, 319, 320, 321, 322, 323, 324, 327, 328, 329
  Alternate Teaching Strategy T24, T25, T27–T29
  ✏ **Writing** 330B
  💿 Phonics **CD-ROM**

- **ON-LEVEL**

  We Win!
  Teaching Strategies 318–324, 327–329
  Alternate Teaching Strategy T24, T25, T27–T29
  ✏ **Writing** 330B
  📖 **Patterned Book** *Hello, Winter!*
  💿 Phonics **CD-ROM**

- **CHALLENGE**

  📖 **Patterned Book** *Hello, Winter!*
  Teaching Strategies 318, 319, 320, 321, 322, 323, 324, 327, 328, 329
  ✏ **Writing** 330B
  💿 Phonics **CD-ROM**

- **LANGUAGE SUPPORT**

  Teaching Strategies 318, 319, 320, 321, 322, 323, 324, 327, 328, 329
  Alternate Teaching Strategy T24, T25, T27–T29
  ✏ **Writing** 330B
  💿 Phonics **CD-ROM**

The Vet Van

- **EASY**

  The Vet Van
  Teaching Strategies 330, 331, 332, 333, 334, 335, 336, 339, 340, 341
  Alternate Teaching Strategy T26, T27, T30, T33
  ✏ **Writing** 342B
  💿 Phonics **CD-ROM**

- **ON-LEVEL**

  The Vet Van
  Teaching Strategies 330–336, 339–341
  Alternate Teaching Strategy T26, T27, T30, T33
  ✏ **Writing** 342B
  📖 **Patterned Book** *That Is Not Violet!*
  💿 Phonics **CD-ROM**

- **CHALLENGE**

  📖 **Patterned Book** *That Is Not Violet!*
  Teaching Strategies 330, 331, 332, 333, 334, 335, 336, 339, 340, 341
  ✏ **Writing** 342B
  💿 Phonics **CD-ROM**

- **LANGUAGE SUPPORT**

  Teaching Strategies 330, 331, 332, 333, 334, 335, 336, 339, 340, 341
  Alternate Teaching Strategy T26, T27, T30, T33
  ✏ **Writing** 342B
  💿 Phonics **CD-ROM**

Jen and Yip

- **EASY**

  Jen and Yip
  Teaching Strategies 342, 343, 344, 345, 346, 347, 348, 351, 352, 353
  Alternate Teaching Strategy T27, T29, T32–T36
  ✏ **Writing** 354B
  💿 Phonics **CD-ROM**

- **ON-LEVEL**

  Jen and Yip
  Teaching Strategies 342–348, 351–353
  Alternate Teaching Strategy T27, T29, T32–T36
  ✏ **Writing** 354B
  📖 **Patterned Book** *Six Yellow Ducks*
  💿 Phonics **CD-ROM**

- **CHALLENGE**

  📖 **Patterned Book** *Six Yellow Ducks*
  Teaching Strategies 342, 343, 344, 345, 346, 347, 348, 351, 352, 353
  ✏ **Writing** 354B
  💿 Phonics **CD-ROM**

- **LANGUAGE SUPPORT**

  Teaching Strategies 342, 343, 344, 345, 346, 347, 348, 351, 352, 353
  Alternate Teaching Strategy T27, T29, T32–T36
  ✏ **Writing** 354B
  💿 Phonics **CD-ROM**

Zack and Jan

- **EASY**

  Zack and Jan
  Teaching Strategies 354, 355, 356, 357, 358, 359, 360, 363, 364, 365
  Alternate Teaching Strategy T24–T36
  ✏ **Writing** 366B
  💿 Phonics **CD-ROM**

- **ON-LEVEL**

  Zack and Jan
  Teaching Strategies 354–360, 363–365
  Alternate Teaching Strategy T24–T36
  ✏ **Writing** 366B
  📖 **Patterned Book** *Patterned Book Choice*
  💿 Phonics **CD-ROM**

- **CHALLENGE**

  📖 **Patterned Book** *Patterned Book Choice*
  Teaching Strategies 354, 355, 356, 357, 358, 359, 360, 363, 364, 365
  ✏ **Writing** 366B
  💿 Phonics **CD-ROM**

- **LANGUAGE SUPPORT**

  Teaching Strategies 354, 355, 356, 357, 358, 359, 360, 363, 364, 365
  Alternate Teaching Strategy T24–T36
  ✏ **Writing** 366B
  💿 Phonics **CD-ROM**

Hop with a Hog

We Win!

The Vet Van

Jen and Yip

Zack and Jan

INFORMAL

Informal Assessment

- Phonics and Decoding, 306W, 308C, 310C, 312C, 316C, 318I, 320C, 322C, 324C, 328C, 330I, 332C, 334C, 336C, 340C, 342I, 344C, 346C, 348C, 352C, 354I, 356C, 358C, 360C, 364C
- Comprehension, 307B, 309B, 309C, 315A, 317A, 319B, 321B, 321C, 327A, 329A, 331B, 333B, 333C, 339A, 341A, 343B, 345B, 345C, 351A, 353A, 355B, 357B, 357C, 363A, 365A
- High-Frequency Words, 311C, 317C, 323C, 329C, 335C, 341C, 347C, 353C, 359C, 365C
- Beginning Reading Concepts, 307C, 319C, 331C, 343C, 355C

Performance Assessment

- Research and Inquiry Project, 306O, 366C
- Interactive Writing, 318A–318B, 330A–330B, 342A–342B, 354A–354B, 366A–366B
- Listening, Speaking, Viewing Activities, 306U, 308A, 310A, 312A, 316A, 318B, 318G, 320A, 322A, 324A, 328A, 330B, 330G, 332A, 334A, 336A, 340A, 342B, 342G, 344A, 346A, 348A, 352A, 354B, 354G, 356A, 358A, 360A, 364A, 366B
- Portfolio
  Writing, 318A, 330A, 342A, 354A, 366A
  Cross-Curricular Activities, 307B, 309B, 311B, 313/314D, 317B, 319B, 321B, 323B, 325/326D, 329B, 331B, 333B, 335B, 337/338D, 341B, 343B, 345B, 347B, 349/350D, 353B, 355B, 357B, 359B, 361/362D, 365B

Practice

- **Phonics and Decoding**
  /h/*h*, 306, 308, 310, 322; /b/*b*, 310; /w/*w*, 318, 320, 322; /v/*v*, 330, 334; /ks/*x*, 332, 334; /kw/*qu*, 342; /j/*j*, 344; /y/*y*, 346; /z/*z*, 348
  Blending, 312, 316, 324, 328, 336, 340, 352, 354, 356, 358, 360, 364
- **Comprehension**
  Cause and Effect, 309, 315, 333, 339, 357
  Make Inferences, 321, 327, 345, 351, 363
- **High-Frequency Words**
  with, was, not, of, 311, 317, 323, 329, 335, 341, 347, 353, 359, 365
- **Beginning Reading Concepts**
  307, 319, 331, 343, 355

FORMAL

Unit 6 Assessment

- **Phonics and Decoding**
  Initial /h/*h*
  Initial /b/*b*
  Initial /w/*w*
  Initial /v/*v*
  Final /x/*x*
  Initial /qu/*qu*
  Initial /j/*j*
  Initial /y/*y*
  Initial /z/*z*
  Blending with Short *a, e, i, o, u*
- **Comprehension**
  Cause and Effect
  Make Inferences
- **High-Frequency Words**
  with, was, not, of
- **Beginning Reading Concepts**
  Shapes
  Categories

Diagnostic/Placement Evaluation

- Individual Reading Inventory
- Running Record
- Phonics and Decoding Inventory
- Grade K Diagnostic/Evaluation
- Grade 1 Diagnostic/Evaluation
- Grade 2 Diagnostic/Evaluation
- Grade 3 Diagnostic/Evaluation

Test Preparation

- Standardized Test Preparation Practice Book

Assessment Checklist

Student .... Grade ....

Teacher ....

	Hop with a Hog	We Win!	The Vet Van	Jen and Yip	Zack and Jan	Assessment Summary
LISTENING/SPEAKING						
Participates in oral language experiences						
Listens and speaks to gain knowledge of culture						
Speaks appropriately to audiences for different purposes						
Communicates clearly (gains increasing control of grammar)						
READING						
Demonstrates knowledge of concepts of print						
Uses phonological awareness strategies, including						
• Identifying, segmenting, and combining syllables						
• Producing rhyming words						
• Identifying and isolating initial and final sounds						
Uses letter/sound knowledge, including						
• Applying letter-sound correspondences to begin to read						
• Phonics and Decoding: initial /h/ *H, h*						
• Phonics and Decoding: initial /w/ *W,w*						
• Phonics and Decoding: initial /v/ *V,v*; Final /ks/ *X,x*						
• Phonics and Decoding: initial /kw/ *Qu,qu*; /j/ *J,j*; /y/ *Y,y*; /z/ *Z,z*						
• Blending with *a, i, o, u, e*						
Develops an extensive vocabulary, including						
• High-frequency words: *with, was, not, of*						
Uses a variety of strategies to comprehend selections						
• Cause and Effect						
• Make Inferences						
Responds to various texts						
Recognizes characteristics of various types of texts						
Conducts research using various sources						
Reads to increase knowledge						
WRITING						
Writes his/her own name						
Writes each letter of the alphabet						
Uses phonological knowledge to map sounds to letters to write messages						
Gains increasing control of penmanship						
Composes original texts						
Uses writing as a tool for learning and research						

+ Observed   − Not Observed

Introducing the Theme

Choices

We can make good choices and decisions every day.

PRESENT THE THEME Read the theme statement to children. Invite each child to tell about one decision he or she already made today.

READ THE POEM Read the poem "Tommy" aloud. Ask children to suggest ways to act out the poem. Then have children act out the poem as you read it again.

TOMMY

I put a seed into the
   ground
and said, "I'll watch
   it grow."
I watered it and
   cared for it
As well as I could
   know.

One day I walked in
   my back yard,
And oh, what did I
   see!
My seed had
   popped itself
   right out,
without consulting
   me.

Gwendolyn Brooks

 Student Listening Library

DISCUSS THE POEM Ask children why they think Tommy's decision to plant a seed and care for it was a good decision. Discuss ways in which growing the seed most likely improved Tommy's environment.

THEME SUMMARY Each lesson relates to the unit theme *Choices* as well as to the global theme *Making Decisions*. These thematic links will help children to make connections from their own choices and decisions to the literature of the unit.

Literature selections presented within the first two lessons are also related to the subtheme *Good Choices*. Lead children to see that choices they make can help make the world a better place.

Selections for the third and fourth lessons are more closely tied to the subtheme *Let's Decide*. These stories provide examples of exploring options before making a decision.

The fifth lesson gives children the opportunity to reread their favorite literature selections and discuss the main theme of *Choices*.

Research and Inquiry

Theme Project: Clean-Up!
Have children generate a list of areas in the community that tend to look unsightly. They will choose one site as the basis for a project about cleaning up the community.

List What They Know Assist children in making a list of reasons why they chose the particular site. Discuss things people do to keep a community clean, making it a better place to live.

Ask Questions and Identify Resources Next, ask children to brainstorm some questions they would need to answer in order to prepare their presentations. Questions can be as basic as, "Where can we get garbage bags?" The local sanitation department should be a good source of information.

Create a Presentation Have children make a poster that depicts their site as it now appears and after the clean-up that they recommend.

CENTER Activities

Setting Up the Centers

Independent Learning Centers will help to reinforce children's skills across all areas of the curriculum. Here's what you will need to help you set up the centers in this unit.

Reading/Language Arts Center

- drawing paper, construction paper, mural paper
- markers, box
- letter cards, number cards, alphabet strips
- nature pictures
- audiocassette player
- Student Listening Library Audiocassette

For suggested activities, see pages 307B, 343B, 355B, 365B.

Math Center

- variety of library books
- chart paper, index cards, drawing paper
- counters, paper clips, connecting cubes

For suggested activities, see pages 311B, 325/326D, 349/350D, 353B.

Science Center

- outline of food pyramid
- markers, scissors, paste, magazines

For suggested activities, see page 317B.

Social Studies/ Cultural Perspectives Center

- picture cards representing various occupations
- desert books and pictures
- mural paper, markers, tape
- drawing paper, paper squares, flat pieces of cardboard
- milk cartons, tubes, recycled objects

For suggested activities, see pages 319B, 323B, 331B, 335B, 337/338D, 361/362D.

Art/Drama Center

- poster paper, drawing paper, construction paper
- markers, paints, paintbrushes, crayons
- audiocassette player, headphones, tape of flute music
- templates of planet Earth
- silver glitter, paste, white chalk
- paper cups, tempera paint, paint sample squares
- envelopes, pictures of wild animals
- hardening clay

For suggested activities, see pages 309B, 313/314D, 321B, 329B, 333B, 341B, 347B, 357B, 359B.

Managing the Centers

MANAGEMENT TIP To make set-ups easier, give each child a colored circle. Post simple instructions at each center, such as "blue circle = markers; red circle = drawing paper." Children will then know what their responsibilities are for gathering materials for the centers.

INSTRUCTIONAL TIP Try to keep a small table or other small surface area open to work with children who may need some special one-on-one help or instruction.

ASSESSMENT TIP As you walk from center to center, ask children to describe to you what they are doing and record their responses. Ask critical thinking questions so that children will begin to think about why they are working on a particular activity.

CLEAN-UP TIP The end of the year is always a good time to begin discarding unwanted or unusable items. Ask children to assist you in sorting through center bins and boxes to throw away dried markers and paste, unusable paper and fabric scraps, over-used magazines, and so on.

Hop with a Hog

Children will read and listen to a variety of stories about ways decisions impact upon daily lives.

**Decodable Story,
pages 313–314 of the
Pupil Edition**

Listening
Library
Audiocassette

**Patterned Book,
page 317B**

Annie's Pet
by Barbara Brenner

**Teacher Read Aloud,
page 311A**

**ABC Big Book,
pages 307A–307B**

Listening
Library
Audiocassette

**Literature Big Book,
pages 309A–309B**

Listening
Library
Audiocassette

**Pupil Edition,
pages 306–317**

**Big Book of Real-Life Reading,
page 40**

**Big Book of Phonics Rhymes and
Poems, pages 23, 24**

 **Listening
Library
Audiocassette**

**Practice Book,
pages 316–317**

- **Phonics Kit**
- **Language Support Book**
- **Alternate Teaching Strategies,** pp T24–T27

**McGraw-Hill School
TECHNOLOGY**

Phonics CD-ROM Provides extra phonics support.

interNET CONNECTION Research & Inquiry Ideas.

Visit www.mhschool.com

Hop with a Hog

READING AND LANGUAGE ARTS

 **DAY 1**

- Phonological Awareness
- Phonics *initial /h/h*
- Comprehension
- Vocabulary
- Beginning Reading Concepts
- Listening, Speaking, Viewing, Representing

DAY 1

Focus on Reading Skills

Develop Phonological Awareness, 306U-306V
"Happy Henry" *Big Book of Phonics Rhymes and Poems*, 23

 **Introduce Initial /h/h,** 306W-306
Practice Book, 306
Phonics/Phonemic Awareness Practice Book

 CD-ROM

 **Read the Literature**

Read *The Big Box: An ABC Book* **Big Book,** 307A-307B
Shared Reading

Build Skills

☑ Shapes: Circle, Triangle, 307C-307
Practice Book, 307

DAY 2

The Earth and I
FRANK ASCH

Focus on Reading Skills

Develop Phonological Awareness, 308A-308B
"My Hamster" *Big Book of Phonics Rhymes and Poems*, 24

 **Review Initial /h/h,** 308C-308
Practice Book, 308
Phonics/Phonemic Awareness Practice Book

 **CD-ROM**

Read the Literature

Read *The Earth and I* **Big Book,** 309A-309B
Shared Reading

Build Skills

☑ Cause and Effect, 309C-309
Practice Book, 309

- Cross Curriculum

 Language Arts, 307B

 Art, 309B

- Writing

 Writing Prompt: Write about the idea for the Big Box that you like best.

 Journal Writing, 307B
Letter Formation, 306W

 Writing Prompt: Write about one way help to make the earth a better place.

 Journal Writing, 309B
Letter Formation, 308C

 = **Skill Assessed in Unit Test**

DAY 3

Annie's Pet

Focus on Reading Skills

Develop Phonological Awareness, 310A-310B
"Happy Henry" and "My Hamster" *Big Book of Phonics Rhymes and Poems,* 23-24

Review /h/h,/b/b, 310C-310
Practice Book, 310
Phonics/Phonemic Awareness Practice Book

 **CD-ROM**

Read the Literature

 Read "Annie's Pet" Teacher Read Aloud, 311A-311B
Shared Reading
Read the Big Book of Real-Life Reading, 40-41
☑ Library/Media Center

Build Skills

☑ High-Frequency Words: *with,* 311C-311
Practice Book, 311

 Activity Math, 311B

 Writing Prompt: Write about what type of pet you have or would like to have.

DAY 4

Hop with a Hog

Focus on Reading Skills

Develop Phonological Awareness, 312A-312B
"Hen and Hog"
**Review Blending with Short *a, e, i, o, u,*** 312C-312
Practice Book, 312
Phonics/Phonemic Awareness Practice Book

Phonics CD-ROM

Read the Literature

Read "Hop with a Hog" Decodable Story, 313/314A-313/314D

☑ Initial /h/h; Blending
☑ Cause and Effect
☑ High-Frequency Words: *with*
☑ Concepts of Print

Build Skills

☑ Cause and Effect, 315A-315
Practice Book, 315

Activity Music, 313/314D

Writing Prompt: Write about your favorite part of the story.

Letter Formation,
Practice Book, 313-314

DAY 5

Hop with a Hog

Focus on Reading Skills

Develop Phonological Awareness, 316A-316B
"The Big Sack"
**Review Blending with Short *a, e, i, o, u,*** 316C-316
Practice Book, 316
Phonics/Phonemic Awareness Practice Book

Phonics CD-ROM

Read the Literature

Reread "Hop with a Hog" Decodable Story, 317A
Read "Hen Had Her Ham" Patterned Book, 317B
Guided Reading
☑ Initial /h/h; Blending
☑ Cause and Effect
☑ High-Frequency Words: *with*
☑ Concepts of Print

Build Skills

☑ High-Frequency Words: *with, go, the, me, and,* 317C-317
Practice Book, 317

Activity Science, 317B

Writing Prompt: What are some good choices? Write about some good food choices that you make every day.

Interactive Writing, 318A-318B

Develop Phonological Awareness

Listen

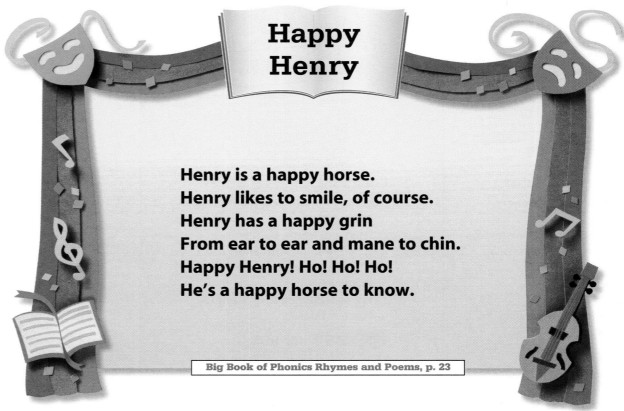

Happy Henry

Henry is a happy horse.
Henry likes to smile, of course.
Henry has a happy grin
From ear to ear and mane to chin.
Happy Henry! Ho! Ho! Ho!
He's a happy horse to know.

Big Book of Phonics Rhymes and Poems, p. 23

Objective: Enhance Awareness of Sounds

LISTEN TO THE POEM

- Read the poem "Happy Henry" to the children. Say the words *Henry* and *Ho,* and point out that the words begin with the same sound.
- Have children say *Ho, ho, ho* using whispering voices and calling voices. Then have children say the words slowly and quickly.

JOIN IN A READING

- Explain to children that you will read the poem again. Children will listen carefully and join in on the words *Ho, ho, ho.*
- Have children decide which type of voice they would like to use.
- Experiment with different types of voices, volume, and speed.

Objective: Listen for Initial /h/

SEGMENTING

- Say the word Henry, emphasizing the initial /h/. Have children segment the sound.

> **H—enry**

- Say the word *happy*, and determine that it begins with the same sound. Have children segment the sound.

ADD THE SOUND /h/

- Tell children you will say a word from the poem without the /h/ sound. Ask children to add the /h/ sound and say the word.

> **enry appy orse o**

RAISE A HAND FOR *H*

- Have children listen to the following sentences and raise a hand when they hear a word that begins with /h/.

> **Henry helps himself to hay.**
> **Henry is going home.**

From Phonemic Awareness to Phonics

Objective: Identify Initial /h/ *H,h*

IDENTIFY THE LETTER FOR THE SOUND.

- Explain to children that the letters *H, h* stand for the sound /h/. Say the sound, and have children say it with you.

- Display the Big Book of Phonics Rhymes and Poems, page 23. Point to the letters in the corner. Identify them, and have children say the /h/ sound.

REREAD THE POEM

Reread the poem. Have children raise a hand when they hear a word that begins with /h/.

LOOK FOR *H*

- Ask children to find a line in the poem where every word begins with *H* or *h*. Then have children read the fifth line with you.

- Have children identify and count the number of times the letters *H, h* appear.

- Point out the capital and lower-case letters.

Happy Henry

Henry is a happy horse.
Henry likes to smile, of course.

Henry has a happy grin,
From ear to ear and mane to chin.

Happy Henry! Ho, ho, ho!
He's a happy horse to know.

Big Book of Phonics Rhymes and Poems, p. 23

OBJECTIVES

Children will:

- **identify the letters *H, h***
- **identify /h/ *H, h***
- **form the letters *H, h***

....

MATERIALS

- **letter cards from the Word Play Book**

TEACHING TIP

INSTRUCTIONAL Give children index cards, and have them fold the card in half. Have them write uppercase *H* by using the long sides as guidelines for the vertical lines and then connecting them with a line drawn across the middle of the card. Show them how to write *h* on the back of the card, using both vertical and horizontal lines as guides.

ALTERNATE TEACHING STRATEGY

....

INITIAL /h/h

For a different approach to teaching this skill, see page T24.

▶ **Visual/Auditory/ Kinesthetic**

Introduce Initial /h/h

TEACH

Identify /h/ H, h Tell children they will learn to write the sound /h/ with the letters *H, h*. Ask them to say the /h/ sound. Then say, "Hello Hal, how are you?" Write the sentence on the chalkboard, and read it aloud, tracking print with your hand. Ask children to raise their "h" letter cards when they hear a word that begins with *h*. Have them greet one another using the sentence but substituting their names. Continue to have children raise their letter cards when they hear a word that begins with h.

Form H, h Display letters *H, h* and, with your back to the children, trace them in the air. Ask children to do the same. Talk about how the letters are similar and how they are different. Ask children to write four *H*s and four *h*s on drawing paper folded into fourths.

PRACTICE

Complete the Pupil Edition Page Read the directions on page 306 to the children, and make sure they clearly understand what they are asked to do. Identify each picture, and complete the first item together. Then work through the page with children, or have them complete the page independently.

ASSESS/CLOSE

Identify and Use H, h Place pictures of the following objects on the chalk ledge. Ask children to write a letter h on the back of their drawing paper for each picture that shows an object whose name begins with *h: hat, hammer, bed, chair, horn, hand*. Invite volunteers to name the objects, and check to see that children have written four *h*s.

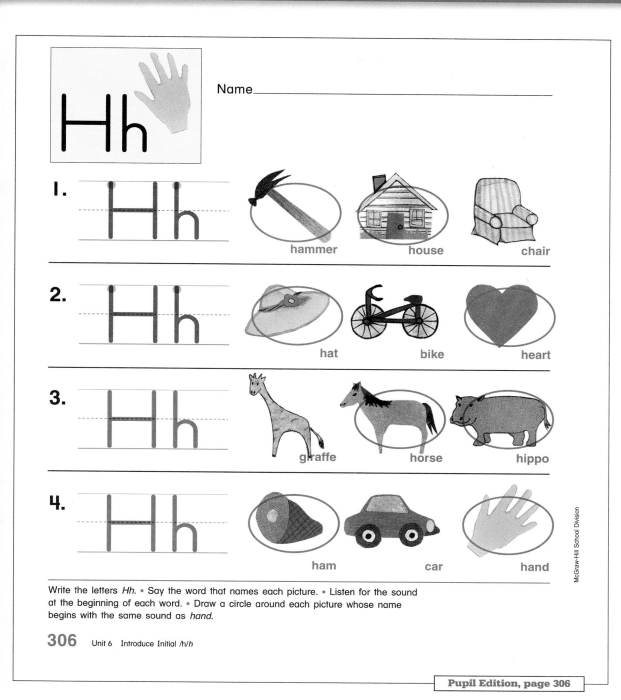

1. Hh — hammer, house, chair

2. Hh — hat, bike, heart

3. Hh — giraffe, horse, hippo

4. Hh — ham, car, hand

Write the letters *Hh*. • Say the word that names each picture. • Listen for the sound at the beginning of each word. • Draw a circle around each picture whose name begins with the same sound as *hand*.

306 Unit 6   Introduce Initial /h/h

McGraw-Hill School Division

1. Hh — saw, hammer *color*

2. Hh — hippo, pig *color*

3. Hh — ladder, house *color*

Write the letters *Hh*. Say the word that names each picture. Color the picture whose name begins with the same sound as *hen*.

At Home: Together, think of words that name things that begin with /h/. Have the child draw a picture of one of these things.

306

Unit 6
Introduce Initial /h/h   6

PRACTICE BOOK page 306

Meeting Individual Needs for Phonics

EASY	ON-LEVEL	CHALLENGE	LANGUAGE SUPPORT
Invite children to repeat the nursery rhyme "Humpty Dumpty" with you. Emphasize words that begin with /h/, and ask children to clap when they hear these words. You can show children a copy of the rhyme, and have them point to each initial *H,h*.	**Brainstorm** a list of animals that begin with *h*, such as: *hippo, horse, hen, hog, hawk, hamster.* Children can draw the animals, write letter *h* labels, then make books of *h* animals, and finally write *H, h* on the covers.	**Play** a version of "Simon Says" in which children only mime the action if it begins with /h/. Call out a variety of commands, for example: *Hammer a nail. Pick an apple. Hold a book. Put on a hat. Ride a bike. Wave hello.*	**Say,** "Hold your hand in front of your mouth." When children have done this, have them repeat the sentence, noticing what happens when they make the /h/ sound. Say these words: *pen, happy, bike, heart, hippo, red.* Have children say /h/ if the word begins with /h/.

306

OBJECTIVES

Children will:

- recognize the ABC story structure
- recognize words with initial *h*

JUDY NAYER lives in New York City. She is an editor and the author of more than 100 children's books.

SUSAN SWAN lives in Texas. For 30 years, Ms. Swan has created 3-D paper sculptures which appear in children's books. She created all the different boxes in this book.

LANGUAGE SUPPORT

ESL Introduce the word *imagination*, and discuss what it means. Ask children to name instances when they use their imaginations, such as playing or making up stories.

Read the Big Book

Before Reading

Build Background

EVALUATE PRIOR KNOWLEDGE Hold up an empty box and have children identify it. Then ask what children could make out of the box. Make a picture or word list. Explain that, in the story, children are using their imaginations to create ideas.

Preview and Predict

DISCUSS AUTHOR AND ILLUSTRATOR Display the Big Book cover and read the title. Discuss what children see on the cover. Identify the author and the illustrator, and ask children how each person contributed to the book. Share some background information about them.

TAKE A PICTURE WALK Take a picture walk through several spreads of the book. Discuss what children see, and how the alphabet is a part of the story.

MAKE PREDICTIONS Ask children to predict what the story might be about.

Set Purposes

Ask children what they want to find out about the box. Explain how they can name the letter on each page, and use the picture and the letter to say the words.

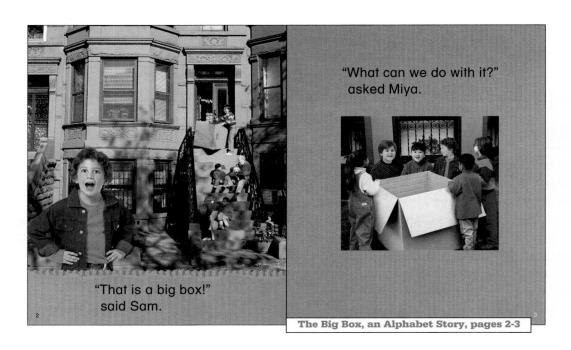

"What can we do with it?" asked Miya.

"That is a big box!" said Sam.

The Big Box, an Alphabet Story, pages 2-3

During Reading

Read Together

- Before you begin to read, point to the first word in the first sentence. Explain that this is where you will begin to read. Continue to track print as you read the story. *Tracking Print*

- After you read page 4, point out the key word on each page, and relate it to the letters at the top of the page. Make sure that children understand that the word *alphabet* begins with the /a/ sound. *Concepts of Print*

- After you read page 6, ask if the box has really turned into these objects. Make sure children understand that the children in the story are using their imaginations. *Make Inferences*

- Make the /h/ sound, and have children say it with you. After you read page 11, have children say the word with that sound. *(house)* Ask them to say other words that begin with that sound. *Phonics*

"We can make a **zebra** with black and white stripes," said Ann.

The Big Box, an Alphabet Story, page 29

After Reading

Return to Predictions and Purposes

Ask children if they found out what they wanted to know about the box. Return to the list that children made earlier and see if any of the ideas were the same.

Literary Response

JOURNAL WRITING Ask children to draw and write about what they would turn the box into.

ORAL RESPONSE Ask questions such as:

- *Is your idea the same or different from an idea in the story?*

- *What size box would you use?*

ABC Activity

Line up lower case letter cards in random order. Invite volunteers to put the cards in the correct order.

Cross Curricular: Language Arts

WHAT LETTER AM I? Write letters of the alphabet on small paper squares and place them in a box. Have partners play a guessing game. One child takes out a letter and gives a clue, such as: *This letter comes just after c.*

The partner guesses and confirms by checking the letter. Children take turns.

▶ **Interpersonal**

Review Shapes: Circle, Triangle

OBJECTIVES

Children will:

- identify circles and triangles

MATERIALS

- *The Big Box:* an ABC Book
- paper circles and triangles

TEACHING TIP

INSTRUCTIONAL

You may wish to discuss the story in the Big Book *The Big Box* before you begin the lesson. Ask volunteers to retell the story and to name some of their favorite parts of the story.

PREPARE

Describe Familiar Shapes
Hold up a large paper triangle. Ask volunteers to point out the sides and corners. Then ask children to find things shaped like triangles in the classroom. Make a picture or a word list. Repeat with a paper circle.

TEACH

Recognize a Shape
Display the Big Book, *The Big Box*, and review the story. Ask children to point to the picture of the box on the cover and to describe it. Then look through the book, and have children look for circles and triangles in the illustrations.

PRACTICE

Complete the Pupil Edition Page
Read the directions on page 307 to the children, and make sure they clearly understand what they are asked to do. *Identify each picture, and complete the first item.* Then work through the page with children, or have them complete the page independently.

ASSESS/CLOSE

Review the Page
Check children's work on the Pupil Edition page. Note areas where children need extra help.

Name_____

Find the circles in the picture. • Color them yellow. • Find the triangles in the picture.
• Color them blue.

Unit 6   Review Shapes: Circle, Triangle   **307**

ALTERNATE TEACHING STRATEGY
·····································

For a different approach to teaching this skill, see page T25.

▶ **Visual/Auditory/Kinesthetic**

Practice 307

Name_____

Find the circles in the picture. Color them orange. Find the triangles in the picture. Color them blue.

26 Unit 6
Review Shapes: Circle, Triangle

At Home: Take turns finding circular shapes in several rooms: door knobs and cup rims. Then find square and rectangular shapes: windows, envelopes and books.

307

PRACTICE BOOK page 307

Meeting Individual Needs for Beginning Reading Concepts

EASY	ON-LEVEL	CHALLENGE	LANGUAGE SUPPORT
Be aware that some children may have difficulty distinguishing between shapes. Give children chenille wire shapes to touch and describe. Then talk about how the shapes are alike and different. Ask children to sort the shapes into two groups.	**Display** several different sizes of pipe cleaners or paper circles and triangles. Give clues about a shape, and invite children to guess the shape. Then have children give clues to you. Talk about how the shapes are alike and different.	**Cut** circular and triangular shapes from sponges. Have pairs of children dip the sponges into paint and make sponge-painting shape patterns onto long paper strips.	**Display** several paper circles and triangles and have children describe each. Talk about which box is the largest and which is the smallest.

Develop Phonological Awareness

 Listen

MY HAMSTER

I have a hamster at my house.
It's really a hamster, and not a mouse,
My hamster is tan and very hairy.
It has teeth, but isn't scary.
I have to feed it twice a day.
When I get home from school, we play.

Big Book of Phonics Rhymes and Poems, 24

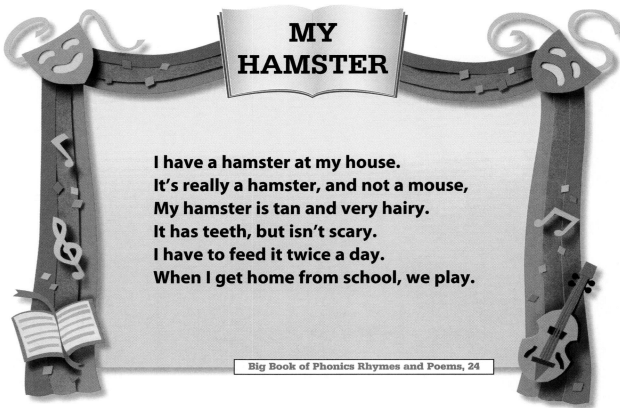

Objective: Listen for Syllables

LISTEN FOR THE NUMBER OF SYLLABLES

- Read the poem aloud. Then explain to children that you are going to name other pets. Tell children you will say the names very slowly. Ask children to count the syllables with you.
- Read the first line of the poem and say, "I have a rab-bit at my house." Pause between syllables of the word. Ask how many syllables the word *rabbit* has.

PUT THE SYLLABLES TOGETHER

- Ask children to blend the syllables and say the word *rab-bit*.

- Continue the game, using other animal names.

> cat, iguana, puppy, goldfish

Objective: Listen for Initial /h/

REREAD THE POEM

- Reread the poem "My Hamster," and emphasize words with the initial /h/ sound.

Have children repeat the sound after you.

- Then have volunteers suggest names for the hamster that begin with /h/. Have children say the names by stretching the /h/ sound.

> **Henry   Hannah   Harriet   Howard   Helen**

SEGMENTING

- Tell children that you will say some of the names without the /h/ sound at the beginning. Say the incomplete names: *arriet, oward, elen.*
- Children add the initial /h/ sound and say the name.

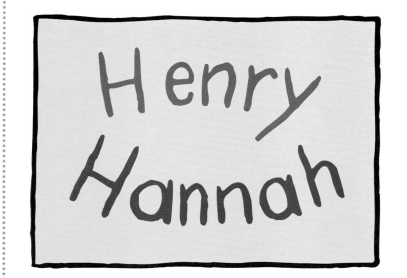

Read Together

From Phonemic Awareness to Phonics

Objective: Identify /h/ *H,h*

RELATE THE LETTER TO THE SOUND

- Explain to children that the letters *H,h* stand for the sound /h/. Display page 24 in the Big Book of Phonics Rhymes and Poems and point to the letters in the corner. Have children repeat the sound.

LISTEN FOR THE SOUND

- Read the poem again, stopping at each word that begins with /h/. Children repeat the word after you.

FIND THE WORDS WITH H,h

- Have children find all of the words with *H,h* in the poem. Make a tally mark for each *H,h* that they find.
- Count together and find how many words have *H,h.*

Hh

My Hamster

I have a hamster at my house.
It's really a hamster, not a mouse.

My hamster is tan and very hairy.
It has teeth but isn't scary.

I have to feed it twice a day.
When I get home from school
we play.

Big Book of Phonics Rhymes and Poems, 24

308B

OBJECTIVES

Children will:
- identify the letters *H, h*
- identify /h/ *H, h*
- form the letters *H, h*

MATERIALS
- letter cards from the Word Play Book

ALTERNATE TEACHING STRATEGY

INITIAL /h/h

For a different approach to teaching this skill, see page T24.

▶ **Visual/Auditory/ Kinesthetic**

Review Initial /h/h

TEACH

Identify /h/ *H, h* Tell children they will review the sound /h/ and the letters *H, h*. Write the letters on the chalkboard, and have children make the sound. Explain that you want to name your imaginary pet hamster a name that begins with *H*. Ask children to raise their hands when they hear a name that begins with *H* and say: *Harriet, Henry, Ruth, Howard, Hilda, Josh*. Then write the "h" names on the chalkboard. Invite children to vote on an *H* name for your hamster.

Form *H, h* Give children cutouts in the shape of a *heart*, and ask a volunteer to name the shape. Then have children write *H* on one side of each heart and *h* on the other side. Say the following words. Children hold up the hearts when they recognize a word that begins with /h/: *head, hand, neck, hip, face, hair*.

PRACTICE

Complete the Pupil Edition Page Read the directions on page 308 to the children, and make sure they clearly understand what they are being asked to do. Identify each picture, and complete the first item together. Then work through the page with children, or have them complete the page independently.

ASSESS/CLOSE

Identify and Use *H, h* Ask children to clap every time they hear a word that begins with /h/, and tell this silly story: Happy the hippo hit a home run. She was hot. The crowd hopped up and down. Have children write *H, h*, and assess their writing.

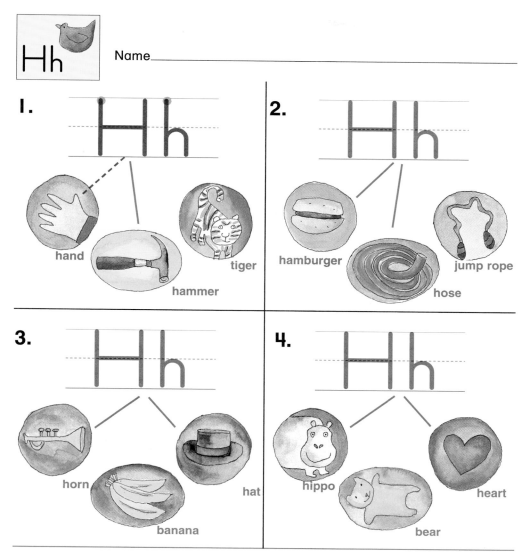

Hh Name_____

1. Hh
hand
hammer
tiger

2. Hh
hamburger
hose
jump rope

3. Hh
horn
banana
hat

4. Hh
hippo
bear
heart

Write the letters *Hh*. • Say the word that names each picture. • Draw a line from the *Hh* to each picture whose name has the same beginning sound as *hen*.

McGraw-Hill School Division

308 Unit 6 Review Initial /h/h

Pupil Edition, page 308

ADDITIONAL PHONICS RESOURCES

Practice Book, *page 308*
Phonics Workbook

McGraw-Hill School
TECHNOLOGY

Phonics CD-ROM
Activities for practice with Initial Letters

PRACTICE BOOK page 308

Meeting Individual Needs for Phonics

EASY	ON-LEVEL	CHALLENGE	LANGUAGE SUPPORT
Give each child two index cards: one with *H* written on it and the other with *h* written on it. Then have children use clay, pipe cleaners, sand, noodles or other materials to create tactile letters. Afterwards, ask them to talk about how the letters are alike and how they are different.	**Invite** children to complete the following sentences using words that begin with h: *I like to play ___ and seek. I wear a ___ on my head. Jack and Jill went up a ___. Can you ___ that tune?* Ask them to write an h for each word that completes a sentence.	**Write** on the chalkboard and read aloud these initial *h* words: *hen, hum, hop, him, hat.* Ask children to make up sentences using the words. Invite them to make up stories using all the *h* words and to think of more *h* words to use. Write the sentences as they dictate.	**Some** ESL children make the /h/ sound using other letters than h. In Spanish, for example, the sound can be made with *j* or *g*, as in *Juana, Jaime, girasol (sunflower)*. Talk about these differences, and clarify that in English /h/ is almost always written with letter h.

308

TESTED OBJECTIVES

- recognize words with initial *h*
- understand cause and effect

FRANK ASCH is the author and illustrator of many popular books. He lives with his wife and son in a small town in Vermont. To help with this book, he asked students to complete the phrase "Earth and I..." He received many responses, and was moved by the feelings that children expressed about their relationship with Earth.

LANGUAGE SUPPORT

ESL The concept of "taking care of Earth" may be difficult for some children to understand. Ask children to talk about how they take care of yards, gardens, pets, and their homes.

Read the Big Book

Before Reading

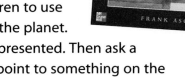

Build Background

EVALUATE PRIOR KNOWLEDGE. Display a globe, and explain that a globe represents our planet, Earth. Then display a world map, and talk about how the map and the globe both represent Earth.

WHAT MAKES UP EARTH? Invite children to use the globe and the map to understand the planet. Show how landforms and water are represented. Then ask a volunteer to close her or his eyes and point to something on the globe. Then the child decides if he or she pointed to land or water.

Preview and Predict

DISCUSS AUTHOR AND ILLUSTRATOR Display the Big Book cover, read the title, and talk about what children see on the cover. Read the author's name. Explain that Mr. Asch is both the author and the illustrator, and share some background information about the author with the children.

Take a **picture walk** through the first four spreads of the book, and talk about what children see.

Invite children to predict what the story might be about and what might happen next.

Set Purposes

Tell children: *I can see by looking at the illustrations that the boy is observing the earth around him. Let's find out how the boy and the earth enjoy each others' companionship and friendship.*

Then I listen to her.

6

The Earth and I, pages 6-7

7

During Reading

Read Together

• Before you begin to read, point to the first word in the first sentence. Explain that this is where you will begin to read. Continue to track print as you read the story. *Tracking Print*

• Explain that when something happens in a story, it often causes something else to happen. After you read page 18, ask: *What happens when the boy grows vegetables in his garden?* (He has food to eat.) *Understand Cause and Effect*

• Make the /h/ sound, and have children say it with you Read pages 30-31, and ask which word begins with that sound. Ask how many times the children hear the word. (happy; two) *Phonics and Decoding*

She listens to every word.

The Earth and I, page 5

After Reading

Return to Predictions and Purposes

Return to the predictions that children made. Ask if reading the story answered their questions.

Literary Response

JOURNAL WRITING Fold a sheet of drawing paper in half. On one side, have children draw a picture to show one way the boy cared for the earth. On the other side, children show how the earth cared for the boy. Have them write about their pictures.

ORAL RESPONSE Have children respond to questions, such as:

• *What do you do to care for the earth?*

• *How does the earth care for you?*

 **CENTER Activity**

Cross Curricular: Art

EARTH-FRIENDLY POSTERS
Talk about how recycling helps the earth. Invite children to make posters to show how people can recycle items at school and at home. Make a display of the posters.

▶ **Spatial**

Introduce Cause and Effect

OBJECTIVES

Children will:

- identify cause and effect in a story

....

MATERIALS

- *The Earth and I,* Big Book

TEACHING TIP

MANAGEMENT You may wish to have children who are having difficulty completing their Pupil Edition pages independently work with partners to complete a page. Children can record answers on their own pages, but discuss each example first.

PREPARE

Understand Cause and Effect
Turn off the lights in the classroom. Ask children to explain why the room is dark. (Because you switched off the light switch.) Explain that the *effect* was that the room got dark. The cause was switching off the light switch.

TEACH

Find Examples in the Story
Reread page 14 together, and ask children what happens when the boy grows vegetables. Explain that when one thing happens in a story, it can cause something else to happen. Invite children to find other examples, such as: *What happens when the boy sings? What happens when the boy cleans up the litter?* Create a chart, listing the cause and effect of each event that you and children discuss from the story.

PRACTICE

Complete the Pupil Edition Page
Read the directions on page 309 to the children, and make sure they clearly understand what they are asked to do. Identify each picture, and complete the first item together. Then work through the page with children or have them complete the page independently.

ASSESS/CLOSE

Review the Page
Review children's work, and note children who are experiencing difficulty. Have children explain their answers to help you pinpoint their misunderstanding.

Name _____

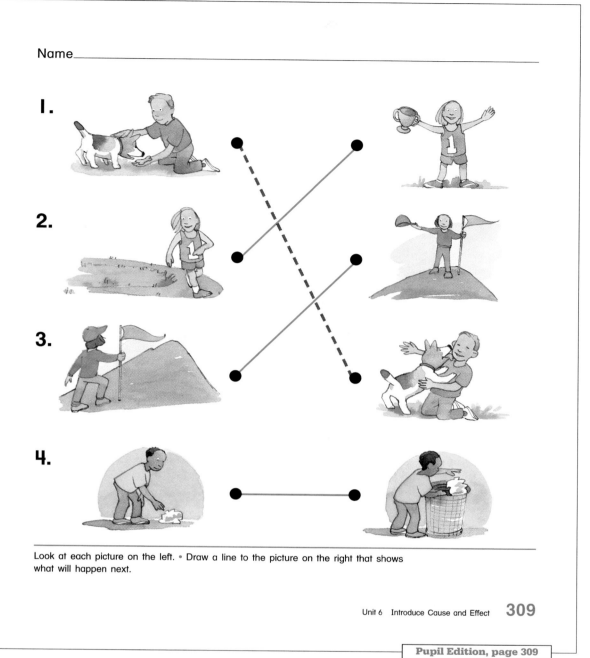

Look at each picture on the left. • Draw a line to the picture on the right that shows what will happen next.

Pupil Edition, page 309

ALTERNATE TEACHING STRATEGY

CAUSE AND EFFECT

For a different approach to teaching this skill, see page T26.

▶ **Visual/Auditory/Kinesthetic**

Practice **309**

Name _____

Look at the first picture in each row. Circle the picture that shows why it happened.

Unit 6
Introduce Cause and Effect

At Home: Ask, Why do we tie our shoes? What would happen, or could happen, if we didn't tie them?

309

PRACTICE BOOK page 309

Meeting Individual Needs for Comprehension

EASY	ON-LEVEL	CHALLENGE	LANGUAGE SUPPORT
Ask children to name tasks that they do every day, such as brushing teeth, eating, sleeping, and so on. Make a picture list. Then have children explain what happens when children do that task.	**Show** pictures of people doing different actions. Ask children what might happen because of these actions. Have children dictate their ideas to you as you make a list of effects.	**Talk** about how to take care of classroom plants. Make a picture or word list of what the plants need to grow. Then make a list of the effects of this care.	**Have** children perform simple tasks to show cause and *effect*. For example, children can build a tower of blocks and then gently push the tower down. Help children explain what happens using this language pattern: *The tower of blocks fell because I pushed it.*

309

Develop Phonological Awareness

Listen

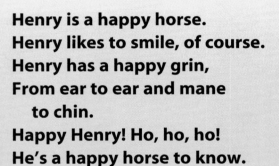

Happy Henry
a poem

Tub Time
a poem

Henry is a happy horse.
Henry likes to smile, of course.
Henry has a happy grin,
From ear to ear and mane
    to chin.
Happy Henry! Ho, ho, ho!
He's a happy horse to know.

Rub-a-dub-dub,
Scrub-a-scrub-scrub,
I'm taking a bubble bath
In the tub.
Rub-a-dub-dub,
Scrub-a-scrub-scrub,
I'm pulling the plug out.
Blub, blub, blub.

Big Book of Phonics Rhymes and Poems, p.23 p.11

Objective: Develop Listening Skills

READ THE POEM Read "Happy Henry" aloud. Ask questions to focus on the details.

> **What animal is this poem about?**
> **What is the animal's name?**
> **Why does the author think Henry is happy?**

CLAP FOR HENRY Reread "Happy Henry" and invite children to clap each time they hear *Henry*.

LISTEN AND FIND HENRY Have children stand in a circle and whisper their names. Secretly ask one child to

whisper *Henry* instead. Identify a child as the "listener." Give the listener a paper smiley face to hand to "Happy Henry" when Henry is found. Explain that the listener must find the child who is whispering *Henry*. The listener walks around the circle, listening as children whisper. Once found, the listener gives the child whispering *Henry* the smiley face. Repeat with a new listener and a new *Henry*.

Objective: Listen for /h/ and /b/

LISTEN FOR INITIAL /h/ Read the title "Happy Henry," emphasizing the initial /h/ sound. Have children repeat the words with you, segmenting the initial /h/ sound.

LISTEN FOR FINAL /b/ Read the poem "Tub Time," emphasizing the words with initial and final /b/. Have children repeat the words with you.

RESPOND TO THE SOUND Say sentences and have children raise a hand each time they hear /h/.

> **Hank wore a handsome hat on his head.**
> **Helen feeds the hungry hippopotamus.**

Say sentences and have children pretend to scrub their backs each time they hear /b/.

> **In the bath, I scrub and rub the dirt away.**
> **Bob took a cab to the bank.**

WHICH SOUND IS MISSING? Tell children you will say part of a word. Explain that they must say /h/ or /b/ to complete the word. Say: _ot.

Ask: *What sound is missing, /h/ or /b/?* Have children try both sounds, then decide. Repeat with other word parts and have children make words with /h/ or /b/.

> /h/ ___at, __em, ___id, __op, __ut;
> /b/ ta__, De__, cri__, __eg, __elt

Read Together

From Phonemic Awareness to Phonics

Objective: Identify /h/ H, h and /b/ B, b

IDENTIFY THE LETTERS
Display pages 23 and 11 in the *Big Book of Phonics Rhymes and Poems*. On each page, point to the letters, identify them, and say the sounds they stand for. Have children say each sound with you.

REREAD THE POEMS Reread the poems. Point to each word, emphasizing those with /h/ or /b/.

FIND WORDS WITH *H, h, B, b*
Have children use their fingers to frame words in the poems that have *H, h, B,* or *b*.

Happy Henry   Hh

Henry is a happy horse.
Henry likes to smile, of course.

Henry has a happy grin,
From ear to ear and mane to chin.

Happy Henry! Ho, ho, ho!
He's a happy horse to know.

Tub Time

Rub-a-dub-dub,
Scrub-a-scrub-scrub,
I'm taking a bubble bath
In the tub.

Rub-a-dub-dub,
Scrub-a-scrub-scrub,
I'm pulling the plug out.
Blub, blub, blub.

Big Book of Phonics Rhymes and Poems, p. 23, p. 11

OBJECTIVES

Children will:

- **identify and discriminate between /h/H,h and /b/B,b**
- **write the letters H,h and B,b**

ALTERNATE TEACHING STRATEGY

LETTERS /h/*h* and /b/*b*

For a different approach to teaching this skill, see pages T24 and Unit 5, T32.

▶ **Visual/Auditory/ Kinesthetic**

Review /h/h, /b/b

TEACH

Identify and Discriminate Between /h/H,h and /b/B,b

Tell children they will review the sounds /h/ and /b/ and write the letters *H,h, B,b.* Write the letters and have children say the sounds with you. Say: "How big is a baby hippo? Bigger than a baby hog?" Ask children to identify the words that begin with *h* by raising *hands* and the words that begin with *b* by *bobbing* their heads up and down.

Write H,h and B,b

Write *H,h* on one side of the chalkboard and *B,b* on the other side. Repeat the above sentences, and have children point to one letter or another when they recognize a word that begins with /h/ or /b/. Write the word, and have children write the letter *H, h, B,* or *b.*

PRACTICE

Complete the Pupil Edition Page

Read the directions on page 310 of the Pupil Edition, and make sure children clearly understand what they are being asked to do. Identify each picture, and complete the first item together. Then work the page with children, or have them complete the page independently.

ASSESS/CLOSE

Identify and Use H,h and B,b

Continue to play "How Big Is the Baby?" by naming other animals, such as *horse, hare, bird, butterfly, hen,* and by using other *h* and *b* words to ask if it is bigger: *house, balloon, book, hat, bike, helicopter.* Children record guesses by writing *h* or *b* on letter strips.

Name_____

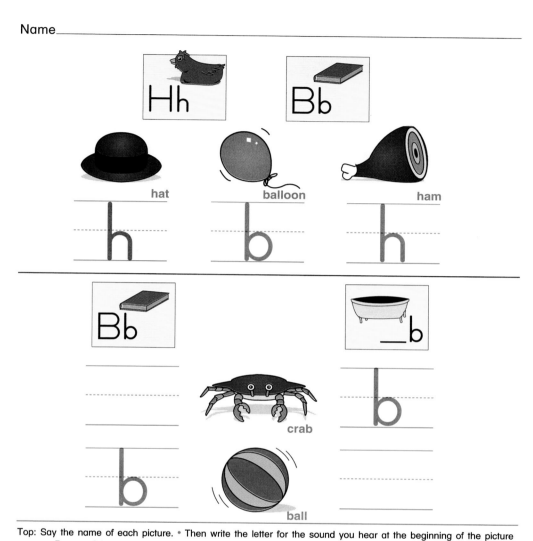

hat   balloon   ham

h   b   h

crab

b   ball

Top: Say the name of each picture. • Then write the letter for the sound you hear at the beginning of the picture name. • Bottom: Say the name of each picture. • If it begins with the sound /b/, write *b* to the left of the picture. • If it ends with the sound /b/, write *b* to the right of the picture.

McGraw-Hill School Division

310   Unit 6   Review   /h/h, /b/b

Pupil Edition, page 310

ADDITIONAL PHONICS RESOURCES

Practice Book, *page 310*
Phonics Workbook

McGraw-Hill School
TECHNOLOGY

Phonics CD-ROM
Activities for practice with
Initial and Final Letters

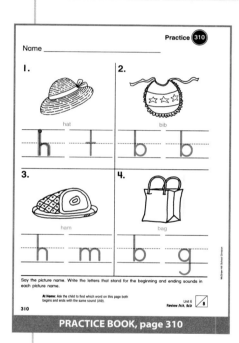

PRACTICE BOOK, page 310

Meeting Individual Needs for Phonics

EASY	ON-LEVEL	CHALLENGE	LANGUAGE SUPPORT
Give each child three *h* and *b* self-stick labels. Line up a *hat, ball, bat, hammer, handkerchief,* and *block* on a table, and have children place *h* and *b* labels on things whose names begin with /h/ or /b/.	**Show** pictures of objects whose names begin with *h* or *b*: *bug, hat, bed, hen, harp, bag*. Have children name the objects and write *b* or *h* on letter strips to show the first letter of each word.	**Lay** out a path of masking tape on the floor. At intervals, tape down an index card that shows *h* or *b*. Children take turns following the path. If they say a word that begins with the letter they land on, they can name another child to take their place.	**Help** ESL children practice /h/ and /b/ sounds by having them repeat the following greeting, inserting names that begin with /b/ or /h/: *Hello, Bill!* Invite children to suggest names, such as: *Bob, Betty, Hal, Helen, Hank.*

Teacher Read Aloud

Annie's Pet
by Barbara Brenner

Annie has 5 dollars to buy a pet, but each time she stops, she ends up with 1 dollar less. Can she get a pet for 0 dollars?

On her birthday, Annie went to the zoo with her parents. That's where she got a great idea. "I have five birthday dollars," she said to her family. "I'm going to buy an animal."

Annie didn't know what kind of animal she wanted. But she knew what she didn't want.

"I don't want a bear," she said. "Bears are too hairy. I don't want a snake. You can't take a snake for a walk."

"Try not to buy too big an animal," said her father.

"You don't want too small an animal," said her mother.

"Get a wild animal," said her brother.

"I don't want a wild animal," said Annie. "I want a pet."

So the very next day, Annie and her mom went off to find the perfect pet for Annie.

They walked down the street until they came to a house. There was a girl with a bird in front of the house.

Continued on page T2

Oral Comprehension

LISTENING AND SPEAKING Ask children what types of pets they have, and how they care for them. Tell children that they will hear a story about a girl who wants to buy a new pet. The story is realistic, because it is something that could happen in real life.

Explain that when Annie does one thing, it makes another thing happen. After you read the story, ask children what happened when Annie spent all of her money.

Activity Have small groups work together to write a different ending for the story. Have them decide what pet Annie finally found. Have children write, dictate, or draw pictures to show their endings.

▶ **Interpersonal/Spatial**

Real-Life Reading

1. Annie wanted to know more about dogs.

2. She had a great idea.

3. She went to the library.

4. The librarian helped her find a book about dogs.

40   41

Big Book of Real-Life Reading, pages 40–41

Objective: Use a Library/Media Center

READ THE PAGE Ask children to describe what a library looks like and why they go there. Ask how a library can help children to find information. Remind children of the story "Annie's Pet," and ask children how the story ended. Explain that Annie needed to find out more about dogs and that children will see pictures of what she did. Discuss the pictures and read the sentences.

ANSWER THE QUESTION Ask why the library was a good place for Annie to get information. Ask: *How can the librarian help you?* Discuss other ways that she could get information.

CENTER Activity

Cross Curricular: Math

WHERE DOES IT GO? Provide as many nonfiction library books for children as there are students in your class. Make sure the subjects are child-friendly, and include animals, space, and vehicles. Point out the cover and title page of each book. Show how children can get information from these parts of a book. Ask children which books they would choose to learn more about cars. Ask the same question regarding cats, horses, and spaceships. Encourage children to choose a book that interests them. Allow time for children to look through their chosen books.

▶ **Logical/Intrapersonal**

OBJECTIVES

Children will:

- **identify and read the high-frequency word *with***

MATERIALS

- **word cards from the *Word Play Book***
- ***Hop with a Hog***

TEACHING TIP

INSTRUCTIONAL

Write the word *with* on the chalkboard. Ask children how many letters are in the word. Continue with other high-frequency words, and make a graph that shows the number of letters in these words.

Introduce High-Frequency Words: *with*

PREPARE

Listen to Words Tell children that they will be learning a new word, *with*. Explain that when you do something *with* somebody else, it means that you do it together. Invite volunteers to tell about things they have done *with* someone else. Say the following sentence: *Annie went with her parents.* Read the sentence again, asking children to raise their hands when they hear the word *with*. Repeat this procedure using the sentence: *She went inside with her cat.*

TEACH

Model Reading the Word in Context Give the word card *with* to each child, and read the word. Reread the sentences, and have children raise their hands when they hear the word.

Identify the Word Write the sentences above on the chalkboard. Then run your hand under the words as you read each sentence. Tell children to hold up their word cards when they hear the word *with*. Then ask volunteers to point to and underline the word *with* in the sentences.

PRACTICE

Complete the Pupil Edition Page Read the directions on page 311 to children, and make sure they clearly understand what they are being asked to do. Complete the first item together. Then work through the page with children or have them complete the page independently.

ASSESS/CLOSE

Review the Page Review children's work, and guide children who are experiencing difficulty or need additional practice.

Name_____

with

1. Ken can sit <u>with</u> Kim.

2. Nan can run <u>with</u> Tim.

3. Ken can hop <u>with</u> Pam.

4. I can nap <u>with</u> the cat!

Read the sentence. • Then draw a line under the word *with* in the sentence.

Pupil Edition, page 311

Meeting Individual Needs for Vocabulary

EASY	ON-LEVEL	CHALLENGE	LANGUAGE SUPPORT
Ask children to name a place they like to go. Then have them form a sentence that tells who they like to go there *with*. Have children continue naming places, and forming sentences for each other.	**Give** each child a letter card: *w, i, t, h*. Put children in groups of four to form the word *with*. Then have each group work together to compose a sentence with the word *with*. Write children's sentences on chart paper.	**Label** sheets of drawing paper with the following sentence: *I like to play with* ___. Tell children to complete the sentence, and illustrate their answers.	**Guide** children to form sentences using *with* to link objects. You can have them think of an object in the classroom or at home: *My coat is with my hat.*

Develop Phonological Awareness

Listen

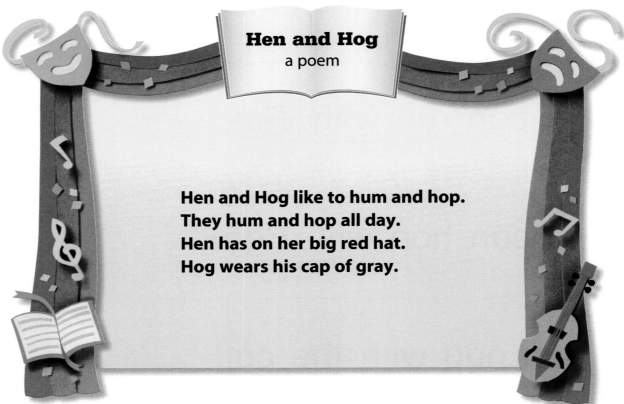

Hen and Hog
a poem

Hen and Hog like to hum and hop.
They hum and hop all day.
Hen has on her big red hat.
Hog wears his cap of gray.

Objective: Listen to Follow Directions

READ THE POEM Read the poem "Hen and Hog." Ask: *What do Hen and Hog like to do?* Invite volunteers to demonstrate how to hum and how to hop. Have children practice both actions.

> **hum   hop**

LISTEN AND FOLLOW DIRECTIONS Tell children you will make a statement and they must listen and follow directions. Say: *Hop if you are wearing red.* Pause while children respond. Say: *Hum if you are five.* Pause while children respond.

Continue with other directions involving hopping or humming.

GIVE DIRECTIONS Once children are familiar with the format, they might enjoy giving directions for others to follow.

> **Jump if you are six.**

Objective: Listen for Blending with Short *a, e, i, o, u* and /h/

LISTEN FOR BLENDING Tell children that when you read the poem "Hen and Hog" you will read one word in a funny way. Read the poem. Segment, then blend the sounds in *hen* each time. After reading the poem, say: /h/-/e/-/n/, hen. Have children repeat, then blend the sounds with you to say hen. Continue with other words from the poem.

> **hat his hop hum**

HOP FOR H Invite three volunteers to stand far apart at the front of the room. Assign the first child /h/, the middle child /a/, and the last child /m/. Have the volunteers hop sideways toward each other as the class says /h/-/a/-/m/. Continue until the volunteers are standing next to each other—and the class is saying *ham*. Finally, have children hop as they say /h/-/am/, ham.

Repeat the activity with new volunteers and other words with short vowels and the letter *h*.

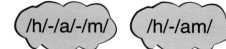

> **hem hip hot hug**

/h/-/a/-/m/   /h/-/am/   ham

Read Together

From Phonemic Awareness to Phonics

Objective: Relate *a, e, i, o, u* to Short Vowel Sounds

LISTEN TO RHYMING WORDS Ask children to listen to a list of rhyming words. Emphasize /at/ as you say each word. Have children repeat the words.

> **hat mat vat**

IDENTIFY THE LETTERS Write *hat, mat,* and *vat* in a column on the board. Point to each letter as you say: /h/-/a/-/t/. Identify the letters. Repeat with mat and vat. Ask a volunteer to circle and identify the letters that are the same in each word.

MAKE RHYMING WORDS Help children brainstorm rhyming words to add to the list.

> **bat fat pat sat tat**

As you write *bat*, emphasize /b/ as you write *b*, then emphasize /at/ as you write and circle the ending letters. Have children say /b/-/at/, then blend the sounds to say *bat*. Continue by adding rhyming words to the list.

hat   fat
mat   pat
vat   sat
bat

312B

OBJECTIVES

Children will:

- identify /a/*a*, /e/*e*, /i/*i*, /o/*o*, /u/*u*
- blend and read short *a, e, i, o, u* words
- write short *a, e, i, o, u* words
- review /h/*h*

MATERIALS

- letter cards from the *Word Building Book*

TEACHING TIP

INSTRUCTIONAL On the chalkboard, write *ha_, he_, hi_, ho_, hu_*. Blend sounds to say each incomplete word with a short vowel /a/, /e/, /i/, /o/, /u/. As children are blending initial *h* words during the lesson remind them of these sounds.

ALTERNATE TEACHING STRATEGY

BLENDING SHORT *a, e, i, o, u*

For a different approach to teaching this skill, see Unit 1, page T32; Unit 2, page T32; Unit 3, page T30; Unit 4, page T32; Unit 5, page T30.

▶ **Visual/Auditory/ Kinesthetic**

Review Blending with short *a, e, i, o, u*

TEACH

Identify *a, e, i, o, u* as Symbols for /a/, /e/, /i/, /o/, /u/

Tell children they will continue to read words with *a, e, i, o, u.*

- Display the *a, e, i, o, u* letter cards and say /a/, /e/, /i/, /o/, /u/. Have children repeat the sounds after you as you point to the cards.

BLENDING Model and Guide Practice

- Place the *h* card before the *a* card. Blend the sounds together and have children repeat after you.

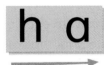 

- Place a *d* letter card after the *h* and *a* cards. Blend to read *had.*

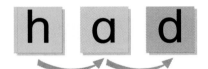 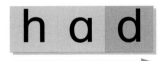

Use the Word in Context

- Ask children to use *had* in a sentence, reminding them that this word tells about something in the past. Say: *I had fun yesterday.*

Repeat the Procedure

- Use the following words to continue modeling and for guided practice with short *a, e, i, o, u: him, hop, hug, hat, hum, hog, hit.*

PRACTICE

Complete the Pupil Edition Page

Read aloud the directions on page 312. Identify each picture, and complete the first item together. Then work through the page with children, or have them complete the page independently.

ASSESS/CLOSE

Write Short *a, e, i, o, u* Words

Observe children as they complete page 312. Then ask them to write five words that have short *a, e, i, o,* or *u* in the middle and begin with h.

Name_____

1. h a t   hat

2. h o p   hop

3. h u g   hug

4. h i t   hit

McGraw-Hill School Division

Blend the sounds and say the word. • Write the word. • Draw a circle around the picture that goes with the word.

312   Unit 6   Review Blending with Short *a, e, i, o, u*

Pupil Edition, page 312

ADDITIONAL PHONICS RESOURCES

Practice Book, *page 312*
Phonics Workbook

McGraw-Hill School
TECHNOLOGY

Phonics CD-ROM
Activities for Practice with Blending and Segmenting

Practice 312

Name _____

1. h e n   hen   2. h u t   hut

3. h o p   hop   4. h i d   hid

Blend the sounds and say the word. Write the word. Draw a line under the picture that goes with the word.

At Home: Write *hop.* Take turns changing *hop* to *hip.* Change *hip* to *dip.* Change *dip* to *rip.* Together, decide if you made real words.

312

Review Blending with Short *a, e, i, o, e*   Unit 5

8

PRACTICE BOOK page 312

Meeting Individual Needs for Phonics

EASY	ON-LEVEL	CHALLENGE	LANGUAGE SUPPORT
Display letter cards *b, g,* and *h* on the chalkboard ledge. Have children point to and name the letter *h* and make the /h/ sound. Then ask them to repeat after you and blend sounds to read the following words: *hen, hop, had, him, hug, hat.*	**Give** children word cards: *hut, hog, ham, hit, hug, hat, hum, him.* Ask them to blend and read one word. Then invite them to read two other words that are like the first one in some way (other than initial *h*). Ask them how the words are alike.	**Go** around in a circle, having each child say *Hog had a ____* and draw from a hat a word card such as: *hen, hut, ham, hop, hat, hug.* Ask them to read the word aloud and say something about it such as: *Hog had a ham and it was huge.*	**Ask** children to chant the initial *h* short vowel sounds *ha-, he-, hi-, ho-, hu-* several times each as you point to them on the chalkboard. Then have them chant these words: *hat, hen, him, hot, hum.*

312

Guided Instruction

BEFORE READING

PREVIEW AND PREDICT Take a brief **picture walk** through the book, focusing on the illustrations.

Ask:

- Who is this story about? Where does it take place?

- Do you think the story is realistic, or is it make-believe? Why?

SET PURPOSES Children may be curious about this story. Alow them to ask questions about any pictures they may find interesting or unusual.

TEACHING TIP

To put book together:

1. Tear out the story page.

2. Cut along dotted line.

3. Fold each section on fold line.

4. Assemble book.

INSTRUCTIONAL If possible, find picture books in the library about medieval times and castles to share with the class.

Hop with a Hog

He can tug the big hog.

3

Don has a big hog.

2

The hog has a hat
with a red dot.

4

Guided Instruction

DURING READING

☑ **Initial *h***

☑ **Cause and Effect**

☑ **Concepts of Print**

☑ **High-Frequency Word: *with***

(1) **CONCEPTS OF PRINT** Model how to run your finger from left to right under each word as you read. Read the title, and then have children repeat the words after you as they track print.

(2) **INITIAL *h*** Have eight volunteers read the words on each page of the story that begin with *h*. (at least two words on each page) Make a class list of words beginning with *h*.

(3) **USE ILLUSTRATIONS** Ask children to share experiences they may have had using a mirror. Help them recognize that the mirror on page 4 shows a reflection of Don and the hog.

(4) **HIGH-FREQUENCY WORDS** Ask children to find the word *with*. Model tracking print and read the word *with*. Invite children to do the same.

LANGUAGE SUPPORT

ESL Explain that the word *hit* may have different meanings. If something or someone is a big hit, it shows that it was successful. Tell children that the hog and Don sang and danced for the king and queen, who enjoyed the entertainment.

Guided Instruction

DURING READING

⑤ INITIAL *h* Ask children to find the word that begin with *h.* (hum, hog) Ask them to think of classroom objects or classmates' names that begin with *h.*

⑥ CAUSE AND EFFECT Explain that when something happens in a story, it can cause something else to happen. Ask children to look at page 8 and tell why Don is hugging the hog. *(because their show went so well)*

ASSESSMENT

CAUSE AND EFFECT

HOW TO ASSESS Have children point out any action in the story and tell what caused it. *(For example, clapping and smiles caused by enjoyment of entertainment.)* You may wish to ask children to use the pictures in their book to aid their recall.

FOLLOW UP Have pairs of children act out a simple cause and effect action/reaction. Ask other children to tell what was the cause and what was its corresponding effect.

Don can hum for the hog.

5

Don and the hog are a big hit.

7

The hog can hop
with Don.

6

Don and the hog
hug and hug!

8

Guided Instruction

AFTER READING

RETURN TO PREDICTIONS AND PURPOSES
Ask children if their predictions about the story were correct. Ask if the story could really happen and what part the children enjoyed the most.

RETELL THE STORY Have children work in small groups to retell the story. Children visualize the events in the story and take turns telling about them.

LITERARY RESPONSE To help children respond to the story, ask:

Where were Don and his hog going?

What kind of show did Don do with his hog?

Invite children to draw and write about a castle. You may wish to provide books with photographs or illustrations.

CENTER Activity

Cross Curricular: Music

DRAWING MUSIC Use a tape player with headphones, and provide tapes with flute or lute music. Have children listen and describe what they hear. You may ask them to listen and use crayons or markers to draw a design as they listen. The colors and lines in the design can reflect how the music makes the children feel.

 OBJECTIVES

Children will:

- recognize cause and effect to understand a story

MATERIALS

- *Hop with a Hog*

TEACHING TIP

INSTRUCTIONAL Explain that court jesters entertained people during medieval times. Provide photographs or illustrations from reference books, if possible. Talk about the clothes that court jesters wore, and how they told stories, played music, and danced.

Review Cause and Effect

PREPARE

Recall the Story
Ask children to recall the story *Hop with a Hog*. Ask how the jester and the hog performed for the king and queen. Ask: "Why did the king and queen applaud? What was funny or entertaining about the performance?"

TEACH

Relate Story Events to Understand Cause and Effect
Reread the story together. Explain that sometimes when one thing happens, it makes something else happen. Have children look at page 3, and ask why Don is having difficulty pushing the pig. Explain the cause and effect relationship: The pig eats a lot, and is very large. He is heavy, and it is difficult for Don to push the wagon. Continue with page 8, asking children why Don and the hog are hugging.

PRACTICE

Complete the Pupil Edition Page
Read the directions on page 315 to the children, and make sure they clearly understand what they are asked to do. Identify each picture, and complete the first item together. Then work through the page with children or have them complete the page independently.

ASSESS/CLOSE

Review the Page
Review children's work, and guide children who are experiencing difficulty.

Name_____

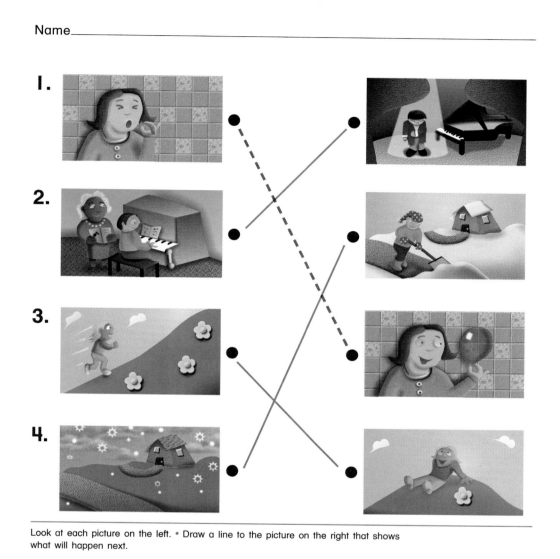

Look at each picture on the left. • Draw a line to the picture on the right that shows what will happen next.

Pupil Edition, page 315

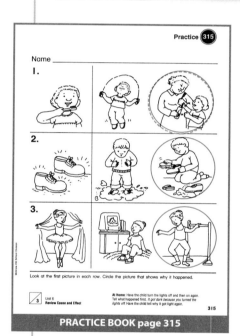

PRACTICE BOOK page 315

Meeting Individual Needs for Comprehension

EASY	ON-LEVEL	CHALLENGE	LANGUAGE SUPPORT
Ask children what happens when they play in the mud. Engage them to discuss the cause and effect of what happens in different kinds of play. Continue eliciting their responses to other familiar situations.	**Give** each child a small glass of water. Ask them to comment on what would happen to the taste if they added sugar, salt, or lemon to the water. Have them add one item, and ask them to describe how the taste of the water has changed.	**Ask** children to pretend that the electricity has gone out at home. Ask how they might prepare food, what they might use for light, and how they could keep warm. Point out the cause and effect relationships of each electrical appliance and how it is used.	**Reread** a favorite story to the class. Guide children to identify cause and effect relationships. Ask for their ideas on how different effects could come from different actions in the story.

315

Develop Phonological Awareness

Listen

The Big Sack
a poem

Duck and Cat run in the sack,
Hen and Pup go, too.
Cub and Pig hop in that bag.
Then Bug runs in to tug and tag.
Hog sees the sack and in he dips.
The pets run around and the big sack rips.

Objective: Focus on Sequence

READ THE POEM Display picture cards of the animals named in the poem "The Big Sack." Read the poem, and point to each animal as it is named.

RECITE THE POEM Once children are familiar with the poem, invite them to join in reciting the poem by saying the name of the animal you are pointing to.

LISTEN FOR SEQUENCE Ask children to close their eyes. Rearrange some of the pictures. Explain that, as you reread the poem, children must decide if the animals on the cards are in the same order as the animals in the poem.

After reading the poem, have children select cards that are out of order. Reread the poem, and invite children holding a card to place it where it belongs in the line of cards.

Objective: Listen for Blending with Short *a, e, i, o, u*

LISTEN FOR SEGMENTED WORDS Invite children to listen as you read "The Big Sack." Explain that you will say one word differently. Then read the poem, segmenting each sound in *cub* as you read the word. After reading, invite children to name the word you said differently. If a clue is needed, say /c/-/u/-/b/, and have children repeat the sounds. With the class, blend the sounds to say *cub*. Repeat with other words in the poem.

> cat   hen   pig   hog   duck

WHO'S IN THE SACK? Mention to children that, before hog got in the sack and ripped it, others got in the sack, too. Invite children to listen and guess who else is in the sack.

Say: *One more got in the sack. Do you know who? Listen and I will tell you. /r/-/a/-/t/ got in the sack, too!*

Pause while children repeat the sounds, then blend the sounds to determine who got in the sack. Repeat by segmenting other names, including names of children in the class.

> Hal   Dog   Ken   Deb   Pam   Cas   Fred

From Phonemic Awareness to Phonics

Objective: Relate *a, e, i, o, u* to Short Vowel Sounds

LISTEN FOR RHYMING WORDS Read the poem "The Big Sack," and invite children to name words in the poem that rhyme.

IDENTIFY THE LETTERS Write *bug* and *tug* in a column on the board. Point to each letter in *bug* as you say /b/-/u/-/g/. Identify the letters. Repeat with *tug*. Invite a volunteer to underline the letters that are the same in both words. Identify the letters *u* and *g* and ask children to say the sounds these letters stand for: /u/, /g/, /ug/.

MAKING RHYMING WORDS Write the following letters on index cards: *b, t, d, h, l, m, r,* and write *-ug* on seven index cards. Hand out the cards, and tell children to make words that rhyme with *bug* by matching letter cards with *-ug* cards.

> hug   lug   mug   rug

Ask partners to segment, then blend, the sounds to say their words; for example, /d/-/ug/, dug.

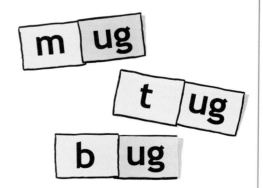

OBJECTIVES

Children will:

- identify /a/*a*, /e/*e*, /i/*i*, /o/*o*, /u/*u*

- blend and read short *a, e, i, o, u* words

- write short *a, e, i, o, u* words

- review /h/*h*, /b/*b*, /g/*g*, /k/*k,ck*, /l/*l*, /p/*p*, /r/*r*, /f/*f*, /k/*c*, /t/*t*, /m/*m*, /s/*s*, /d/*d*, and /n/*n*

MATERIALS

- letter cards from the *Word Building Book*

TEACHING TIP

INSTRUCTIONAL When children encounter words with initial letters *c* and *k* in the same activity, such as *cap* and *kit*, point out that both letters make the /k/ sound. Write several words with initial *c* and *k* on the chalkboard. Say the words, then invite volunteers to identify the first letter.

ALTERNATE TEACHING STRATEGY

BLENDING SHORT
a, e, i, o, u

For a different approach to teaching this skill, see Unit 1, page T32; Unit 2, page T32; Unit 3, page T30; Unit 4, page T32; Unit 5, page T30.

▶ **Visual/Auditory/ Kinesthetic**

Review Blending with short *a, e, i, o, u*

TEACH

Identify *a, e, i, o, u* as Symbols for /a/, /e/, /i/, /o/, /u/

Tell children they will continue to read words with *a, e, i, o, u.*

- Display the *a, e, i, o, u* letter cards and say /a/, /e/, /i/, /o/, /u/. Have children repeat the sounds as you point to the cards.

BLENDING Model and Guide Practice

- Place the *h* card before the *u* card. Blend the sounds together and have children repeat after you.

- Place the *m* letter card after the *h* and *u* cards. Blend to read *hum*.

Use the Word in Context

- Have children use *hum* in a sentence. Ask them if they know a birthday or holiday song, a lullaby or nursery rhyme, and invite them to hum it.

Repeat the Procedure

- Use the following words to continue modeling and guided practice with short *a, e, i, o, u*: *hen, ham, hut, cut, hip, hot, kid.*

PRACTICE

Complete the Pupil Edition Page

Read aloud the directions on page 316. Identify each picture, and complete the first item together. Then work through the page with children, or have them complete the page independently.

ASSESS/CLOSE

Build Short *a, e, i, o, u* Words

Observe children as they complete page 316. Show two consonant letter cards and have children select a medial vowel card.

Name_____

1. hat (ham)

    ham

2. (men) mop

    men

3. (duck) luck

    duck

4. dog (bib)

    bib

Draw a circle around the word that names the picture. • Say the word. • Then write the word.

McGraw-Hill School Division

Pupil Edition, page 316

ADDITIONAL PHONICS RESOURCES

Practice Book, *page 316*

Phonics Workbook

McGraw-Hill School

TECHNOLOGY

Phonics CD-ROM

Activities for Practice with Blending and Segmenting

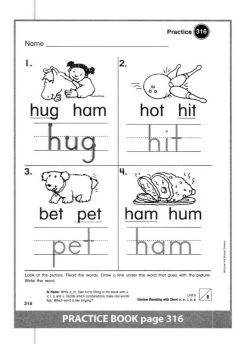

Practice 316

Name _____

1. hug ham

    hug

2. hot hit

    hit

3. bet pet

    pet

4. ham hum

    ham

Look at the picture. Read the words. Draw a line under the word that goes with the picture. Write the word.

At Home: Write *h_m.* Take turns filling in the blank with *a, e, i, o,* and *u.* Decide which combinations make real words. Ask: Which word is like singing?

316   Unit 6
Review Blending with Short *a, e, i, o, u*   8

PRACTICE BOOK page 316

Meeting Individual Needs for Phonics

EASY	ON-LEVEL	CHALLENGE	LANGUAGE SUPPORT
Write these words on the chalkboard: *hop, hat, bet, hut, kid, cot, hip, hen, bad, gum.* Ask children to sort the words into groups that have the same middle letter. Show children how to write headings *a, e, i, o, u* on a sheet of paper and list the words in columns.	**On** the chalkboard write *a, e, i, o, u.* Give children letter cards *h, b, g, k, ck, l, p, r, f, c, t, m, s, d, n.* Circle a vowel and ask children to use their letter cards to make a word.	**Display** the word cards *ham, met, tip, pod, dug* in random order and ask children to arrange them so each word begins with the last letter of the word before it (as shown). Invite children to continue adding words, such as: *gum, mad, dip, pot, tack, kid.*	**Have** children repeat each short *a, e , i, o, u* word you write on the chalkboard, blending to read aloud: *fan, bat, pet, dip, rip, mop, lock, hug, cut.* Show gestures to pantomime the words and ask children to act them out as they read them.

316

Reread the Decodable Story

Hop with a Hog

☑ **Hop with a Hog**
☑ **Initial** *h*
☑ **Cause and Effect**
☑ **High-Frequency Word:**
   with

Hop with a Hog

Guided Reading

SET PURPOSES Have children discuss what their purpose is for rereading the story. Children may wish to find out more about the story.

REREAD THE BOOK As you reread the story, keep in mind any problems children experienced during the first reading. Use the following questions to guide reading.

① **INITIAL** *h* Ask children to look again at page 8, blend sounds, and read the last word: *h-u-g hug*. Ask what other word in the sentence starts with *h*. *(hog)*

② **CAUSE AND EFFECT** Have children describe the action on page 3. *(Don is tugging the hog.)* Ask children why he might need to do that. *(The hog and cat are very heavy.)*

RETURN TO PURPOSES Ask children if they found out what they needed to know from the story. See if they have any unanswered questions.

LITERARY RESPONSE Have children fold drawing paper into thirds. Ask them to draw what happens first, next, and last in the story.

INFORMAL ASSESSMENT

INITIAL /h/H,h
HOW TO ASSESS Choose *h* words from the story, and have children blend to read. Note if they are able to recognize sounds for letters and blend.

FOLLOW UP Use letter cards to blend *h* words from the story: *hop, hog, hug.*

Read the Patterned Book

Hen Had Her Ham

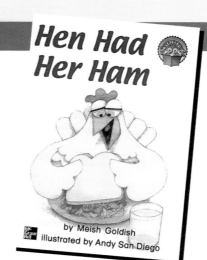

☑ Initial *H, h*
☑ Cause and Effect
☑ High-Frequency Word: *with*
☑ Concepts of Print

by Meish Goldish
illustrated by Andy San Diego

Guided Reading

PREVIEW AND PREDICT Read the title and the author's and the illustrator's name. Take a **picture walk** through pages 2-4, noting the setting of the story and the characters. Ask whether the story seems to be real or fantasy. Have children make a prediction about what will happen in the story.

SET PURPOSES Have children decide what they want to find out from the story. Tell children you will read to find out what will happen to the hen. Tell them that the story contains words with the letter *H, h.*

READ THE BOOK Use the following prompts while the children are reading, or after they have read independently. Remind them to run their fingers under each word as they read.

Pages 2-3: Point to the word that begins with *w. Let's read it together:* with. *High-Frequency Words*

Pages 4-5: Model: *I can use what I know about short a to read the word* had. *Each letter makes its own sound. Let's blend these sounds together,* h-a-d had. *Can you think of another word that rhymes with had? Phonics and Blending*

Pages 6-7: *Can you find a word on page 6 that is also on page 7? (Hen, had, her with) Let's say the letters together to see if the word is the same. Concepts of Print*

Page 8: *Sometimes one event in a story can lead to something else. Why does Hen need water? (The peppers were too hot to eat.) Cause and Effect*

RETURN TO PREDICTIONS AND PURPOSES Ask children if they found out what they needed to know from the story. See if their predictions were correct.

LITERARY RESPONSE The following questions will help focus children's responses:

• *What item from the story would you put on a ham sandwich?*

• *What kind of sandwich would you like to make? Write about it in your journal, and draw a picture.*

LANGUAGE SUPPORT

 **ESL** Write the following words with corresponding pictures on index cards: *ham, hot, Hen.* Blend the sounds and read the words together. Then reread the story with the children.

CENTER Activity

Cross Curricular: Science

PYRAMID OF FOOD Draw a food pyramid with each section labeled (*carbohydrates, fruits, vegetables, meat, dairy, sweets and fats*) Explain which foods go in each section. Have children draw other foods that fit in each section. Share the food pyramid with the class.

▶ Spatial

317C *Hop with a Hog*

OBJECTIVES

Children will:

- identify and read the high-frequency word *with*

MATERIALS

- word cards from the *Word Play Book*
- *Hop with a Hog*

TEACHING TIP

INSTRUCTIONAL Write the high-frequency word *with* on the chalkboard and have children give you a special signal when they hear or see the word throughout the day.

Review with, go, the, me, and

PREPARE

Listen to Words Tell children that they will review the word *with*. Read the following sentence, and have children raise hands when they hear the word *with*: *The hog danced with the knight.*

TEACH

Model Reading the Word in Context Reread the decodable book. Ask children to listen for the word *with*.

Identify the Word Tell children to first look at their word cards, and then to look for the word in the story. Read the sentences, tracking print, and ask children to come up and point to the word *with*. Have volunteers put a stick-on dot below the word.

Review High-Frequency Words Hold up word cards for the following: *the, a, my, that, and, I, is, said, we, are, you, have, to, me, go, do, for, he, she, has.* Children read the words together.

PRACTICE

Complete the Pupil Edition Page Read the directions on page 317 to children, and make sure they clearly understand what they are being asked to do. Complete the first item together. Then work through the page with children or have them complete the page independently.

ASSESS/CLOSE

Review the Page Review children's work, and guide children who are experiencing difficulty or need additional practice.

Name_____

1.

Ben said, "Go with me."

_____

2.

Pam said, "You can go with me."

_____

3.

I ran to the den with Pam and Ben.

_____

Read each sentence. • Draw a circle around the word *with* where you see it in each sentence. **1.** Draw a line under the word *go*. **2.** Draw a line under the word *me*. **3.** Draw a line under the words *the* and *and*.

Unit 6   Review *with, go, the, me, and*   **317**

ALTERNATE TEACHING STRATEGY

HIGH-FREQUENCY WORDS: *with*

For a different approach to teaching the skill, see page T27.

▶ **Visual/Auditory/ Kinesthetic**

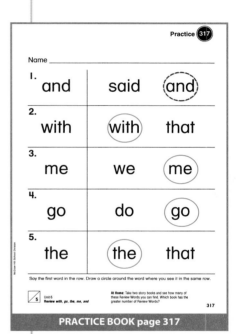

PRACTICE BOOK page 317

Meeting Individual Needs for Vocabulary

EASY	ON-LEVEL	CHALLENGE	LANGUAGE SUPPORT
Give each child a word card and read the word *with*. Then say sentences that do or do not use the word *with*. Children hold up their word cards if they hear the word.	**Have** children think of something else that Hog could do *with* the knight. Have children draw a picture and then dictate a sentence to you describing it.	**Have** groups of children rewrite the story, changing the character of Hog to a different animal. Children can write text or dictate sentences to you. Have them use the word *with* in each sentence. If they write, have them underline the word *with*.	**Show** pictures of different types of food. Have children name foods they like to eat together: *eggs with toast, peanut butter with jelly, bread with butter,* and so on.

317

GRAMMAR/SPELLING
CONNECTIONS
Model subject-verb agreement, complete sentences, and correct tense so that students may gain increasing control of grammar when speaking and writing.

Interactive Writing

Write a Poster

Prewrite

LOOK AT THE STORY PATTERN Reread the story *The Earth and I*. Discuss the story pattern: the boy talks about how he and the Earth are friends. Then talk about how the boy was a friend to the Earth. Make a picture/word list.

Draft

CREATE A POSTER If possible, show examples of posters, and explain that a poster gives information in words and pictures. Tell children that they will work with a partner to make a poster showing how people can save the Earth.

- Begin by giving pairs of children large sheets of drawing paper. Have them help you write the title on each: *Save the Earth*.

- Have children use the list and brainstorm ways that people can improve the environment. Children plan their posters. Help them write text, and have them illustrate the posters.

Publish

COMPLETE THE POSTER Have children make any changes, and complete the posters.

The Earth and I are friends.
We grow trees together.

Presentation Ideas

PRESENT THE POSTER Have pairs of children present their poster to the rest of the children. Children read the text, explain their pictures, and answer questions. Then display the posters.

PARTNERS

▶ **Representing/Viewing**

ROLE PLAY AN IDEA Have one child act out an idea from his or her poster. Others guess the idea.

GROUP

▶ **Representing/Viewing**

COMMUNICATION TIPS

- **Speaking** Encourage children to track print when they read text on their posters. Remind them to speak loudly and clearly.

TECHNOLOGY TIP

Explore environmental concerns on the Internet with children.

LANGUAGE SUPPORT

ESL Read the class posters, and clarify any words that are confusing.

Meeting Individual Needs for Writing

EASY	ON-LEVEL	CHALLENGE
Draw a Picture Show children a globe or a picture of Earth. Children draw a picture of the planet and label it.	**Write a Verse** Sing the following to the tune of "Happy Birthday": *We can save the Earth* (two times) *We can (pick up our trash)* *We can save the Earth.* Have children write and sing new verses to the song.	**Journal Entry** Have children pretend to be the Earth. Have them write a journal entry explaining how they feel when people work to save the environment.

We Win

The variety of literature in this lesson will offer children several opportunities to read and listen to stories about choices that enrich lives.

We Win!

Decodable Story, pages 325–326 of the Pupil Edition

Listening Library Audiocassette

Hello, Winter!

by Suzanne Martinucci
illustrated by Bruce Armstrong

Patterned Book, page 329B

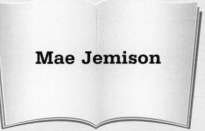

Mae Jemison

Teacher Read Aloud, page 323A

WRITTEN BY JUDY NAYER
ILLUSTRATED BY SUSAN SWAN

ABC Big Book, pages 319A–319B

Listening Library Audiocassette

The Earth and I

FRANK ASCH

Literature Big Book, pages 321A–321B

Listening Library Audiocassette

**Pupil Edition,
pages 318–329**

**Big Book of Real-Life Reading,
page 42**

**Big Book of Phonics Rhymes and
Poems, pages 57, 58**

 Listening
Library
Audiocassette

ADDITIONAL RESOURCES

**Practice Book,
pages 318–319**

- **Phonics Kit**
- **Language Support Book**
- **Alternate Teaching Strategies,** pp T28–T29

McGraw-Hill School
TECHNOLOGY

Phonics CD-ROM Provides
extra phonics support.

interNET CONNECTION Research & Inquiry Ideas.

Visit www.mhschool.com

We Win!

READING AND LANGUAGE ARTS

- **Phonological Awareness**
- **Phonics** *initial /w/w*
- **Comprehension**
- **Vocabulary**
- **Beginning Reading Concepts**
- **Listening, Speaking, Viewing, Representing**

DAY 1

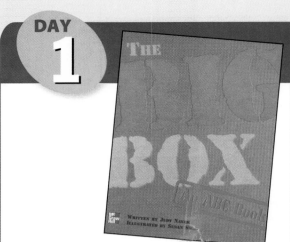

DAY 2

Focus on Reading Skills
Develop Phonological Awareness, 318G-318H
"Wee Willie Winkie" *Big Book of Phonics Rhymes and Poems,* 57

 Introduce Initial /w/w, 318I-318
Practice Book, 318
Phonics/Phonemic Awareness
Practice Book

 **Phonics** CD-ROM

Read the Literature
Read *The Big Box: An ABC Book* **Big Book,** 319A-319B
Shared Reading

Build Skills
☑ Shapes: Square, Rectangle, 319C-319
Practice Book, 319

Focus on Reading Skills
Develop Phonological Awareness, 320A-320B
"Wally Walrus" *Big Book of Phonics Rhymes and Poems,*58

Review Initial /w/w, 320C-320
Practice Book, 320
Phonics/Phonemic Awareness
Practice Book

 **Phonics** CD-ROM

Read the Literature
Read *The Earth and I* **Big Book,** 321A-321B
Shared Reading

Build Skills
☑ Make Inferences, 321C-321
Practice Book, 321

- **Cross Curriculum**

 Cultural Perspectives, 319B

 **Art,** 321B

- **Writing**

 Writing Prompt: If you had a big box, what would you make it into?

 Journal Writing, 319B
Letter Formation, 318I

 Writing Prompt: Write about something you like to do with the earth.

 Journal Writing, 321B
Letter Formation, 320C

DAY 3

Mae Jemison

Focus on Reading Skills

Develop Phonological Awareness, 322A-322B

"Wee Willie Winklie" and "Wally Walrus" *Big Book of Phonics Rhymes and Poems,* 57-58

 **Review /h/h,/b/b,** 322C-322

Practice Book, 322

Phonics/Phonemic Awareness
Practice Book

Phonics CD-ROM

Read the Literature

Read "Mae Jemison" Teacher Read Aloud, 323A-323B
Shared Reading

Read the Big Book of Real-Life Reading, 42-43
☑ Library/Media Center

Build Skills

☑ High-Frequency Words: *was,* 323C-323
Practice Book, 323

 Activity Cultural Perspectives, 323B

 Writing Prompt: Would you like to travel in a space shuttle? Write about what it would be like.

DAY 4

We Win!

Focus on Reading Skills

Develop Phonological Awareness, 324A-324B

"Pet Pals"

 **Review Blending with Short** *a, e, i, o, u,* 324C-324

Practice Book, 324

Phonics/Phonemic Awareness
Practice Book

Phonics CD-ROM

Read the Literature

Read "We Win!" Decodable Story, 325/326A-325/326D

☑ Initial /w/w; Blending
☑ Make Inferences
☑ High-Frequency Words: *was*
☑ Concepts of Print

Build Skills

☑ Make Inferences, 327A-327
Practice Book, 327

 **Activity** Math, 325/326D

 Writing Prompt: What do you think Ken did at the end of this story?

Letter Formation,
Practice Book, 325-326

DAY 5

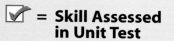

We Win!

Hello, Winter!

by Suzanne Martinucci
illustrated by Bruce Armstrong

Focus on Reading Skills

Develop Phonological Awareness, 328A-328B

"A Pup Named Tag"

 **Review Blending with Short** *a, e, i, o, u,* 328C-328

Practice Book, 328

Phonics/Phonemic Awareness
Practice Book

Phonics CD-ROM

Read the Literature

Reread "We Win!" Decodable Story, 329A
Read "Hello, Winter!" Patterned Book, 329B
Guided Reading
☑ Initial /w/w; Blending
☑ Make Inferences
☑ High-Frequency Words: *was*
☑ Concepts of Print

Build Skills

☑ High-Frequency Words: *was, with, I, he, she,* 329C-329
Practice Book, 329

 **Activity** Art, 329B

 Writing Prompt: Write about a good choice that you can make to keep the earth healthy and strong.

Interactive Writing, 329A-329B

Develop Phonological Awareness

Listen

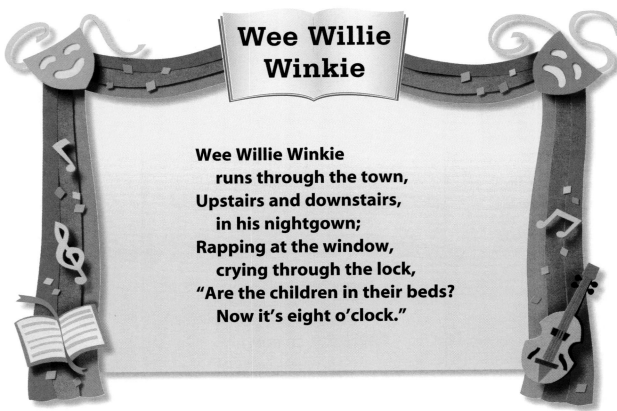

Wee Willie Winkie

Wee Willie Winkie
runs through the town,
Upstairs and downstairs,
in his nightgown;
Rapping at the window,
crying through the lock,
"Are the children in their beds?
Now it's eight o'clock."

Objective: Listen for Rhyming Words

READ THE POEM Read the poem "Wee Willie Winkie," emphasizing the rhyming words. Then reread the poem, omitting the rhyming words. Have children say the rhyming words when you get to them.

> town   nightgown   lock   o'clock

IDENTIFY OTHER RHYMING WORDS Say the following three words: down, ball, frown. Ask a volunteer to say the words that rhyme. (down, frown) Continue this activity with the following words:

> rock, tock, car; tall, block, dock; dog, flock, sock

PLAY A RHYMING GAME Have children sit in a circle. Say the word Wee. Tell children that wee means very small. Hold up a small beanbag. Tell children they will play a rhyming game with this little wee beanbag. The way to play is to say a word that rhymes with Wee and then pass the beanbag to the person next to you. Play the game until all children have had a chance.

> me   be   three   she   tea
> flee   we   see   agree

Objective: Listen for Initial /w/

LISTEN FOR SOUNDS Say the name *Will*. Emphasize the /w/ sound. Have children repeat the sound after you. Then read the title of the poem. Ask which words begin with /w/. (Wee Willie Winkie) Then say the following words. Show children how to make a *W* with their fingers. Then have them make a *W* if they hear a word that begins with /w/.

wait wall tan win bat call

CLAP FOR SYLLABLES Reread the word *Wee*. Have children clap to identify how many syllables it has. (one) Then say the name *Willie*. Have children clap to identify how many syllables. (two) Continue with the name *Winkie*.

Then say the following words that begin with /w/. Have children clap to determine how many syllables each word has. Compare the number of syllables in each word.

whale water watermelon
white wonder Washington

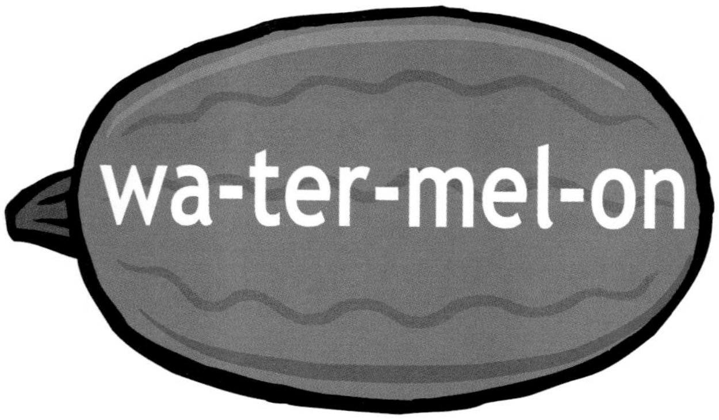
wa-ter-mel-on

Read Together

From Phonemic Awareness to Phonics

Objective: Identify Initial /w/W,w

IDENTIFY THE LETTER FOR THE SOUND Explain to children that the letter *w* stands for the /w/ sound. Display the *Big Book of Phonics Rhymes and Poems*, page 57. Point to the letters in the corner and identify them. Have children say the sound with you.

REREAD THE POEM Reread the poem. Ask volunteers to point to the *w's* in the poem. Point out if the letters are capital or lowercase. Have children put a stick-on note below each *W, w* word. Then reread the poem and have children make the /w/ sound every time you get to a word that begins with *W, w*.

Wee Willie Winkie
window

COUNT HOW MANY LETTERS Write the words that begin with *W, w* on the chalkboard. Have children count how many letters are in each word. Ask children which word is the longest. Then ask which word is the shortest. Have children brainstorm other *w* words. Encourage children to think of long words.

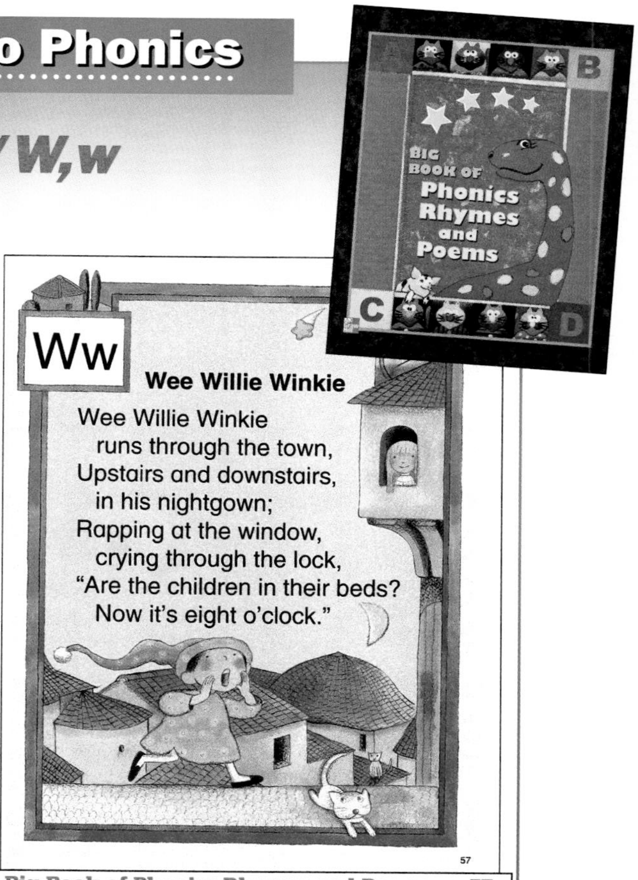
B
Big Book of Phonics Rhymes and Poems
C
D
Ww
Wee Willie Winkie
Wee Willie Winkie
runs through the town,
Upstairs and downstairs,
in his nightgown;
Rapping at the window,
crying through the lock,
"Are the children in their beds?
Now it's eight o'clock."
57
Big Book of Phonics Rhymes and Poems, p. 57

OBJECTIVES

Children will:

- identify the letters *W,w*
- identify /w/ *W,w*
- form the letters *W,w*

MATERIALS

- letter cards and picture cards from the Word Building Book

TEACHING TIP

INSTRUCTIONAL

Children may need to review *M,m* and talk about how the letters are the same as and different from *W,w*. Give them tactile letters cut from rigid foam or heavy cardboard. Help them sort the letters to show *m* and *w*.

ALTERNATE TEACHING STRATEGY

INITIAL /w/ *w*

For a different approach to teaching this skill, see page T28.

▶ **Visual/Auditory/ Kinesthetic**

Introduce Initial /w/w

TEACH

Identify /w/ W, w
Tell children they will learn to write the sound /w/ with the letters *W, w*. Write the letters on the chalkboard, and have children make the sound with you. Ask them to say the sound /w/ and to wave when they hear a word that begins with /w/. Speak slowly, emphasizing the initial *w's: Wanda washed with warm…* . Then stop, and invite children to guess the next word. (water)

Form W, w
Display *W, w* letter cards, and, with your back to the children, trace the letters in the air. Have them do the same. Give children rolls of modeling clay, and ask them to shape the letters on top of large, laminated letter cards *W* and *w*. Then ask them to write both forms of the letter *w* on letter strips. Point out that the two forms are the same but the sizes are different.

PRACTICE

Complete the Pupil Edition Page
Read the directions on page 318 of the Pupil Edition, and make sure children clearly understand what they are being asked to do. Identify each picture, and complete the first item together. Then work through the page with children, or have them complete the page independently.

ASSESS/CLOSE

Identify and Use W, w
Show pictures of the following: *watch, hat, wagon, wig, ball*. Ask children to name each object pictured, then ask them to say which objects' names do and do not begin with *w*. Ask them to write a *w* on a letter strip for each *w* picture.

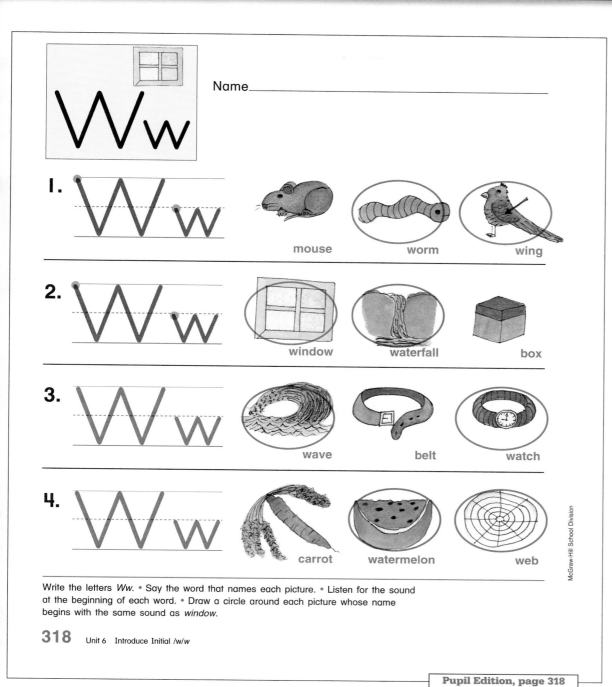

Name_____

1. W w — mouse · worm · wing

2. W w — window · waterfall · box

3. W w — wave · belt · watch

4. W w — carrot · watermelon · web

Write the letters *Ww.* • Say the word that names each picture. • Listen for the sound at the beginning of each word. • Draw a circle around each picture whose name begins with the same sound as *window.*

318   Unit 6   Introduce Initial /w/*w*

McGraw-Hill School Division

Pupil Edition, page 318

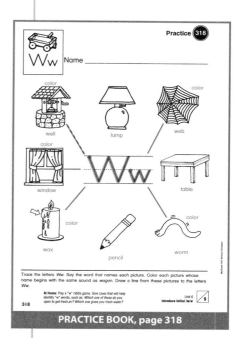

ADDITIONAL PHONICS RESOURCES

Practice Book, *page 318*
Phonics Workbook

McGraw-Hill School
TECHNOLOGY

Phonics CD-ROM
Activities for practice with Initial Letters

Practice **318**

W w   Name _____

well · lamp · web
window · W w · table
wax · pencil · worm

Trace the letters *Ww.* Say the word that names each picture. Color each picture whose name begins with the same sound as *wagon.* Draw a line from these pictures to the letters *Ww.*

At Home: Play a "w" riddle game. Give clues that will help identify "w" words, such as: Which one of these do you open to get fresh air? Which one gives you fresh water?

318

Unit 6
Introduce Initial /w/*w*

PRACTICE BOOK, page 318

Meeting Individual Needs for Phonics

EASY	ON-LEVEL	CHALLENGE	LANGUAGE SUPPORT
Have children roll out modeling clay in the shape of a worm. Then have them use their worm to form the letter *w.* You may also wish to have groups of four children form a *w* with their bodies.	**Have** children answer rhyming riddles for words that begin with /w/. For example, what rhymes with dragon and starts with /w/? (wagon) Use these words: *cake/wake, talk/walk, ball/wall, gave/wave, day/way.* Write each new word and have children circle the *w.*	**Play** "Charades" using action words that begin with *w.* Have children form two teams. Give one team a word, and help them think up a way to act it out silently. The other team has to guess. Then they reverse roles. Children keep score by writing *w* for each correct guess.	**Chant** the following words with repeated initial *w's* to reinforce children's recognition of initial /w/ words: *W-w-we w-w-want to make a w-w-wish. W-w-we w-w-wish to . . .* Invite children to suggest something they would like to do. Write *w* on chart paper, and have children trace the letter.

318

Children will:

- use story details
- recognize words with initial *w*
- understand alphabetical order

TEACHING TIP

Help children recognize which uppercase and lowercase letters are formed the same way. Use an alphabet chart and compare the letters for *a* and *b*. Then have children look at *c* and ask: *Are these two letters formed the same way? Are they the same size?*

Read the Big Book

Before Reading

Develop Oral Language

Sing "The Alphabet song" together. The song is on page 2 of the Big Book of Phonics Rhymes and Chimes. Then ask a volunteer to point to the letters on an alphabet chart as you sing the song again.

Remind children that they read a story about friends who had a box. Ask them to recall some of the ideas they had.

Set Purposes

Model: We read a story about some friends who wanted to make something out of a box. As we read the story today, let's look at the materials the children would need to make something. Let's also look for the words on each page that begin with the same letter on the page.

"We can make a **quilt** for a bed," said Gina.

20

"We can make a **robot**," said Matt.

21

The Big Box, pages 20-21

During Reading

Read Together
- Before you begin to read, point to the first word in the first sentence. Explain that this is where you will begin to read. Continue to track print as you read the story. *Tracking Print*

- Before you read page 4, ask a child to locate the letter on the page and identify it. Then have the child find the word on the page that begins with the same letter. Continue through the story. *Phonics*

- After you read page 5, discuss the illustration of the boat. Ask what materials children would need to make the boat. Continue with other pictures in the book. *Use Illustrations*

- Make the /w/ sound and have children make the sound with you. After you read page 26, ask children to say two words that begin with that sound. (we, wagon) *Phonics*

"We can make a **castle**," said Matt.

After Reading

Literary Response

JOURNAL WRITING Ask children to pretend that they have a shoebox. Have them draw and write about what they would make from it.

ORAL RESPONSE Ask questions, such as:

- *What materials would you need?*

- *How would you play with the box?*

ABC Activity
Put magnetic letters in a box. Have children sit in a circle. One child closes his or her eyes, takes a letter, and guesses what it is. Children take turns.

INFORMAL ASSESSMENT

Place letter cards upside-down on the table. Child picks up a card, says the letter, and tells the letter that comes next.

CULTURAL PERSPECTIVES

QUILTS Share that quilts have been made for hundreds of years in Asia, Africa, and Europe. In the U.S., American women used to make quilts to celebrate special occasions.

▶ **Intrapersonal**

Activity Provide each child with a square piece of paper and magic markers. Ask each child to draw a self-portrait. Place self-portraits face down in the shape of a square. Tape the squares together along the borders. Carefully turn the quilt over and display the classroom quilt.

OBJECTIVES

Children will:

• identify squares and rectangles

MATERIALS

• *The Big Box:* an ABC Book

TEACHING TIP

MANAGEMENT

Assemble paper shapes in a variety of sizes and colors. Sort them according to shape, and store each kind of shape in a separate container. Label each container with a paper shape.

Review Shapes: Square, Rectangle

PREPARE

Describe Familiar Shapes
Hold up a large paper square and have children describe it. Let volunteers count the sides and corners. Have children find other squares in the classroom. Then repeat with a paper rectangle.

TEACH

Recognize Shapes
Display the Big Book, *The Big Box*, and recall the story. Take a picture walk through the book, and have children find squares and rectangles. Make a picture or a word list together. Then see if you can find similar objects in the classroom or school.

PRACTICE

Complete the Pupil Edition Page
Read the directions on page 319 to the children, and make sure they clearly understand what they are asked to do. *Identify each picture, and complete the first item.* Then work through the page with the children, or have them complete the page independently.

ASSESS/CLOSE

Review the Page
Check children's work on the Pupil Edition page. Note areas where children need extra help.

Name_____

Find the squares in the picture. • Color them one color. • Find the rectangles in the picture. • Color them another color.

Unit 6   Review Shapes: Square, Rectangle   **319**

Pupil Edition, page 319

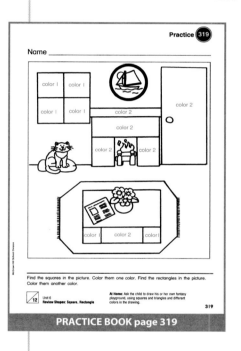
Meeting Individual Needs for Beginning Reading Concepts

EASY	ON-LEVEL	CHALLENGE	LANGUAGE SUPPORT
Have children use clay to make squares and rectangles. Demonstrate how to roll out the clay. Then use craft sticks or plastic knives to cut around the faces of blocks. Ask children to tell about the sides and corners.	**Children** sort paper squares and rectangles into two groups. Ask how the two groups are alike and how they are different.	**Have** pairs of children trace the faces of boxes of different sizes. Ask them to identify the shapes they make.	**Children** may have difficulty distinguishing squares from rectangles. Help children distinguish between shapes by having them use their fingers to trace around the sides of pipe cleaners. Encourage children to use the words *long* and *short* to tell about the sides.

319

Develop Phonological Awareness

Listen

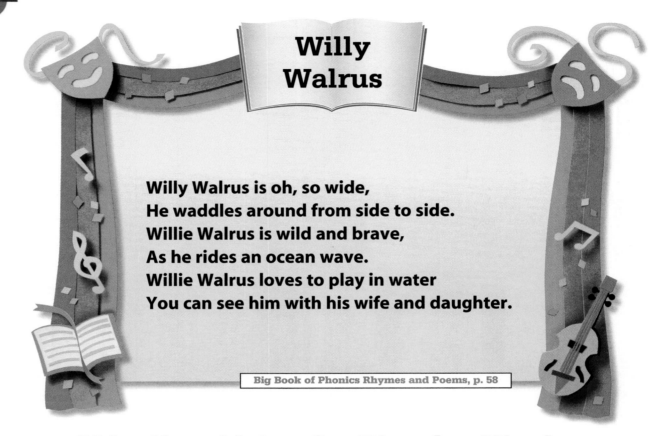

Willy Walrus

Willy Walrus is oh, so wide,
He waddles around from side to side.
Willie Walrus is wild and brave,
As he rides an ocean wave.
Willie Walrus loves to play in water
You can see him with his wife and daughter.

Big Book of Phonics Rhymes and Poems, p. 58

Objective: Listen for Rhyming Words

LISTEN TO THE POEM

- Read the poem "Willie Walrus" to children.
- Then reread the poem, emphasizing the rhyming words.

> **wide side   brave wave   water daughter**

- Read the poem again, omitting the last word in lines 2, 4, and 6. Ask children to chime in and say them.

SUBSTITUTE NEW WORDS

- Read the poem again. Then explain to children that you will substitute new rhyming words. Point out that the words might not make sense.

- Read the poem, two lines at a time. Substitute the following words:

> **side—> ride   wave —> cave   water —> otter**

- Children say the words that were substituted.

Objective: Listen for Initial /w/

SEGMENTING

- Say the word *wide* and emphasize the initial /w/ sound. Then say the word *Willie*, and determine that both words begin with the same sound.
- Then read each line of the poem slowly. Children hold up fingers to show how many times they hear a word that begins with /w/.

RECOGNIZE THE SOUND

- Say the following words. Children raise a hand if the word begins with /w/.

> **wet   wild   west   best   fin   win**

DIFFERENTIATE INITIAL SOUNDS

- Tell children you will say two words and they need to repeat the word that has the /w/ sound.

> **slide/wide   ball/wall   rent/went**
> **worm/germ   wind/find   fill/will**

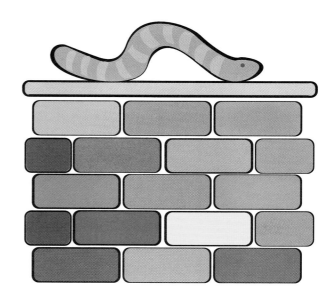

Read Together

From Phonemic Awareness to Phonics

Objective: Identify Initial /w/ *w, W*

IDENTIFY THE LETTER FOR THE SOUND

- Explain to children the letter *w* stands for the sound /w/. Say the sound and have children repeat it.
- Then display page 58 in the Big Book of Phonics Rhymes and Poems. Point to the letters in the corner of the page and identify them. Point out that the uppercase and lowercase letters are formed the same way. Have children repeat the sound after you.

REREAD THE POEM

- Read the poem again, pointing to each word. Have children *wave* when you read a word that begins with /w/.

WHICH LETTER IS W?

- Write the letters *W, w* on small pieces of paper.
- Volunteers take a letter and find a word in the poem that begins with *W* or *w*.

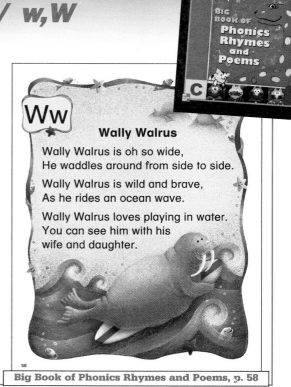

Ww

Wally Walrus

Wally Walrus is oh so wide,
He waddles around from side to side.

Wally Walrus is wild and brave,
As he rides an ocean wave.

Wally Walrus loves playing in water.
You can see him with his wife and daughter.

58

Big Book of Phonics Rhymes and Poems, p. 58

Review Initial /w/ w

OBJECTIVES

Children will:

- identify and use /w/ *W, w*
- write and discriminate between *W, w*

....

MATERIALS

- letter cards from the *Word Building Book*

TEACHING TIP

INSTRUCTIONAL Have children read all the words under *w* on your classroom Word Wall. Encourage them to add *w* words after this lesson.

ALTERNATE TEACHING STRATEGY

....

INITIAL /w/*w*

For a different approach to teaching this skill, see page T28.

▶ **Visual/Auditory/ Kinesthetic**

TEACH

Identify /w/ *W, w* Tell children they will review the sound /w/ and write the letters *W, w*. Write the letters and make the /w/ sound. Write this sentence on the chalkboard: *Walt will wait with us.* Read the sentence aloud, tracking the print with your hand. Have volunteers underline the *w*'s. Ask children to *wiggle* their fingers when they hear a word that begins with /w/. Repeat using this sentence: *We will wait with Walt.*

Write and Discriminate Between *W* and *w* Write *W* and *w* on the chalkboard some distance apart. Write the following words on the board, and read them aloud: *win, West, web, wet, Wednesday.* Ask children to point to the *w* each word begins with; then write *W* or *w*.

PRACTICE

Complete the Pupil Edition Page Read the directions on page 320 in the Pupil Edition, and make sure children clearly understand what they are being asked to do. Identify each picture, and complete the first item together. Then work through the page with children, or have them complete the page independently.

ASSESS/CLOSE

Identify and Use *W, w* Write and read aloud this story: *It was cold on Wednesday. It was windy, too. We wore our winter coats to keep warm.* Ask children to show a red counter for each word that begins with *W* and a blue counter for each word that begins with *w*. Then have them write *W* or *w* for each counter. Read the story again so that children can check their work.

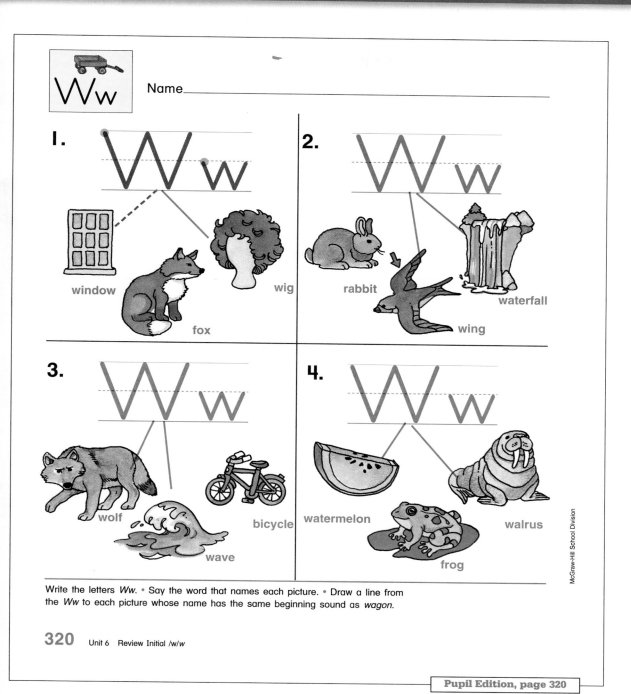

Ww Name_____

1.
window
fox
wig

2.
rabbit
wing
waterfall

3.
wolf
wave
bicycle

4.
watermelon
frog
walrus

Write the letters *Ww*. • Say the word that names each picture. • Draw a line from the *Ww* to each picture whose name has the same beginning sound as *wagon*.

McGraw-Hill School Division

320   Unit 6   Review Initial /w/w

Pupil Edition, page 320

ADDITIONAL PHONICS RESOURCES

Practice Book, *page 320*
Phonics Workbook

McGraw-Hill School
TECHNOLOGY

 **Phonics** CD-ROM
Activities for practice with Initial Letters

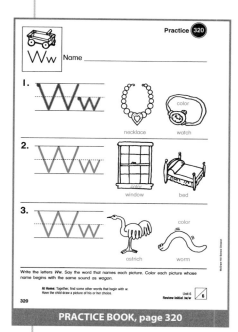

Practice **320**

Ww Name_____

1. necklace   watch (color)

2. window   bed (color)

3. ostrich   worm (color)

Write the letters *Ww*. Say the word that names each picture. Color each picture whose name begins with the same sound as *wagon*.

At Home: Together, find some other words that begin with *w*. Have the child draw a picture of his or her choice.

320   Unit 6
Review Initial /w/w

PRACTICE BOOK, page 320

Meeting Individual Needs for Phonics

EASY	ON-LEVEL	CHALLENGE	LANGUAGE SUPPORT
Read the Mother Goose nursery rhyme "Wee Willie Winkie" aloud to children. Write it in large letters on the chalkboard, and read it again as you track the print with your hand. Ask children to circle the words that begin with the letters *W, w*.	**Write** and read aloud these sentences: *The bird flaps its ___. Water is ___. Can the dog ___ its tail? Did you ___ the game?* Have children say words that begin with *w* to complete each sentence, then write a *w* for every *w* word they use.	**Have** children write sentences about things they do in a week. Tell children to use words that start with /w/. For example: *I walk to school. I watch TV. I wash my hands. I went to the store.*	**Show** picture cards, and have children "win" cards that have pictures whose names begin with /w/: *window, water, wasp, walrus.* Have them trace tactile letters for *W, w*.

320

TESTED OBJECTIVES

- recognize words with initial *w*
- make inferences

TEACHING TIP

Talk about what it means to be a good friend. Make a picture/word list that explains children's ideas.

Read the Big Book

Before Reading

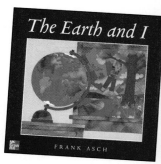

Develop Oral Language Teach children the following finger play. Have children stand in a circle.

Morning Verse

Down is the earth,	(Touch the ground.)
Up is the sky.	(Rise with arms above.)
There are my friends,	(Gesture outward.)
And here am I.	(Cross arms over chest.)
Good morning, good morning.	

Remind children about the boy who cared for the earth in the story "The Earth and I."

Set Purposes *Model: We read a story about a boy who cared for the earth. When we read this time, let's think about how the boy was a good friend.*

The Earth and I are friends.

28

The Earth and I, page 28

Before Reading

Read Together
- Before you begin to read, point to the first word in the first sentence. Explain that this is where you will begin to read. Continue to track print as you read the story. *Tracking Print*

- How are the boy and the earth friends? (They spent time together.) As you continue through the story, ask: *How do the boy and the earth show their friendship? Use Story Details*

- Discuss with children the pictures on pages 12–14. Say: *I notice that these pages do not have any words. How do the pictures help to tell the story? Use Illustrations*

- Invite children to look at page 7. *Why is the boy sad? How do you know he is sad?* (He sees how people have littered earth; his expression is sad and worried.) *Make Inferences*

- Make the /w/ sound and have children say it with you: Read pages 7 and 8, and ask which words begin with that sound. Ask children to point to and to repeat the words. *Phonics and Decoding*

The Earth and I, page 12

After Reading

Retell the Story
Have volunteers pretend to be the earth. Have them say how the boy was its friend. If necessary, revisit illustrations in the book.

Literary Response
JOURNAL WRITING Have children draw a picture of how they could be a friend to the earth. Invite them to write about their pictures.

ORAL RESPONSE Ask children to share and describe their pictures with the class.

CENTER Activity

Cross Curricular: Art

MY OWN EARTH In advance, cut out several templates to represent the earth. Have children trace and cut out the earth. Provide paints, brushes, and markers so children can decorate their planet.

Display the cut-out earths on a bulletin board or other prominent place.

▶ **Spatial**

OBJECTIVES

Children will:

- make inferences to understand a story

....

MATERIALS

- *The Earth and I*

TEACHING TIP

INSTRUCTIONAL Talk about how body language helps us know how others are thinking and feeling. Stand and fold your arms, looking angry. Ask children how you might be feeling. Invite volunteers to show other facial and body signals, and have classmates identify their feelings.

Introduce Make Inferences

PREPARE

Recall the Story
Ask children to recall the story *The Earth and I*. Invite volunteers to tell about what they remember.

Look at the Illustrations
Take a picture walk through the book, having children describe some of their favorite parts of the story. Use the illustrations to elicit children's ideas on what the boy is thinking and feeling.

TEACH

Use Details to Make Inferences
Explain to children that authors use words and pictures to let us know how characters are feeling. Read page 23, and have children explain why the boy is sad. Continue with other examples in the story.

PRACTICE

Complete the Pupil Edition Page
Read the directions on page 321 to children, and make sure they clearly understand what they are asked to do. Identify each picture, and complete the first item together. Then work through the page with children, or have them complete the page independently.

ASSESS/CLOSE

Review the Page
Review children's work, and note children who are experiencing difficulty.

Name

1.     

2.    

3.     

Look at the picture on the left. • Draw a circle around the face that shows how the person in the picture is feeling.

Pupil Edition, page 321

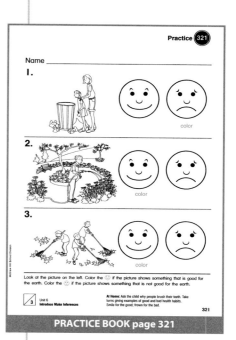

ALTERNATE TEACHING STRATEGY

MAKE INFERENCES

For a different approach to teaching the skill, see page T29.

▶ **Visual/Auditory/ Kinesthetic**

PRACTICE BOOK page 321

Meeting Individual Needs for Comprehension

EASY	ON-LEVEL	CHALLENGE	LANGUAGE SUPPORT
Point out that animals and plants as well as people are friends of the Earth. Turn to pages 26–27 and have children describe how the animals and boy might be feeling, and why.	**Choose** a picture book that children are familiar with. Take a picture walk, and retell the story with children. Then have them reflect on the text and illustrations to describe how the characters might be feeling, and what they might be thinking.	**Discuss** the pages, focusing on how the text and illustrations give us information about the story. Then, have children write and illustrate a new page for the story. Write down their ideas for new text. Ask them how their new page has added to or changed the story.	In a class discussion, create a list of familiar emotions: happy, sad, angry, scared, surprised. Invite pairs of children to act out emotions with facial expressions and body gestures. Classmates can guess the emotions.

Develop Phonological Awareness

Listen

Wee Willie Winkie
a poem

My Hamster
a poem

Wee Willie Winkie
runs through the town,
Upstairs, and downstairs,
in his night gown;
Rapping at the window,
crying through the lock,
"Are the children in their
    beds?
Now it's eight o'clock."

A hamster lives at my house.
It's a hamster, not a mouse.
My hamster is tan and hairy.
It has teeth but isn't scary.
I have to feed it twice a day.
And in the afternoon, we play.

Big Book of Phonics Rhymes and Poems, p. 57, p. 24

Objective: Listen to Sounds in Speech

READ THE POEM Read "Wee Willie Winkie" aloud. Reread the question. Discuss how your voice goes up. Have children say the question after you.

ASK MORE QUESTIONS Invite children to suggest other nighttime activities the children might be doing. Help them state the activities as questions.

> Are the children brushing their teeth?
> Are the children reading stories?

PARTNER INTERVIEWS Help children brainstorm questions they might ask each other.

> What is your favorite color?
> Do you have a pet?
> How do you get to school?

Have partners ask each other the questions. Show children how their voices go up when they ask a question.

Objective: Listen for /w/ and /h/

LISTEN FOR INITIAL /W/ Read the title "Wee Willie Winkie," emphasizing the initial /w/ sound. Have children repeat the words after you.

LISTEN FOR INITIAL /H/ Read the poem "My Hamster," emphasizing words with the initial /h/ sound. Have children repeat the words.

> **hamster   house   hairy   has   have**

PASS WILMA'S HAT Place some small cubes or blocks in a woman's hat. Tell children you will say a word. Explain the following:

If the word begins with /h/ or /w/, the child with the hat takes out one block and passes the hat to the next child. If the word does not begin with /h/ or /w/, the child

passes the hat to the next child, without removing an object.

> **wait   bait   sing   hand   wiggle   heel   wade**
> **walk   tag   hose   well   seep   nap   hill**

Play continues until all blocks have been removed from Wilma's hat.

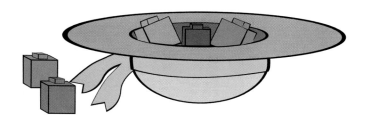

From Phonemic Awareness to Phonics

Objective: Identify /w/ W, w and /h/ H, h

IDENTIFY THE LETTERS
Display pages 57 and 24 in the *Big Book of Phonics Rhymes and Poems*. On each page, point to the letters, identify them, and say the sound they stand for. Have children say each sound with you.

REREAD THE POEMS Reread the poems. Point to each word, emphasizing words with /w/ or /h/.

FIND WORDS WITH *W, w, H, h*
Have children place self-stick dots under the words in the poems that begin with *W, w, H,* or *h*.

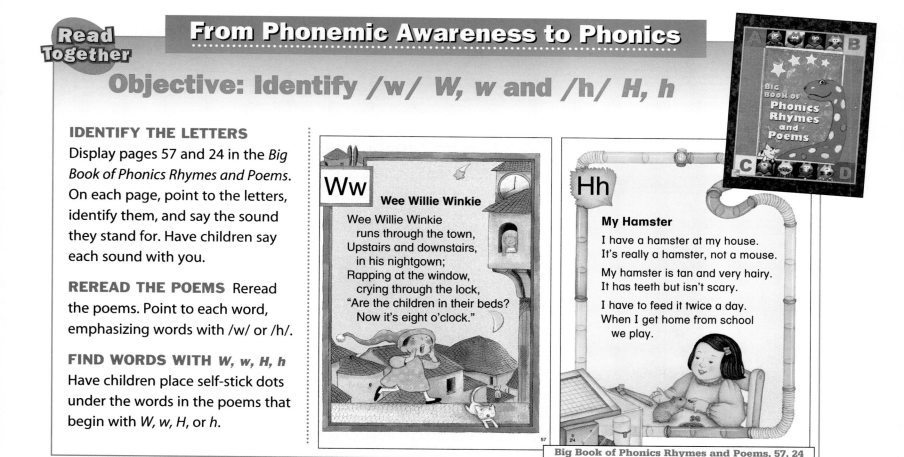

Ww

Wee Willie Winkie

Wee Willie Winkie
   runs through the town,
Upstairs and downstairs,
   in his nightgown;
Rapping at the window,
   crying through the lock,
"Are the children in their beds?
   Now it's eight o'clock."

Hh

My Hamster

I have a hamster at my house.
It's really a hamster, not a mouse.

My hamster is tan and very hairy.
It has teeth but isn't scary.

I have to feed it twice a day.
When I get home from school
   we play.

Big Book of Phonics Rhymes and Poems, 57, 24

322B

Children will:

- identify and discriminate between /w/*W,w* and /h/*H,h*

- write and use letters *W,w* and *H,h*

MATERIALS

- picture cards from the Word Building Book

TEACHING TIP

INSTRUCTIONAL Have children hold their fingers up in front of their mouths, and ask them to say the words *hair* and *happy*. Ask children to tell what they observed. Help children understand that the sound /h/ causes us to release a breath of air. Have children experiment with other /h/ words to test their observation.

ALTERNATE TEACHING STRATEGY

INITIAL /w/*w* AND /h/*h*

For a different approach to teaching this skill, see page T24, T28.

▶ **Visual/Auditory/ Kinesthetic**

Review /w/W, /h/h

TEACH

Identify and Discriminate Between /w/W,w and /h/H,h

Tell children they will review the sounds /w/ and /h/ at the beginning of words and write letters *W,w, H,h*. Make the following word cards and place them on the chalkboard ledge: *hid, Willy, wet, hum, hat, Helen, win, wag*. On the chalkboard, write *H,h* on one side and *W,w* on the other side. Ask children to point to the letter that each word begins with. Point to each word card as you read it aloud.

Write W,w and H,h

Have children write *W, w* or *H, h* on letter strips to show the arrangement of first letters on the above word cards. Then rearrange the word cards, and have children write the new order of initial *w* and *h*.

PRACTICE

Complete the Pupil Edition Page

Read the directions on page 322 to the children, and make sure they clearly understand what they are being asked to do. Identify each picture, and complete the first item together. Then work through the page with children, or have them complete the page independently.

ASSESS/CLOSE

Identify and Use W,w and H,h

Tell this story: *Hana won a ham. She had ham on Wednesday.* Ask children to circle a *w* or *h* on their letter strips every time they hear a word that begins with one of the letters.

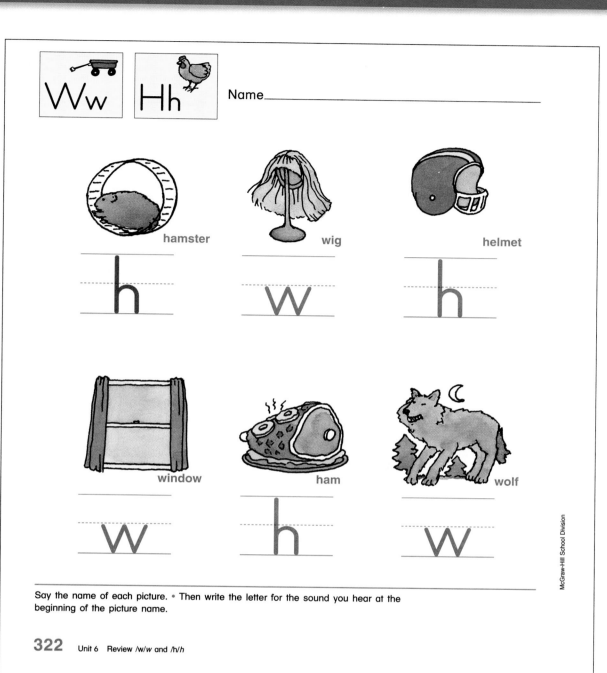

Ww **Hh** Name _____

hamster   wig   helmet

h   w   h

window   ham   wolf

w   h   w

Say the name of each picture. • Then write the letter for the sound you hear at the beginning of the picture name.

322   Unit 6   Review /w/w and /h/h

McGraw-Hill School Division

Pupil Edition, page 322

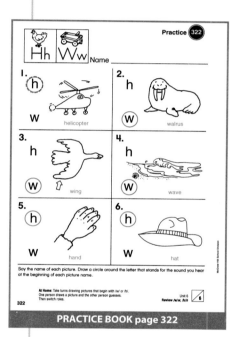
Meeting Individual Needs for Phonics

EASY	ON-LEVEL	CHALLENGE	LANGUAGE SUPPORT
Give children tactile letters *H,h* and *W,w*. Have them talk about how the capital and lowercase forms are alike and how they are different. Say words that begin with *h* or *w* such as *hen, wet, wag, hug, had, win*. Ask them to hold up the letter that shows how each word begins.	**Ask** children to use words that begin with *w* or *h* to complete the following sentences: *Rain is* (wet). *She* (hit) *a home run. He wears a* (wig)(hat) *on his head. See the dog* (wag) *his tail. The spider spins a* (web). *I* (hum) *a tune.* Children write the initial letter for each word they say.	**Have** children write letter cards for *h* and *w*. Ask pairs of children to combine their *h* and *w* letter cards and place the cards face down between them. One child turns a card face up and the partner says a word that begins with that letter. Then partners switch roles.	**Ask** ESL children to repeat these words and pantomime them with you: *hop, hug, wag, win, hum*. Explain the meanings of the words as you teach children the pantomime gestures. Then ask children to use each word in a sentence.

322

Teacher Read Aloud

Listen

Mae Jemison

D o you ever dream of becoming an astronaut? Would you like to look down at Earth from outer space? When Mae Jemison was a young girl, she dreamed about traveling to space. On summer nights, she would gaze up at the stars and wish that she was closer to them. When she grew up, she made her dream come true. In 1992, Mae Jemison became the world's first female African American astronaut.

Mae Jemison grew up in Chicago, Illinois. As a young girl, she was a good student. She loved science. She also was a great dancer.

When it came time for Mae to go to college, she had to make a hard decision. Would she study to become a doctor or a dancer?

After giving it a lot of thought, Mae made up her mind. She chose to become a doctor.

Mae loved working as a doctor. She even worked in Africa for two years, helping sick people to get well. But she never forgot her dream of going to space. So she applied to become an astronaut.

Continued on page T3

Oral Comprehension

LISTENING AND SPEAKING Ask children what jobs they might like to have when they grow up. Explain that you will read a true story about Mae Jemison. Mae was the first female African American to become an astronaut.

After you read, ask: *What kind of person do you think Mae is? What words might describe her? What questions would you like to ask her?*

Activity Have children draw themselves in an occupation they might like to have some day. Encourage children to use their imagination and show any occupation they want in their drawings.

▶ **Spatial**

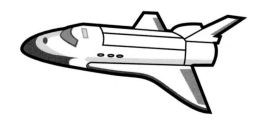

Real-Life Reading

1. Peter dreams of becoming an astronaut.

2. One day he went to the library to learn about space.

3. The librarian showed Peter CD-ROM about space.

4. Peter saw a spaceship take off. He learned a lot.

42

43

Big Book of Real-Life Reading, pages 42-43

Objective: Use the Library/Media Center

READ THE PAGE Ask children how they could find out more about space. Make a list of their ideas. Then explain that children can use a library and computers to find information. Discuss the pictures and read the corresponding text. Ask them to talk about when they used CD-ROMs to find information. If children are unfamiliar with CD-ROMs, explain what they look like and how they work.

ANSWER THE QUESTION After children discuss the pictures, ask: *How are CD-ROMs different from books? What would you like to find out about by using a CD-ROM?* Explain that most public libraries have computers with CD-ROMs that children can use. Ask: *Would you like to learn more about space like the boy in the book? What other things would you like to learn more about by using a CD-ROM?*

CULTURAL PERSPECTIVES

SCULPTURES Share that the story takes place in Africa. Africa is the second largest continent in the world. Explain to children that Africa includes different African cultures, and that its people have many traditional art forms. African sculpture is one of Africa's greatest traditions.

Activity Help children make art sculptures. Using a flat piece of cardboard as the base, build the sculpture by gluing together recycled milk cartons, tubes, and other objects. When the sculpture is done, paint the sculpture.

▶ **Kinesthetic/Logical/Mathematical**

Children will:

- identify and read the high-frequency word *was*

....

MATERIALS

- word cards from the *Word Play Book*
- *We Win!*

TEACHING TIP

MANAGEMENT Provide dashed letters, ruled paper, and starting dots for children who need help to write words. Be aware of children who have different levels of fine motor skills.

Introduce High-Frequency Words: *was*

PREPARE

Listen to Words   Tell children that they will be learning a new word: *was.* Explain that the word *was* can help children say something about a person or thing. Give examples of using *was* by describing one person or thing several different ways. Example: *Sam was brave. Sam was a firefighter. Sam was eating lunch.* Say the following sentence: *Gina was smart.* Read the sentence again, and ask children to raise hands when they hear the word *was.* Repeat with the sentence: *Gina was a doctor.*

TEACH

Model Reading the Word in Context   Give a word card to each child, and read the word. Reread the sentences, and have children raise their hands when they hear the word.

Identify the Word   Write the sentences above on the chalkboard. Track print and read each sentence. Children hold up their word cards when they hear the word *was.* Then ask volunteers to point to and underline the word *was* in the sentences.

Write the Word   Review how to write the letters *w, a,* and *s.* Then have children practice writing the word *was.*

PRACTICE

Complete the Pupil Edition Page   Read the directions on page 323 to children, and make sure they clearly understand what they are being asked to do. Complete the first item together. Then work through the page with children or have them complete the page independently.

ASSESS/CLOSE

Review the Page   Review children's work, and note children who are experiencing difficulty or need additional practice.

Name_____

1.

The hog was in the mud.

2.

The duck was wet.

3.

The pig was in the pen.

4.

The cat was in the den.

Read the sentence. • Then draw a line under the word *was* in the sentence.

Unit 6   Introduce High-Frequency Words: *was*   **323**

Pupil Edition, page 323

ALTERNATE TEACHING STRATEGY
....

HIGH-FREQUENCY WORDS: *was*

For a different approach to teaching the skill, see page T27.

▶ **Visual/Auditory/ Kinesthetic**

Practice **323**

Name_____

1. The cat was on the mat.

2. The cub was in the tub.

3. The hen was in the pen.

4. The bug was on the rug.

Read the sentence. Then draw a line under the word *was* in the sentence.

▨ Unit 6
4 Introduce High-Frequency Words: *was*

At Home: Show the child the sentence starter *I was*. Then take turns finishing the sentence with words or pictures.

323

PRACTICE BOOK page 323

Meeting Individual Needs for Vocabulary

EASY	ON-LEVEL	CHALLENGE	LANGUAGE SUPPORT
Laminate copies of the word *was* on posterboard. Have children use eraseable markers to trace the word. Then have them read the word and repeat.	**Give** children letter cards for *w, a,* and *s.* Have children form the word *was.* Have them use the word in a sentence.	**Label** a sheet of drawing paper with the sentence: *Last week, I was ___.* Help them complete the sentence, read it, and illustrate it.	**Help** children understand that the word *was* tells about something that happened earlier, sometime in the past. Have children complete this sentence by telling what they were doing, wearing, and eating yesterday: *Yesterday, I was ____.*

323

Develop Phonological Awareness

Listen

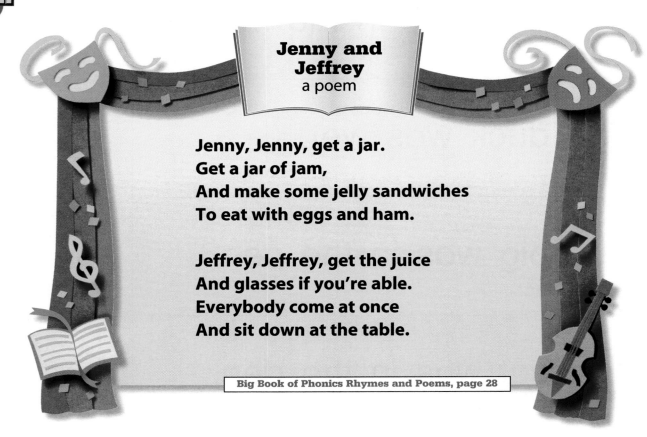

Jenny and Jeffrey
a poem

Jenny, Jenny, get a jar.
Get a jar of jam,
And make some jelly sandwiches
To eat with eggs and ham.

Jeffrey, Jeffrey, get the juice
And glasses if you're able.
Everybody come at once
And sit down at the table.

Big Book of Phonics Rhymes and Poems, page 28

Objective: Identify and Make Rhymes

LISTEN FOR THE RHYMING WORDS
Read the poem "Jenny and Jeffrey" aloud. Then reread the first verse. Ask children to listen and say the word that rhymes with *jam* (ham.) Then reread the second verse and ask children to identify the two words that rhyme. As you read, emphasize the words *able* and *table.*

> jam ham able table

BRAINSTORM RHYMING WORDS Then have children think of other words that rhyme with *jam*. Accept nonsense words but encourage children to think of real words

> jam ham Pam ram Sam yam

SUBSTITUTE RHYMING WORDS Then substitute a rhyming word in the fourth line and read the new verse aloud. Talk about this new nonsense verse. Repeat by substituting other rhyming words.

> Jenny, Jenny, get a jar.
> Get a jar of jam.
> And make some jelly sandwiches
> To eat with eggs and *ram.*

Objective: Listen for /j/

LISTEN FOR THE SOUND Say the title of the poem "Jenny and Jeffrey." Emphasize the initial /j/ sound and point out that both names begin with the same sound. Have children repeat the sound.

Reread the poem and ask what Jenny was supposed to get. (a jar of jam) Emphasize the /j/ sound. Then ask what Jeffrey was supposed to get. (the juice)

JUMP FOR THE SOUND Say the following words. Emphasize the /j/ sound. Have children jump if they hear the /j/ sound.

> joke   run   job   boy   jar   cab   joy

SEGMENT THE SOUND Tell children you will play a guessing game. You will say a word in a funny way and children need to listen to figure out what the word is. Then say the word /j/-/u/-/mp/. Have children repeat the word with you slowly at first and then more quickly.

Then ask a volunteer to say the word. Repeat this game with the following words:

> joy   just   job   jeans   joke   jolly

From Phonemic Awareness to Phonics

Objective: Identify Initial /j/ J, j

IDENTIFY THE LETTER FOR THE SOUND Explain that the letter *j* stands for the /j/ sound. Display the *Big Book of Phonics Rhymes and Poems*, page 28. Point to the letters in the corner and identify them. Have children say the /j/ sound with you.

REREAD THE POEM Reread the poem. Frame each word with initial *J, j* and have the children say the words with you.

MATCH WORDS WITH INITIAL J Make word cards to match words in the poem with

initial *j*. Invite volunteers to match the cards with the words in the poem. Read them together.

DIFFERENTIATE INITIAL SOUNDS Give each child a letter card with *J, j* on it. Say the words *jar, box*. Ask children to hold up their letter cards and say the word that begins with the /j/ sound. Repeat this activity with:

> joke/poke   Kelly/jelly
> ham/jam   car/jar
> moose/juice   cob/job

Jenny and Jeffrey

Jj

Jenny, Jenny, get a jar.
Get a jar of jam.
And make some jelly sandwiches
To eat with eggs and ham.

Jeffrey, Jeffrey, get the juice
And glasses if you're able.
Everybody come at once
And sit down at the table.

Big Book of Phonics Rhymes and Poems, p. 28

324B

OBJECTIVES

Children will:

- identify /a/*a*, /e/*e*, /i/*i*, /o/*o*, /u/*u*
- blend and read short *a, e, i, o, u* words
- write short *a, e, i, o, u* words
- review /w/*w*

MATERIALS

- letter cards from the *Word Building Book*

TEACHING TIP

INSTRUCTIONAL When working with words that begin with *w*, be careful not to include any words that begin with *wh*, such as *what, when, where, why,* or *which*. If children suggest any of these words, briefly explain that they will learn about these words at another time.

ALTERNATE TEACHING STRATEGY

BLENDING SHORT *a, e, i, o, u*

For a different approach to teaching this skill, see Unit 1, page T32; Unit 2, page T32; Unit 3, page T30; Unit 4, page T32; Unit 5, page T30.

▶ **Visual/Auditory/ Kinesthetic**

Review Blending with short *a, e, i, o, u*

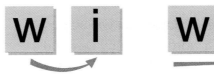

TEACH

Identify *a, e, i, o, u* as Symbols for /a/, /e/, /i/, /o/, /u/

Tell children they will continue to read words with *a, e, i, o, u*.

- Display the *a, e, i, o, u* letter cards and say /a/, /e/, /i/, /o/, /u/. Have children repeat the sounds as you point to the cards.

BLENDING Model and Guide Practice

- Place the *w* card before the *i* card. Blend the sounds together and have children repeat after you.

- Place the *n* letter card after the *w* and *i* cards. Blend to read *win*.

Use the Word in Context

- Ask children to use *win* in a sentence, perhaps telling how to play a familiar game.

Repeat the Procedure

- Use the following words to continue modeling and guided practice with short *a, e, i, o, u*: *wig, wag, web, bat, wet, wed, tag.*

PRACTICE

Complete the Pupil Edition Page

Read the directions on page 324 to children, and make sure they clearly understand what they are being asked to do. Identify each picture, and complete the first item together. Then work through the page with children or have them complete the page independently.

ASSESS/CLOSE

Build Short *a, e, i, o, u* Words

Observe children as they complete page 324. Then ask them to use their letter cards *g, b, t, d, n* to build five words that have short *a, e, i, o,* or *u* in the middle and begin with *w*.

Name_____

1.

w e b

web

2.

w a g

wag

3.

w i g

wig

4.

w i n

win

Blend the sounds and say the word. • Write the word. • Draw a circle around the picture that goes with the word.

324   Unit 6   Review Blending with Short *a, e, i, o, u*

McGraw-Hill School Division

Pupil Edition, page 324

ADDITIONAL PHONICS RESOURCES

Practice Book, *page 324*
Phonics Workbook

McGraw-Hill School
TECHNOLOGY

Phonics CD-ROM
Activities for Practice with Blending and Segmenting

PRACTICE BOOK page 324

Meeting Individual Needs for Phonics

EASY	ON-LEVEL	CHALLENGE	LANGUAGE SUPPORT
Write initial *w* CVC words on the chalkboard and ask children questions about them, such as: *What letter is in the middle? What sound does it show? What sound does the word begin with? End with?* Then have children say the word aloud.	**Ask** children to write, then read aloud words that begin with *w* to complete these sentences: *Look at the spider's (web). That dog sure can (wag) his tail! Did your team (win) the game?*	**Help** children make up a story using the following words. Introduce the words one at a time, and write them on the chalkboard: *wet, wag, web, win.* Record the story and invite the class to illustrate it.	**Children** may have difficulty discriminating between lowercase *d* and lowercase *b*. Write the words *wed* and *web* on the chalkboard. Blend the sounds to say the words. Show pictures of a wedding and a spider's web to help children see the difference.

324

Guided Instruction

BEFORE READING

PREVIEW AND PREDICT Take a brief **picture walk** through the book, focusing on the illustrations.

- What game are the children playing? Who is winning?

- Do you think the story is realistic, or is it make-believe? Why?

SET PURPOSES Discuss with children what they want to find out as they read the story. They may want to know who will win the game.

TEACHING TIP

To put book together:

1. Tear out the story page.

2. Cut along dotted line.

3. Fold each section on fold line.

4. Assemble book.

INSTRUCTIONAL Ask children if they play or watch baseball games. Have them share their experiences, and briefly talk about the rules. Talk about what it means when a game is tied.

We Win!

Ken was up at bat.

3

Ken had on a red cap.

2

Ken had a hit and ran!

4

Guided Instruction

DURING READING

☑ **Concepts of Print**

☑ **Make Inferences**

☑ **High-Frequency Word:** *was*

☑ **Initial *H, h***

① CONCEPTS OF PRINT Focus the children's attention on the title page. Read the title and have children repeat the words as you track print. Remind children that a title page helps you to know what a story is going to be about.

② MAKE INFERENCES After you read the text on page 2, make sure children understand that the score is tied and that the game is almost over. Ask what Ken wants to do. Then ask children how they think Ken is feeling.

③ HIGH-FREQUENCY WORDS Have children point to the word on page 3 that begins with *w: was*. Read the word together as you track print. Then have children do the same.

④ PHONICS After you read page 4, ask children to say the words that begin with *h*. (had, hit)

LANGUAGE SUPPORT

ESL The term *up at bat* is an idiomatic expression that may be difficult for second-language children. Demonstrate *up at bat* and ask children to pantomime, using the picture on page 3 as a model.

Guided Instruction

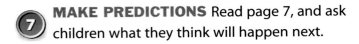

BEFORE READING

5 **CONCEPTS OF PRINT** Ask children to frame the quotation marks on page 5 and explain what they mean. Ask who is speaking. *(Ned)*

6 **CAUSE AND EFFECT** After you read page 6, guide children in a discussion of why Ned did not tag Ken. A cause might have been that Ken was too fast, or that Ned was too slow. The effect was that Ned was unable to tag Ken.

7 **MAKE PREDICTIONS** Read page 7, and ask children what they think will happen next.

8 **MAKE INFERENCES** After you read page 8, ask children how they think Ken feels.

ASSESSMENT

CONCEPTS OF PRINT

HOW TO ASSESS Point to the quotation marks on page 8. Ask children what the marks mean. *(that someone is speaking)* Ask who is speaking. *(Ken)*

FOLLOW UP If children have trouble, have them frame the quotation marks with their hands and say the words.

"I can tag him," said Ned.

5

Ken ran on and on.

7

But Ned did not tag Ken.

6

"We win! We win!" said Ken.

8

Guided Instruction

AFTER READING

RETURN TO PREDICTIONS AND PURPOSES
Remind children of their predictions. Ask if they found out who won the game. *(Ken's team)* Ask if the story could really happen, and if children were surprised at the ending.

RETELL THE STORY Have children retell the story. Children visualize the events in the story and take turns telling what happened.

LITERARY RESPONSE To help children respond to the story, ask:

- What was your favorite part of the story?

- What do you think would have happened if Ken hadn't hit the ball?

Invite children to draw and write about a sport they like to play.

Balls OOOO Strikes OOO Outs OOO												
Inning	1	2	3	4	5	6	7	8	9	R	H	E
Hawks												
Cubs												

CENTER Activity

Cross Curricular: Math

BATTER UP! Create a baseball scoreboard on chart paper that shows two teams, innings, and the number of runs each inning. Then prepare simple rebus number stories on index cards. Children can use counters to solve the problems. They may also wish to create their own problems.

▶ **Logical/Mathematical**

Review Make Inferences

Children will:

- make inferences to understand a story

MATERIALS

- *We Win!*

TEACHING TIP

INSTRUCTIONAL Point out inferences children make concerning daily routines. For instance: *What do you think we are going to do next? Why do you think this?*

PREPARE

Recall the Story

Ask children to recall the story *We Win!* Ask children who the characters are, and why it is important for Ken to hit a home run. You may wish to have volunteers share information about scoring in the game of baseball.

TEACH

Use Story Clues to Make Inferences

Reread pages 2–3 together. Talk about how Ken might be feeling and why. Remind children that they can use the illustrations, text, and what they already know as clues. Continue through each spread of the book, talking about how the characters are feeling, and why they might be feeling that way.

PRACTICE

Complete the Pupil Edition Page

Read the directions on page 327 to the children, and make sure they clearly understand what they are being asked to do. Identify each picture, and complete the first item together. Then work through the page with children or have them complete the page independently.

ASSESS/CLOSE

Review the Page

Review children's work, and note children who are experiencing difficulty.

Name _____

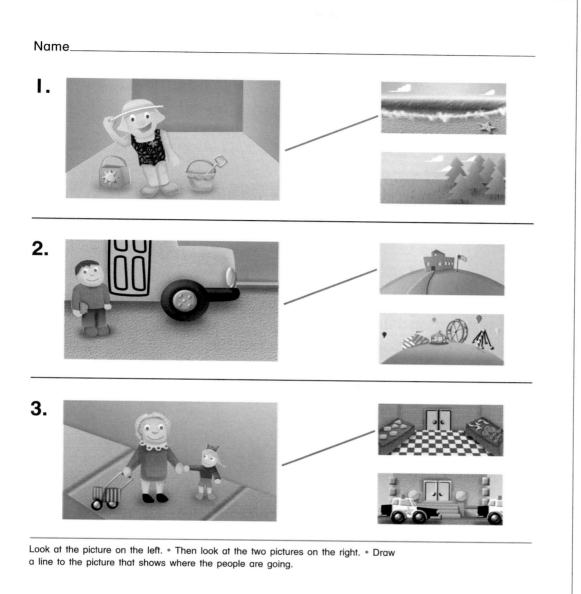

1.

2.

3.

Look at the picture on the left. • Then look at the two pictures on the right. • Draw a line to the picture that shows where the people are going.

Unit 6 Review Make Inferences   **327**

Pupil Edition, page 327

ALTERNATE TEACHING STRATEGY

······························

MAKE INFERENCES
For a different approach to teaching this skill, see page T29.

▶ **Visual/Auditory/Kinesthetic**

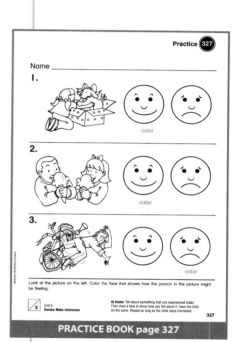

PRACTICE BOOK page 327

Meeting Individual Needs for Comprehension

EASY	ON-LEVEL	CHALLENGE	LANGUAGE SUPPORT
Have children choose a part of the story and act out how Ken is feeling: when he is at bat, when he hits the ball, when he scores, when the team wins the game. Encourage them to use facial expressions and body gestures.	**Help** children to make a word web to show how Ken is feeling. Write *Ken* in the center of the web, and have children write or dictate their ideas to you.	**Write** different situations on index cards. Children sit in a circle, and the first child takes a card. Whisper the situation to the child, and have the child act it out. Others guess the emotion that the player is expressing.	**Talk** about winning and losing during a game, and how it makes a person feel. Children can discuss their feelings.

327

Develop Phonological Awareness

Listen

A Pup Named Tag
a poem

Kim has a pet, a pup named Tag.
Tag can tug and lick and wag.
Tag likes Dad's sock and Mom's red hat.
Tag wags his tail at Nan and Pat.
Tag likes to play outside in the sun.
Tag, the pup, is a lot of fun!

Objective: Listen for Sense

READ THE POEM Read the poem "A Pup Named Tag" several times. Ask: *What kind of animal is Tag?*

> **a pup**

SUBSTITUTE ANIMAL NAMES Invite children to name other animals that might be pets.

> **duck   pig   cat   hamster   turtle**

Read the poem again, but substitute an animal name children suggested for *pup* each time. After reading, discuss why the revised poem does or does not make sense.

SUBSTITUTE NONSENSE WORDS Read the first line of the poem, but substitute nonsense words. Have children listen to identify the nonsense words. Continue with other lines in the poem.

> **Kim—a tup named Pag.**
> **Tag—wick and lag.**

Objective: Listen for Blending with Short *a, e, i, o, u*

LISTEN FOR SEGMENTED WORDS Invite children to listen as you read "A Pug Named Tag." As you read the poem, segment the sounds in *Tag* each time you say it. After reading the poem, ask children to name the segmented word. If a clue is needed, say /t/-/a/-/g/. Have children repeat the sounds and then blend them to say *tag*. Repeat the activity with other words in the poem.

> pet   Kim   sock   fun

WHAT CAN TAG DO? Read the poem and have children name all the things Tag can do.

> tug   lick   wag   play

Tell children Tag can do lots of other things, too. They must listen and guess what Tag can do.

Say: *What does Tag like to do? Here's a clue, just for you! Tag likes to /b/-/e/-/g/ for treats.*

Pause while children repeat, and then blend, the sounds to say *beg*. Have children raise their hands when they know what Tag likes to do. Repeat with other action words as clues.

> run   dig   hunt   eat

From Phonemic Awareness to Phonics

Objective: Relate *a, e, i, o, u* to Short Vowel Sounds

LISTEN TO RHYMING WORDS Read the poem. Invite children to name rhyming words in the poem.

IDENTIFY THE LETTERS Say /t/- /a/- /g/ as you write *Tag* on chart paper. Then identify the letters. Have children repeat the sounds—and then the letters. Repeat with *wag*. Have a volunteer circle and identify letters that are the same in both words. Have children say the segmented—and then the blended sounds.

> /a/-/g/-/ag/

LISTEN FOR RHYMING WORDS Ask children if the words *pat* and *hat* rhyme. Have children repeat after you: "/p/-/at/, /h/-/at/." Guide children in recognizing that the words rhyme because they have the same /at/ ending. Tell children you will say word pairs. Children should pat their shoulders if the word pairs rhyme.

> can/tan   bet/red
> Kim/his   lot/pot
> Pup/cup   lick/sick

OBJECTIVES

Children will:

- identify /a/a, /e/e, /i/i, /o/o, /u/u
- blend and read short a, e, i, o, u words
- write short a, e, i, o, u words
- review /w/w, /h/h, /b/b, /g/g, /k/k,ck, /l/l, /p/p, /r/r, /f/f, /k/c, /t/t, /m/m, /s/s, /d/d, and /n/n

MATERIALS

- letter cards from the *Word Building Book*

TEACHING TIP

INSTRUCTIONAL Ask children to look at a mirror and say /w/ and /h/ several times. Tell them to notice how their lips change shape. Ask them to describe how they look as they make each sound.

ALTERNATE TEACHING STRATEGY

BLENDING SHORT a, e, i, o, u

For a different approach to teaching this skill, see Unit 1, page T32; Unit 2, page T32; Unit 3, page T30; Unit 4, page T32; Unit 5, page T30.

▶ **Visual/Auditory/ Kinesthetic**

Review Blending with short *a, e, i, o, u*

TEACH

Identify a, e, i, o, u as Symbols for /a/, /e/, /i/, /o/, /u/

Tell children they will continue to read words with a, e, i, o, u.

- Display the a, e, i, o, u letter cards and say /a/, /e/, /i/, /o/, /u/. Have children repeat the sounds as you point to the cards.

BLENDING Model and Guide Practice

- Place the w card before the e card. Blend the sounds together and have children repeat after you: we-.

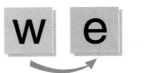 

- Place the t letter card after the w and e cards. Blend to read *wet*.

 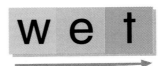

Use the Word in Context

- Have children use *wet* in a sentence, perhaps by identifying something that is or can be wet.

Repeat the Procedure

- Use the following words to continue modeling and for guided practice with short a, e, i, o, u: *hip, hop, wed, hug, cab, gum, lick*.

PRACTICE

Complete the Pupil Edition Page

Read aloud the directions on page 328. Identify each picture, and complete the first item together. Then work through the page with children or have them complete the page independently.

ASSESS/CLOSE

Write Short a, e, i, o, u Words

Observe children as they complete page 328. Then give them letter cards a, e, i, o, u and w, h, b, g, k. Ask children to write five words, each beginning with one of the consonants and having a different medial vowel.

Name

1. web win

web

2. ham hot

hot

3. wig wag

wag

4. bug beg

bug

Draw a circle around the word that names the picture. • Say the word. • Then write the word.

McGraw-Hill School Division

328 Unit 6 Review Blending with Short *a, e, i, o, u*

Pupil Edition, page 328

ADDITIONAL PHONICS RESOURCES

Practice Book, *page 328*

Phonics Workbook

McGraw-Hill School
TECHNOLOGY

Phonics CD-ROM

Activities for Practice with Blending and Segmenting

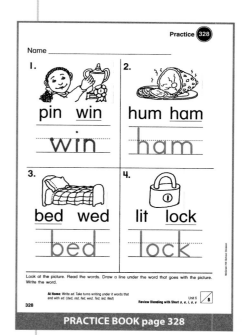

PRACTICE BOOK page 328

Meeting Individual Needs for Phonics

EASY	ON-LEVEL	CHALLENGE	LANGUAGE SUPPORT
Write these words on the chalkboard: *hop, hat, bet, hut, kid, cot, hip, hen, bad, gum.* Ask children to sort the words into groups of words that have the same middle letter. Show children how to write headings *a, e, i, o, u* on a sheet of paper and list the words in columns.	**Write** three columns of letters on the chalkboard: *w, h, l, r, f, t; a, e, i, o, u,* and *b, g, ck, p.* Have children take turns choosing a first letter from the group on the left, a medial vowel, and a letter from the group on the right to make a word.	**Use** all the letter cards under review and invite children to write short *a, e, i, o, u* words on a chart. Seat them in a circle and ask them to make up a story, each child saying a sentence that includes one or more of the words on the chart.	**Give** children opportunities to blend and read words by labeling classroom objects, such as: *hat, cap, bag, sack, rock, kit, cup, mug, pin, pen, map.* Talk about how sometimes different words are used for the same or similar objects.

Reread the Decodable Story

We Win!

☑ **Initial** *w*
☑ **Make Inferences**
☑ **High-Frequency Word:** *was*
☑ **Concepts of Print**

ASSESSMENT

MAKE INFERENCES
HOW TO ASSESS Invite children to choose a page from the story and to talk about how the characters are feeling.

FOLLOW UP If children have difficulty, help them use the illustrations and text as clues.

Guided Reading

SET PURPOSES Tell children that when they read the story again, they can find out more about what happened. Explain that you also want them to look for and read the words that begin with *w*. Remind them that they know the word *was* and will see it again in this story.

REREAD THE BOOK As you guide children through the story, address specific problems they may have had during the first read. Use the following prompts to guide the lesson:

• **MAKE INFERENCES** Ask children how Ken's teammates might be feeling at the end of the story, and why. (happy and excited because they won the game)

• **CONCEPTS OF PRINT** Ask children how many words are in the title. (2) Ask which word has two letters. *(We)*

RETURN TO PURPOSES Ask children if they found out more about what happened in the story. Ask if they found any words that begin with *w*. Ask if anyone found the word *was*.

LITERARY RESPONSE Invite children to draw and write about their favorite part of the story. Ask children the following questions about the story:

• *What was your favorite part of the story? Why?*

• *Have you ever been part of a winning team?*

Read the Patterned Book

Hello, Winter!

☑ Initial *W, w*
☑ Make Inferences
☑ High-Frequency Word: *was*
☑ Concepts of Print

Hello, Winter!
by Suzanne Martinucci
illustrated by Bruce Armstrong

Guided Reading

PREVIEW AND PREDICT Read the title and the author's and the illustrator's name. Ask who writes the words and who draws the illustrations. Take a **picture walk** through pages 2–4, noting the setting of the story, the season, and the characters. Have children make a prediction about what will happen in the story.

SET PURPOSES Have children decide what they want to find out from the story and predict what the children might do. Tell them that the story contains words with initial *W, w*.

READ THE BOOK Use the following prompts while the children are reading or after they have read independently. Remind them to run their fingers under each word as they read.

Pages 2-3: Point to the second word. *Let's read it together: was. Find the same word on page 3. High-Frequency Words*

Pages 4-5: *Look at page 4. How many words begin with w? (3) Phonics*

Pages 6-7: *How do you know the children were warm?* (There is a fire; they are wearing warm clothes and blankets.) *Make Inferences*

Page 8: *How many words are on this page?* (8) *Which word is the longest?* (wonderful) *Which word is the shortest?* (a) *Concepts of Print*

RETURN TO PREDICTIONS AND PURPOSES Ask children if they found out what they needed to know from the story. See if their predictions were correct.

LITERARY RESPONSE The following questions will help focus children's responses:

- What things in the story would you like to do?

- What is your favorite thing to do in the winter? Write about it and draw a picture.

CENTER Activity

Cross Curricular: Art

WINTER WONDERLAND Provide black paper, white chalk, silver glitter, and glue. Children draw pictures of winter scenes on the black paper and use the glitter to create a dramatic winter effect.

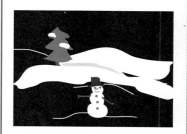

OBJECTIVES

Children will:

- identify and read the high-frequency word *was*

MATERIALS

- word cards from the Word Play Book
- *We Win!*

TEACHING TIP

INSTRUCTIONAL

Continue to use poems and picture books to highlight high-frequency words. Children will develop self-esteem and confidence as they read and recognize these words.

Review *was, with, I, he, she*

PREPARE

Listen to Words Tell children that they will review the word *was*. Read the following sentence, and have children raise hands when they hear the word *was: It was winter.*

TEACH

Model Reading the Word in Context Reread the decodable book. Ask children to listen for the word *was.*

Identify the Word Tell children to first look at their word cards, and then to look for the word in the story. Read the sentences, tracking print, and ask children to come up and point to the word *not*. Have volunteers put a stick-on dot below the word.

Review High-Frequency Words Hold up word cards for the following: *the, a, my, that, I, and, you, said, we, are, is, have, to, me, go, do, for, he, she, has, with*. Have children read the words together.

PRACTICE

Complete the Pupil Edition Page Read the directions on page 329 to children, and make sure they clearly understand what they are being asked to do. Complete the first item together. Then work through the page with children or have them complete the page independently.

ASSESS/CLOSE

Review the Page Review children's work, and guide children who are experiencing difficulty or need additional practice.

Name_____

1.

(He)(was) a dog.

_____

2.

(She)(was) a cat.

_____

3.

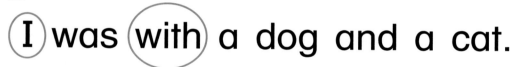
(I) was (with) a dog and a cat.

_____

Read the sentences. Then do the following: **1.** Draw a circle around the words *was* and *he*. **2.** Draw a circle around the words *was* and *she*. **3.** Draw a circle around the words *I* and *with*.

Pupil Edition, page 329

ALTERNATE TEACHING
STRATEGY

HIGH-FREQUENCY
WORDS: *was*

For a different approach to teaching the skill, see page T27.

▶ **Visual/Auditory/ Kinesthetic**

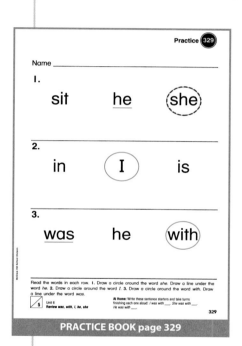

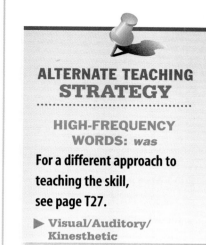

PRACTICE BOOK page 329

Meeting Individual Needs for Vocabulary

EASY	ON-LEVEL	CHALLENGE	LANGUAGE SUPPORT
Label a sheet of drawing paper with children's names: *(Pat) was at bat.* Have children draw pictures of themselves at bat. Talk about the pictures and read the words together.	**Ask** children to think of sentences with the word *was*. Have children dictate their sentences to you. Write the sentences, and then reread them. Have volunteers underline the word *was*.	**Work** with children to create a group story about a sport or game. Have children take turns telling part of the story, and write the text for them. Guide them to tell the story in past tense and use the word *was*. Then have children find the word *was* in the written story and circle it.	**Gather** several short poems that contain the word *was*. Read each poem aloud. Have children hold up their word cards when they hear the word *was*.

329

Interactive Writing

Write a Song

Prewrite

LOOK AT THE STORY PATTERN Reread the book *The Earth and I*. Talk about the language patterns in the story: *I help . . . She helps . . . I sing . . . she sings . . .*

Then have children list things they can do to help the Earth.

Draft

WRITE THE SONG Introduce children to the song "Mister Sun" by Raffi. Tell children they are going to write this song to "Mister Earth."

• Sing the song together. Then have children complete the pattern:

Oh Mister Earth, Earth,

Mr. Earth, Earth,

Please _____.

Write children's ideas on chart paper.

Publish

WRITE THE SONG Sing the new verses together. Make any changes that children agree upon. Then have children write the final verses on chart paper.

Oh, Mister Earth, Earth,
Mr. Earth, Earth,
Please grow some fruit with me.

Presentation Ideas

SING THE SONG After singing the new verses several times, have children record the new song on tape. Keep the written verses displayed in the classroom.

▶ **Representing/ Singing**

ACT OUT THE SONG Invite partners to work together and think of ways to act out verses of the song.

Play the tape, and invite children to sing along as they watch the actors and actresses.

▶ **Singing/Representing**

COMMUNICATION TIPS

- **Singing** Encourage children to listen to each other as they sing, listening to the melody and tempo.

- **Representing** Have children compare different presentations of the role plays. Ask how they were alike and different.

TECHNOLOGY TIP

Help children to input their verses on the computer. Print out the verses and keep copies near the listening area of your classroom.

LANGUAGE SUPPORT

ESL Sing and role play other simple songs about Earth and Nature, such as *Twinkle Twinkle Little Star* and *The Itsy Bitsy Spider*.

Meeting Individual Needs for Writing

EASY

Create a Verse Invite children to choose an element of nature and fill in the blank: *Mr. _____.* You may wish to brainstorm ideas, such as Moon, Snake, River, Spider. Ask them to illustrate their choice.

ON-LEVEL

Write a Note Invite children to write a note to Mr. Sun. Brainstorm questions to ask.

CHALLENGE

Create a New Verse Invite children to think of a new verse to the song. Have them write and sing their verses. Remind children to sound out words as they write.

The Vet Van

Children will read and listen to stories about exploring options and outcomes to help make a good decision.

The Vet Van

Listening Library Audiocassette

Decodable Story, pages 337–338 of the Pupil Edition

That is Not Violet

by Cynthia Rothman
illustrated by Nicole Rutten

Patterned Book, page 341B

The Three Little Pigs

by Joseph Jacobs

Teacher Read Aloud, page 335A

THE BIG BOX

WRITTEN BY JUDY NAYER
ILLUSTRATED BY SUSAN SWAN

Listening Library Audiocassette

ABC Big Book, pages 331A–331B

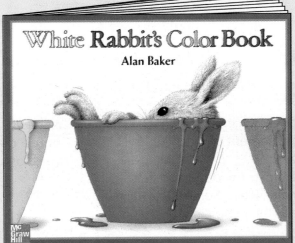

White Rabbit's Color Book

Alan Baker

Listening Library Audiocassette

Literature Big Book, pages 333A–333B

Pupil Edition,
pages 330–341

Big Book of Real-Life Reading,
page 44

Big Book of Phonics Rhymes and
Poems, pages 54–55, 56, 59, 60

 Listening
Library
Audiocassette

ADDITIONAL RESOURCES

Practice Book,
pages 330–341

- **Phonics Kit**
- **Language Support Book**
- **Alternate Teaching Strategies,** pp T30–T33

McGraw-Hill School
TECHNOLOGY

Phonics CD-ROM Provides extra phonics support.

interNET CONNECTION Research & Inquiry Ideas.

Visit www.mhschool.com

The Vet Van

READING AND LANGUAGE ARTS

- **Phonological Awareness**
- **Phonics** *initial /v/v; final /ks/x*
- **Comprehension**
- **Vocabulary**
- **Beginning Reading Concepts**
- **Listening, Speaking, Viewing, Representing**

DAY 1

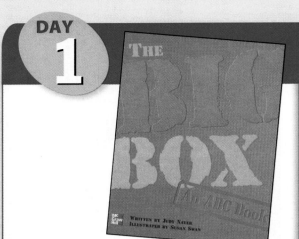

Focus on Reading Skills
Develop Phonological Awareness, 329G-329H
"Very Musical" and "Vickie's Velvet Vest" *Big Book of Phonics Rhymes and Poems,* 54-56
Introduce Initial /v/v, 329I-329
Practice Book, 329
Phonics/Phonemic Awareness
Practice Book

 CD-ROM

Read the Literature
 Read *The Big Box: An ABC Book* **Big Book,** 331A-331B
Shared Reading

Build Skills
☑ Categories, 331C-331
Practice Book, 331

DAY 2

White Rabbit's Color Book
Alan Baker

Focus on Reading Skills
Develop Phonological Awareness, 332A-332B
"I Am Six" and "Max" *Big Book of Phonics Rhymes and Poems,* 59-60
Introduce Final /ks/x, 332C-332
Practice Book, 332
Phonics/Phonemic Awareness
Practice Book

 **CD-ROM**

Read the Literature
 Read *White Rabbit's Color Book* **Big Book,** 333A-333B
Shared Reading

Build Skills
☑ Cause and Effect, 333C-333
Practice Book, 333

- **Cross Curriculum**

 Cultural Perspectives, 331B

 Art, 333B

- **Writing**

 Writing Prompt: Write about how you would turn a big box into a castle.

 Journal Writing, 331B
Letter Formation, 329I

 Writing Prompt: What color bunnies you like best? Write about them.

 Journal Writing, 333B
Letter Formation, 332C

☑ = **Skill Assessed in Unit Test**

DAY 3

The Three Little Pigs

Focus on Reading Skills

Develop Phonological Awareness, 334A-334B
"Very Musical"; "Vickie's Velvet Vest" and "I Am Six"; "Max" *Big Book of Phonics Rhymes and Poems*, 54-56; 59-60

**Review /v/v, /ks/x,** 334C-334
Practice Book, 334
Phonics/Phonemic Awareness Practice Book

Phonics CD-ROM

Read the Literature

Read "The Three Little Pigs" Teacher Read Aloud, 335A-335B
Shared Reading
Read the Big Book of Real-Life Reading, 46-47
☑ Library/Media Center

Build Skills
☑ High-Frequency Words: *not*, 335C-335
Practice Book, 335

 Cultural Perspectives, 335B

 Writing Prompt: If you were a little pig, what would you use to build your house with? Draw a picture and write about your ideas.

DAY 4

The Vet Van

Focus on Reading Skills

Develop Phonological Awareness, 336A-336B
"Pup, Duck, and Fox"
**Review Blending with Short** *a, e, i, o, u,* 336C-336
Practice Book, 336
Phonics/Phonemic Awareness Practice Book

Phonics CD-ROM

Read the Literature
Read "The Vet Van" Decodable Story, 337/338A-337/338D

☑ Initial /v/v; Final /ks/x; Blending
☑ Cause and Effect
☑ High-Frequency Words: *not*
☑ Concepts of Print

Build Skills
☑ Story Structure, 339A-339
Practice Book, 339

Social Studies, 337/338D

 Writing Prompt: Write about what you would like to be when you grow up.

Letter Formation,
Practice Book, 337-338

DAY 5

The Vet Van

That is Not Violet
by Cynthia Rothman
illustrated by Nicole Rutten

Focus on Reading Skills

Develop Phonological Awareness, 340A-340B
"Pup, Duck, and Fox"
**Review Blending with Short** *a, e, i, o, u,* 340C-340
Practice Book, 340
Phonics/Phonemic Awareness Practice Book

Phonics CD-ROM

Read the Literature
Reread "The Vet Van" Decodable Story, 341A
Read "That's Not Violet!" Patterned Book, 341B
Guided Reading
☑ Initial /v/v; Final /ks/x; Blending
☑ Cause and Effect
☑ High-Frequency Words: *not*
☑ Concepts of Print

Build Skills
☑ High-Frequency Words: *not, was, is, do, we, are, with,* 341C-341
Practice Book, 341

Art, 341B

 Writing Prompt: How do you decide what to do during recess or playtime? Write about how you make your decision.

Interactive Writing, 342A-342B

330F

Develop Phonological Awareness

Listen

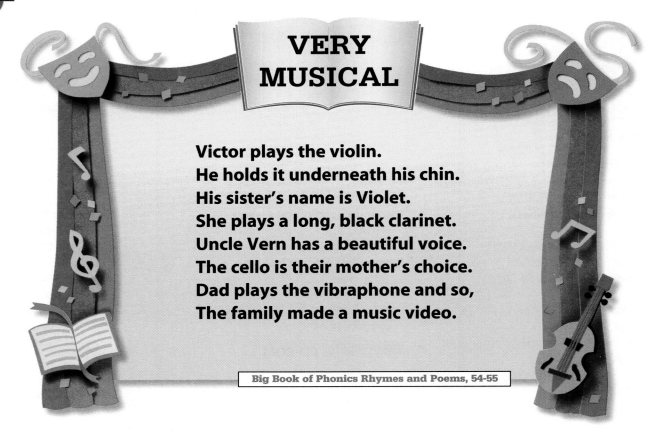

VERY MUSICAL

Victor plays the violin.
He holds it underneath his chin.
His sister's name is Violet.
She plays a long, black clarinet.
Uncle Vern has a beautiful voice.
The cello is their mother's choice.
Dad plays the vibraphone and so,
The family made a music video.

Big Book of Phonics Rhymes and Poems, 54-55

Objective: Identify Long and Short Words

LISTEN TO THE POEM
- Read the poem "Very Musical" aloud.
- Point out that some words in the poem are longer than others.

LISTEN FOR SYLLABLES
- Point to and then say the words *black* and *vibraphone*. Have children clap the syllables with you (*black, vi-bra-phone*).
- Have children determine that there is one syllable in *black* and three syllables in *vibraphone*.
Ask children to identify the longer word (vi-bra-phone).

LISTEN FOR THE LONGER WORD
- Have children listen to pairs of words. Then have them clap the syllables and identify which word of each pair is longer.

chin/violin   voice/video   Vern/beautiful

Objective: Listen for Initial /v/ *V,v*

SEGMENTING

- Say the word *very*, emphasizing the initial sound /v/. Have children repeat the /v/ sound.
- Make the /v/ sound and say "v-v-v-v-ery good." Have children repeat the phrase.
- Say the names and the instruments referred to in the poem. Have children say "very good" if the name or instrument begins with /v/.

Victor violin Violet clarinet Vern voice cello vibraphone

 **Read Together**

From Phonemic Awareness to Phonics

Objective: Identify /v/ *V,v*

IDENTIFY THE LETTER FOR THE SOUND /v/

- Explain to children that the letter *v* stands for the sound /v/. Make the /v/ sound and have children repeat it.
- Display the Big Book of Phonics Rhymes and Poems, page 54, and point to the letters *V, v* in the corner. Identify the letters and say the sound. Have children repeat it.

REREAD THE POEM

- Show children how to make a *v* by holding up their second and third fingers. Then reread the poem slowly. Children hold up fingers for *v* when they hear a word that starts with /v/.

FIND THE WORDS WITH V,v

- Write the letters *V,v* on small stick-on notes. Invite children to place the stick-on notes on words in the poem that begin with *V* or *v*.

Vv

Very Musical

Victor plays the violin.
He holds it underneath his chin.

His sister's name is Violet.
She plays a long, black clarinet.

Big Book of Phonics Rhymes and Poems, 54

330H

OBJECTIVES

Children will:

- identify the letters *V, v*
- identify /v/ *V, v*
- form the letters *V, v*

....

MATERIALS

- letter cards and picture cards from the *Word Building Book*

Introduce Initial /v/ v

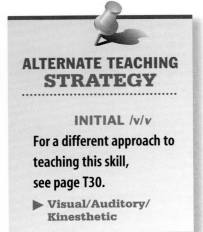

ALTERNATE TEACHING STRATEGY

....

INITIAL /v/v

For a different approach to teaching this skill, see page T30.

▶ **Visual/Auditory/ Kinesthetic**

TEACH

Identify /v/ V, v   Tell children they will learn to write the sound /v/ with the letters *V, v*. Write the letters on the chalkboard, and have children say the /v/ sound with you. Ask them to say the sound /v/ and say, *That is very good.* Ask children to identify the word that begins with /v/. Show pictures of objects whose names do and do not begin with *v* and help children to name the object; for example: *violin, guitar, vacuum cleaner, vase, house, vegetables.* Ask children to hold up their *v* letter cards when they see a picture whose name word with /v/.

Form V, v   Display the letters *V, v*, and, with your back to the children, trace them in the air. Ask children to do the same. Demonstrate how to fold a sheet of paper in half vertically, then open and use the fold line as a guide for writing the letter *V*. Have children write *V* at the top of their papers and *v* at the bottom.

PRACTICE

Complete the Pupil Edition Page   Read the directions on page 330 of the Pupil Edition, and make sure children clearly understand what they are being asked to do. Identify each picture, and complete the first item together. Then work through the page with children, or have them complete the page independently.

ASSESS/CLOSE

Identify and Use V, v   Say the following sentence, and have children hold up their index and middle fingers to show a *V* when they hear a word that begins with the letter *v*: *Vic's van is very fast.* Write the sentence on the chalkboard and ask children to write *V* or *v* for each initial *v* they see.

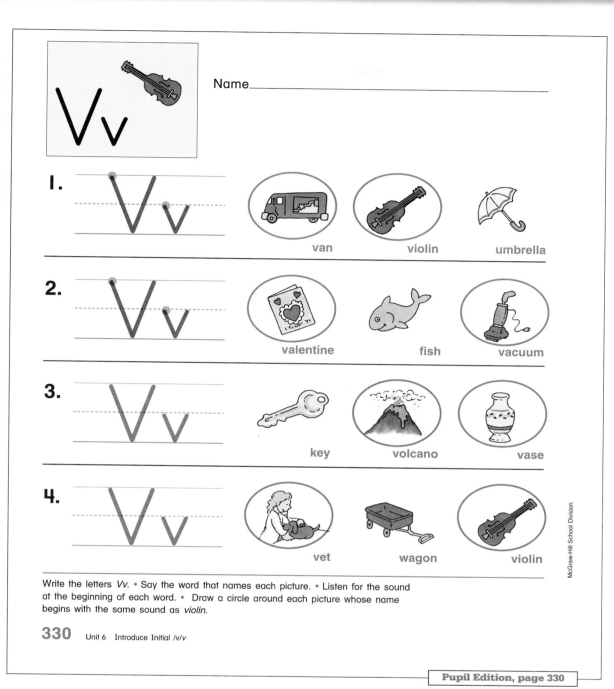

Name

1. Vv

van · violin · umbrella

2. Vv

valentine · fish · vacuum

3. Vv

key · volcano · vase

4. Vv

vet · wagon · violin

Write the letters *Vv*. • Say the word that names each picture. • Listen for the sound at the beginning of each word. • Draw a circle around each picture whose name begins with the same sound as *violin*.

McGraw-Hill School Division

330 Unit 6 Introduce Initial /v/v

Pupil Edition, page 330

ADDITIONAL PHONICS RESOURCES

Practice Book, *page 330*
Phonics Workbook

McGraw-Hill School
TECHNOLOGY

Phonics CD-ROM
Activities for practice with Initial Letters

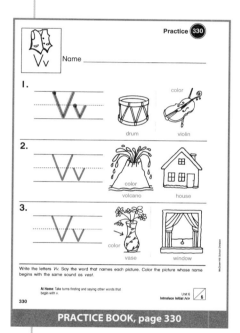

Practice 330

Name

1. Vv

drum · violin · color

2. Vv

volcano · color · house

3. Vv

vase · color · window

Write the letters *Vv*. Say the word that names each picture. Color the picture whose name begins with the same sound as *vest*.

At Home: Take turns finding and saying other words that begin with v.

330

Unit 6
Introduce Initial /v/v 6

McGraw-Hill School Division

PRACTICE BOOK, page 330

Meeting Individual Needs for Phonics

EASY	ON-LEVEL	CHALLENGE	LANGUAGE SUPPORT
Have children fold paper heart shapes in half vertically, then open them, and use the fold as a guide to write *V*. Tell children that /v/ is the sound you hear at the beginning of *valentine*. Have children make the /v/ sound with you. Children can decorate their valentine hearts.	**Invite** children to answer riddles using words that begin with v, such as: *When you speak you use this.* (voice) *It's bigger than a car.* (van) *Broccoli is one kind of these.* (vegetables) *You put flowers in this.* (vase) Have children write a *v* for every answer.	**Ask** children to tell stories about vacations they have taken or would like to take. Encourage them to use *v* words, such as: *visit, very, van, view, video, valley.* Have them dictate and illustrate their stories.	**For** ESL children who have difficulty distinguishing between initial /v/ and /b/, say the two sounds. Ask children what position your lips are in when you make these sounds. Have children practice the sounds, then chant these words: *vet, bet, vest, best, vat, bat.*

330

OBJECTIVES

Children will:

- make inferences
- recognize words with initial *v*
- understand alphabetical order

TEACHING TIP

Keep alphabet books in your reading corner. Invite children to compare structures of the books, and identify letters and key words.

Read the Big Book

Before Reading

Develop Oral Language
Sing "The Monkey Alphabet Song" with children. The song is on page 4 in the Big Book of Phonics Rhymes and Chimes. Then give children letter cards and sing the song again. Children hold up the appropriate card when they hear that letter.

Remind children that they read a story about some friends who found a box. Ask children to name some of the characters in the story.

Set Purposes
Remind children that they read a story about children who use their imaginations. Explain that they will learn more about the children. They will also say the word that begins with each alphabet letter.

"We can make a **game**," said Rob.

"We can make a **house**," said Gina.

The Big Box, pages 10-11

During Reading

Read Together

- Before you begin to read, point to the first word in the sentence. Explain that this is where you will begin to read. Continue to track print as you read the story. *Tracking Print*

- As you read the story, omit words that begin with the highlighted letter. Have children say the word, using the picture and the letter. After children supply the key word, confirm the choice by saying, *That's correct. The word alphabet begins with the letter* a. *Concepts of Print*

- After you read page 5, ask what they know about Rob from the story *(He likes boats.)* Invite children to think about Rob's other ideas in the story, and what his ideas tell us about him. *Make Inferences*

- Make the /v/ sound, and have children say the sound with you. After you read page 25, ask what word begins with that sound. *(van)* Ask children to think of other words that begin with the same sound. *Phonics*

"We can make an **alphabet** box," said Gina.

The Big Box, page 4

After Reading

Literary Response

JOURNAL WRITING Ask children to draw and write about one of the children in the story.

ORAL RESPONSE Ask questions such as:

- *Would you like to have ___ as a friend? Why or why not?*

- *What things did ___ want to make from the box?*

ABC Activity

Show the letter card for a, and have children make the /a/ sound with you. Ask a volunteer to say a word that begins with that sound. Continue through the alphabet.

CULTURAL PERSPECTIVES

STAMPS Share that each country in the world has its own stamps. Stamps show what is important to that country. Stamps show a country's leaders, famous artists, inventors, and natural wildlife.

▶ **Spatial/Linguistic**

Activity Provide each child with a sheet of paper. Ask them to draw a stamp that shows something important to them. Have children display and discuss their stamps.

OBJECTIVES

Children will:

- sort and classify objects

....

MATERIALS

- *The Earth and I*

TEACHING TIP

INSTRUCTIONAL

Before beginning the lesson, review the terms *same* and *different*. Use clothing, classroom objects, and colors to reinforce these concepts.

Review Categories

PREPARE

Play a Game

Play the game "Same and Different." Say: *I am thinking of an animal with four legs and a tail. What animal coud it be?* Accept all reasonable answers and talk about how the animals are the same and how they are different.

TEACH

Find What Belongs

Display the Big Book *The Earth and I*, and ask children to recall the story. Then name a category, such as animals, and take a picture walk through the book to find out what belongs in this category. Make a picture or a word list. Then continue with plants.

PRACTICE

Make Groups

Read the directions on page 331 to the chidlren, and make sure they clearly understand what they are asked to do. Identify each picture, and complete the first item. Then work through the page with children, or have them complete the page independently.

ASSESS/CLOSE

Review the Page

Check children's work on the Pupil Edition page. Note areas where children need extra help.

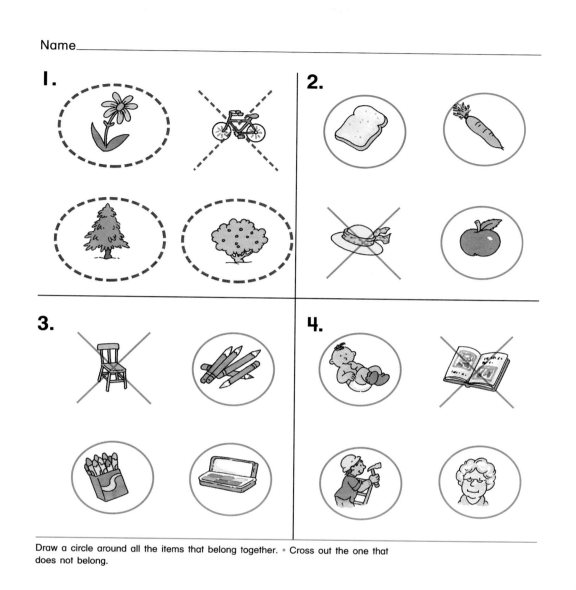

Name_____

1.

2.

3.

4.

Draw a circle around all the items that belong together. • Cross out the one that does not belong.

Unit 6   Review Categories   331

Pupil Edition, page 331

ALTERNATE TEACHING
STRATEGY

For a different approach to teaching this skill, see page T33.

▶ **Visual/Auditory/ Kinesthetic**

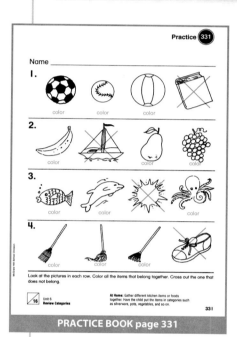

PRACTICE BOOK page 331

Meeting Individual Needs for Beginning Reading Concepts

EASY	ON-LEVEL	CHALLENGE	LANGUAGE SUPPORT
Begin with a very simple category, such as color. Put various crayons on a table, and ask a child to sort by color. Then have the child sort the crayons by size.	**Name** a category, such as food. Have children name items that belong in this category and make a picture or a word list.	**Use** the word list from the On-Level activity, and ask children how they can make different categories of food. Children may list fruits, vegetables, meats, dairy, grains, and so on. Have them classify the items from the list.	**Have** children look outside the classroom window. Ask children to classify by asking: *What animals do you see? What plants? What people do you see?*

Develop Phonological Awareness

Listen

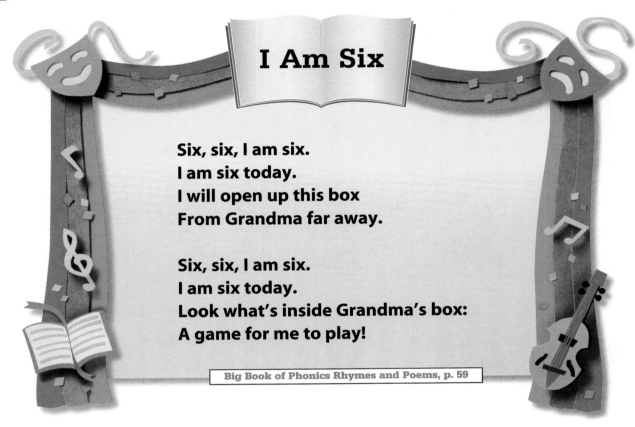

I Am Six

Six, six, I am six.
I am six today.
I will open up this box
From Grandma far away.

Six, six, I am six.
I am six today.
Look what's inside Grandma's box:
A game for me to play!

Big Book of Phonics Rhymes and Poems, p. 59

Objective: Listen to and Compare Sounds

IDENTIFY SOUNDS

- Prepare a large box with several objects inside that you can use to make distinct sounds. Examples: paper to crumble, a box of paper clips, a ruler to tap.
- Read the poem "I Am Six" to children.
- Tell children that they will play a game called "A Box from Grandma."
- Without letting children see into the box, reach in and shake the box of clips. Then crumple the paper. Finally, tap the ruler on the bottom of the box. Have children describe the sounds that they heard.
- Then show them the items that you used to make the sounds, and verify their guesses.

CHANGE THE SEQUENCE OF SOUNDS

- Repeat the activity, making the noises in a different order. Children tell what they heard first, next, and last.

ADD SOUNDS TO THE BOX

- Have children repeat the poem with you. This time add one more sound to the box, showing it to the children first.
- Then repeat the activity.

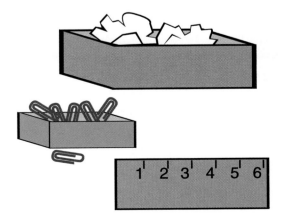

Objective: Listen for Final /ks/

SEGMENTING

- Make the /ks/ sound and have children say it with you. Then say the word box, emphasizing the final sound. Have children repeat the sound after you.

- Explain that sometimes when you take away a sound of a word, you get a new word. Say *box*. Then take away /b/.

> **box —-> ox**

- Ask children if they know what an ox is, and establish that the meaning of the word is different from *box*.

SEGMENT THE INITIAL SOUND

- Say the following words. Have children repeat them, without the initial sound.

> **fox/ox   lox/ox   mix/ix**
> **box/ox   six/ix   fix/ix**

From Phonemic Awareness to Phonics

Read Together

Identify Final /ks/ *x*

IDENTIFY THE LETTER FOR THE SOUND

- Explain to children that the letter x stands for the sound /ks/. Display page 59 in the Big Book of Phonics Rhymes and Poems, and point to the letters in the corner. Identify the letters and have children repeat the sound.

- Read the poem again, stopping at each word that ends with /ks/. Have children repeat the sound /ks/ with you.

FIND WORDS WITH X

- Write a lowercase x on 10 stick-on notes. Have children place the notes over the *x*s in the poem.

- Have children identify and count the number of times the letters X,x appear.

I Am Six

Six, six, I am six.
I am six today.
I will open up this box
From Grandma far away.

Six, six, I am six.
I am six today.
Look what's inside Grandma's box.
A game for me to play!

59

Big Book of Phonics Rhymes and Poems, p. 59

TESTED OBJECTIVES

Children will:
- identify the letter *x*
- identify /ks/ *x*
- form the letter *x*

....

MATERIALS
- letter cards from the Word Play Book

TEACHING TIP

INSTRUCTIONAL Continue to emphasize the order in which strokes are written as children write letters. Have them practice writing the letters with a variety of materials (sand/salt tray, finger paint, crayons, and so on).

ALTERNATE TEACHING STRATEGY

....

FINAL /ks/x

For a different approach to teaching this skill, see page T31.

▶ **Visual/Auditory/Kinesthetic**

Introduce Final /ks/x

TEACH

Identify /ks/ *x* — Tell children they will learn to write the sound /ks/ with the letter *x*. Write the letter, and have them make the sound with you. Ask them to repeat the sound after you, and on the chalkboard write *Max, Mal, Ray, Rex, Tex, Tod*. Read the names, and ask children to hold up their letter cards when they recognize a name that ends in *x*.

Form *x* — Display letter *x* and, with your back to the children, trace it in the air. Ask children to do the same. Then have them trace letter *x*s on their desks with their fingers. Give each child a piece of paper folded into four sections, and ask them to write *x* on each section.

PRACTICE

Complete the Pupil Edition Page — Read the directions on page 332 to the children, and make sure they clearly understand what they are asked to do. Identify each picture, and complete the first item together. Then work through the page with children, or have them complete the page independently.

ASSESS/CLOSE

Identify and Use *x* — Place the following words written on index cards on the chalkboard ledge: *fix, fin, wax, wag*. Point to each word as you read them aloud. Write this sentence on the chalkboard: *Max has to ___ the mop so he can ___ the floor.* Read the sentence several times, and invite children to fill in the missing words using the word cards.

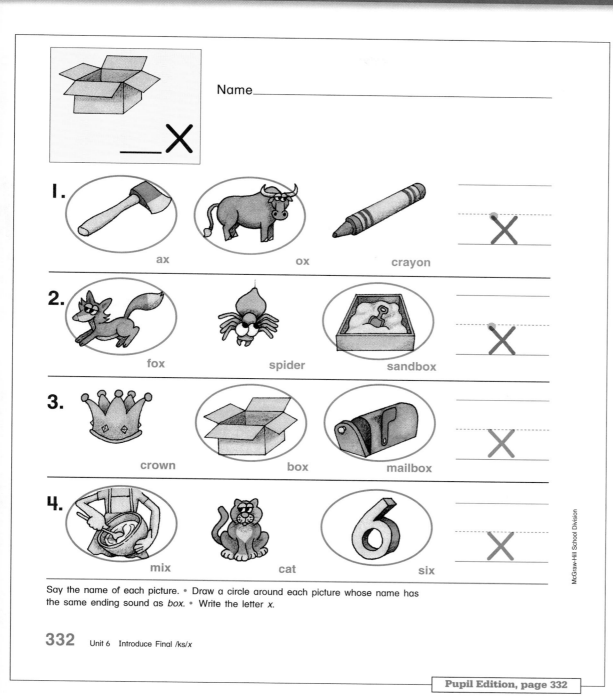

Name_____

__x

1. ax　　　ox　　　crayon　　x

2. fox　　　spider　　　sandbox　　x

3. crown　　　box　　　mailbox　　x

4. mix　　　cat　　　six　　x

Say the name of each picture. • Draw a circle around each picture whose name has the same ending sound as *box*. • Write the letter *x*.

McGraw-Hill School Division

332　Unit 6　Introduce Final /ks/x

Pupil Edition, page 332

ADDITIONAL PHONICS
RESOURCES
Practice Book *page 332*
Phonics Workbook

McGraw-Hill School
TECHNOLOGY

Phonics CD-ROM
Activities for practice with
Initial Letters

Practice 332

__x

Name_____

1. moose　　ox　color　　x

2. six　　eight　color　　x

3. fox　color　　rabbit　　x

Say the name of each picture in each row. Color the picture whose name has the same ending sound as box. Write the letters x.

At Home: Together, think of other words (ax, fix, and so on) that end in x. Ask the child to write x for each word you think of.

Unit 6
Introduce Final /ks/x

332

McGraw-Hill School Division

PRACTICE BOOK page 332

Meeting Individual Needs for Phonics

EASY	ON-LEVEL	CHALLENGE	LANGUAGE SUPPORT
Have children raise their arms and then cross them to show the letter *x*. Invite a volunteer to name items. Ask children to raise their "*x* arms" if they hear /ks/ at the end of the named item. If needed, supply the volunteer with words: *hat, box, lion, fox, ox, pig,* and so on.	**Place** a *box* with the letter *x* on it on a table, and show pictures of the following: *ox, fox, sack,* (numeral) *six, kite, ax*. Help children name the objects; put pictures into the box if they end in *x*. Have them draw *x* pictures and label with *x* self-stick notes.	**Place** a box on a table labeled with the word *box*. Invite children to draw things that end with x on index cards. Then write the letter *x* under each item. Have children share their pictures with each other before putting the cards in the box.	**Write** the word *box* on the chalkboard. Read the word aloud and have children repeat it. Then invite them to put their *x* self-stick notes on boxes they see in the classroom. Remind them to look for boxes of all sizes.

OBJECTIVES

- understand cause and effect

ALAN BAKER lives outside a small village in England. He says, "My illustrations are mostly of plants, animals, and fantasy. I derive much inspiration from travel, which I do a lot of, living very simply, which I think is important in order to really 'see things.'"

LANGUAGE SUPPORT

ESL Use the illustrations and photographs to reinforce color words. Help children identify the colors as necessary, and encourage them to find or name other things that are the same color. You may also wish to use crayons and to have children match things in the classroom that are the same color.

Read the Big Book

Before Reading

Build Background

EVALUATE PRIOR KNOWLEDGE Name primary colors, and have children find objects in the classroom that are of each color. Then invite them to name other things that are that color.

MIX SOME COLORS Display red, blue, and yellow paint. Have volunteers help you mix red and blue paint, and have them discover that they create the color purple. Invite children to name other colors to mix, and make a chart that records colors that they create.

Preview and Predict

DISCUSS AUTHOR AND ILLUSTRATOR Point out that Mr. Baker is both the author and the illustrator, and share some background information.

TAKE A PICTURE WALK Read the title of the book and display the cover. Take a **picture walk** through the first four spreads of the book, and talk about what happens to the rabbit.

MAKE PREDICTIONS Invite children to predict what the rabbit might do next.

Set Purposes

Ask children what they would like to find out about the rabbit and about mixing colors.

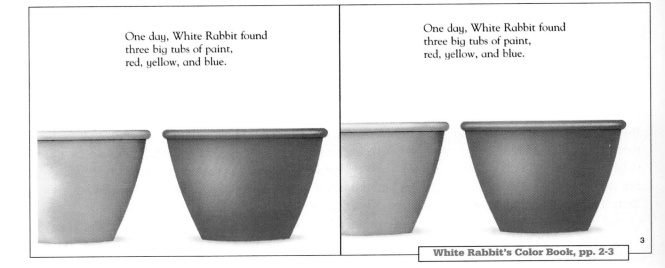

One day, White Rabbit found three big tubs of paint, red, yellow, and blue.

One day, White Rabbit found three big tubs of paint, red, yellow, and blue.

White Rabbit's Color Book, pp. 2-3

During Reading

Read Together

- Before you begin to read, point to the first word in the first sentence. Explain that this is where you will begin to read. Continue to track print as you read the story. *Tracking Print*

- After you read page 8, point to the first question mark. Explain that this mark tells us that the sentence asks a question. Have children reread the sentence with you, raising their voices at the end of the sentence. Then discuss the exclamation point, and reread the sentence with excitement. *Concepts of Print*

- As you read page 8, ask children: *Why did the rabbit turn orange?* Continue to ask questions about the colors, such as: *What happened when Rabbit painted himself red and blue? Understand Cause and Effect*

Red Rabbit, sizzling hot red.

12

White Rabbit's Color Book, p.12

After Reading

Return to Predictions and Purposes

Ask children if their predictions about the story were correct. Then ask if they found out what they wanted to know about color mixing.

Literary Response

JOURNAL WRITING Ask children to draw a picture of Rabbit after he painted himself a new color. Help children to write the colors that were mixed to make the new color.

ORAL RESPONSE Engage children in a discussion about their drawings by asking the following questions:

- *What color is Rabbit in your picture?*

- *What colors would he mix to become that color?*

Cross Curricular: Art

COLOR CREATIONS Provide paper cups with tempera paint, water, paintbrushes, and drawing paper. Have children experiment with color mixing as they paint their own pictures.

Encourage them to try to mix new colors and to record the results.

▶ **Spatial/Kinesthetic**

OBJECTIVES

Children will:

- recognize cause and effect to understand a story

MATERIALS

- *White Rabbit's Color Book*

TEACHING TIP

INSTRUCTIONAL

Use classroom experiences to highlight cause-and-effect relationships. Ask questions such as: *What will happen when the school bell rings?*

Review Cause and Effect

PREPARE

Recall the Story Ask children to recall the story *White Rabbit's Color Book.* Ask children: *Why do you think the rabbit jumped into the paint?*

TEACH

Relate Story Events Read the story and stop after page 8. Ask: *What happened after the rabbit jumped into the paint?* Explain that often when one thing happens, it causes something else to happen. Then continue to read the story, stopping to ask what happens each time the rabbit dips into the paint.

PRACTICE

Complete the Pupil Edition Page Read the directions on page 333 to the children, and make sure they clearly understand what they are being asked to do. Identify each picture, and complete the first item together. Then work through the page with children, or have them complete the page independently.

ASSESS/CLOSE

Review the Page Review children's work, and note children who are experiencing difficulty.

Name_____

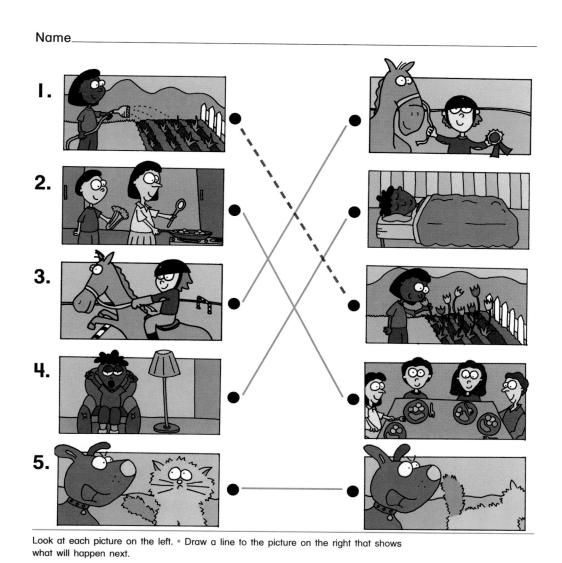

Look at each picture on the left. • Draw a line to the picture on the right that shows what will happen next.

Unit 6   Review Cause and Effect   **333**

Pupil Edition, page 333

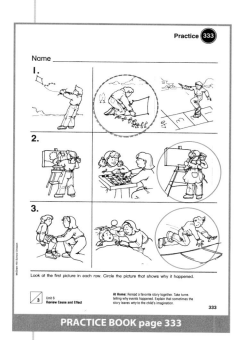

ALTERNATE TEACHING STRATEGY

CAUSE AND EFFECT

For a different approach to teaching this skill, see page T26.

▶ **Visual/Auditory/Kinesthetic**

Practice 333

Name_____

Look at the first picture in each row. Circle the picture that shows why it happened.

Unit 6
Review Cause and Effect

At Home: Reread a favorite story together. Take turns telling why events happened. Explain that sometimes the story leaves cause why to the child's imagination.

333

PRACTICE BOOK page 333

Meeting Individual Needs for Comprehension

EASY	ON-LEVEL	CHALLENGE	LANGUAGE SUPPORT
Prepare small tins with tempera paint in primary colors. Children mix two colors and describe their actions and results. Then have them use their new color to paint something that might be that color.	**Show** pictures of everyday actions and ask children to describe cause-and-effect relationships. Ask questions such as: *What happens when you don't get enough sleep? What happens when you water the plants? What happens when it gets cloudy outside?*	**Draw** a picture of a broken window. Ask children to brainstorm reasons for it being broken. Continue with other examples, such as a dog that is covered with mud.	**Invite** children to turn the light switch on. Then ask: *What happens when you turn on the switch?* Continue with other examples, such as watering flowers or dropping a glass of water.

333

Develop Phonological Awareness

Listen

Vickie's Velvet Vest
a poem

I Am Six
a poem

Vickie has a velvet vest
That's very, very pretty.
Vickie wears her velvet vest
To go into the city.
Vickie went to visit
Aunt Vera and Uncle Joe.
They had a very good dinner
And they saw a funny show.

Six, six, I am six.
I am six today.
I will open up this box
From Grandma far away.
Six, six, I am six.
I am six today.
Look what's inside Grandma's
   box.
A game for me to play.

Big Book of Phonics Rhymes and Poems, pages 56 and 59

Objective: Listen and Count Syllables

READ THE POEMS Read "Vickie's Velvet Vest" and "I Am Six." They say the name *Vickie* aloud. Repeat the name and hold up one finger for each syllable as you say it.

COUNT SYLLABLES Explain that each finger stands for one syllable. Help children determine that there are two syllables in *Vickie*. Repeat with other words.

COUNT THE NUMBER OF SYLLABLES Invite a volunteer to say his or her name aloud. Have the class hold up one finger for each syllable they say. Count the syllables in the child's name.

SUBSTITUTE NAMES reread "Vickie's Velvet Vest" several times. Each time substitute another child's name for *Vickie*. Have children say the new name with you each time it is used in the poem and hold up one finger for each syllable as it is said.

Objective: Listen for /v/ and /ks/

LISTEN FOR INITIAL /v/ Make the /v/ sound and ask children to repeat it with you. Then read the title "Vickie's Velvet Vest," emphasizing the initial /v/ sound. Have children repeat the words with you.

> **Vickie's Velvet Vest**

LISTEN FOR FINAL /ks/ Read the title "I Am Six," emphasizing the final /ks/ in the word *six*. Have children say the /ks/ sound.

RECOGNIZE AND COUNT THE SOUND Provide each child with counters and a cup. Reread "Vickie's Velvet Vest." Have children place one counter in the cup each time they hear a word that begins with /v/. After reading the poem, say the words that begin with /v/ and have children take one counter out of the cup or each word you say. Help children count the counters.

> Vickie's Velvet Vest Vickie velvet
> vest very very Vickie velvet vest
> Vickie visit Vera very

READ "I AM SIX." Invite children to use their counters and cups to help them count the number of times they hear /ks/ at the end of a word.

> six six six six six box
> six six six six box

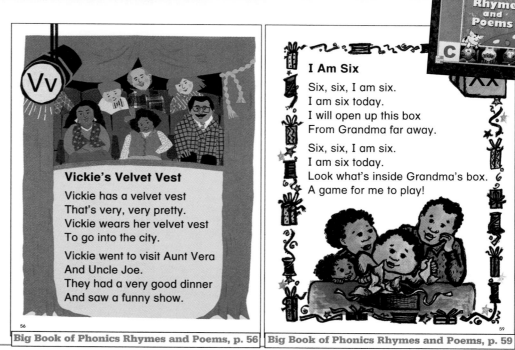

Read Together

From Phonemic Awareness to Phonics

Objective : Identify /v/V,v; /ks/X,x

IDENTIFY THE LETTER Tell children that the letters *V* and *v* stand for /v/ and the letters *X* and *x* stand for /ks/. Have children say the sounds. Display pages 56 and 59 in the *Big Book of Phonics Rhymes and Poems*. Point to *V, v* and *X, x*.

REREAD THE POEMS Reread the poems. Point to each word, emphasizing words with /v/ or /ks/.

FIND THE WORDS WITH V, v, x Have children match letter cards for *V, v,* and *x* to those letters used in the words in the poems.

Vickie's Velvet Vest

Vickie has a velvet vest
That's very, very pretty.
Vickie wears her velvet vest
To go into the city.

Vickie went to visit Aunt Vera
And Uncle Joe.
They had a very good dinner
And saw a funny show.

56

I Am Six

Six, six, I am six.
I am six today.
I will open up this box
From Grandma far away.

Six, six, I am six.
I am six today.
Look what's inside Grandma's box.
A game for me to play!

59

Big Book of Phonics Rhymes and Poems, p. 56 *Big Book of Phonics Rhymes and Poems, p. 59*

334B

OBJECTIVES

Children will:

- identify and discriminate between /v/V,v and /ks/x
- write and use letters V,v and x

MATERIALS

- picture cards and word cards from the *Word Building Book*

TEACHING TIP

INSTRUCTIONAL Point out to children that in this lesson all the *v*'s are first letters of words and all the *x*'s are last letters of words. Explain that in English very few words begin with *x*. You may also wish to point out that, while many words end in the sound /v/ *(have, give, love)*, these words have a silent *e* at the end, so *v* is not the last letter of the word.

ALTERNATE TEACHING STRATEGY

....

LETTERS /v/v AND /ks/x

For a different approach to teaching this skill, see pages T30, T31.

▶ **Visual/Auditory/ Kinesthetic**

Review /v/v, /x/x

TEACH

Identify and Discriminate Between /v/V,v and /ks/x

Tell children they will review the sounds /v/ and /ks/ and write the letters *V,v* and *x*. Ask them to repeat both sounds while you write *V,v* on one side of the chalkboard and *x* on the other. Then ask them to clap when they hear either sound and say: *Val the vet can fix the leg of a fox.* Each time children identify a /v/ or /ks/ sound, write the word under the appropriate letter.

Write and Use V,v and x

Show pictures of the following objects, and ask children to name the objects, using words that begin in *v* or end in *x*: *box, vase, violin, (numeral) six, ax, vegetables.* Have them point to the letter on the chalkboard where each word belongs. Write the words and have children write the letters *v* and *x* on letter strips.

PRACTICE

Complete the Pupil Edition Page

Read the directions on page 334 of the Pupil Edition, and make sure children clearly understand what they are being asked to do. Identify each picture, and complete the first item together. Then work through the page with children, or have them complete the page independently.

ASSESS/CLOSE

Identify and Use V,v and x

Arrange these word cards on the chalkboard ledge: *van, wax, fix, vet, vat, ox.* Have children write the same sequence of initial *v* and final *x* on their letter strips.

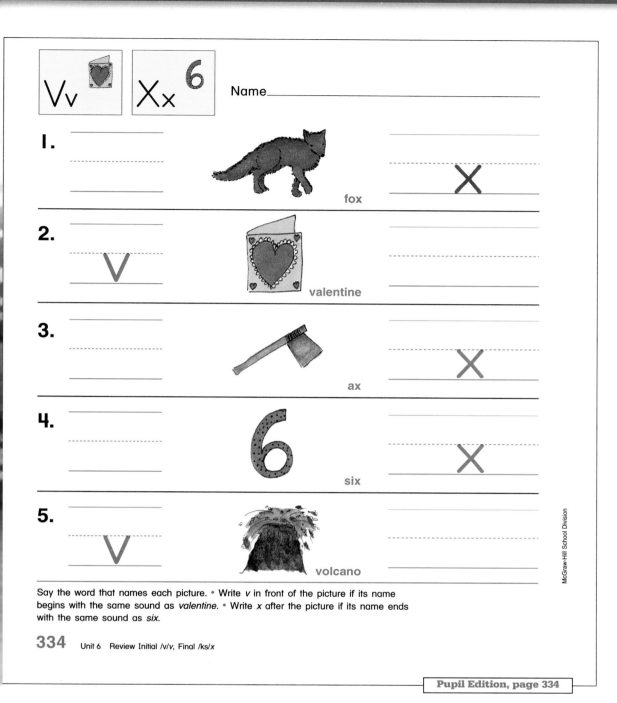

Vv Xx 6   Name_____

1. _____ _____
   _ _ _ _ _ _ _ _   fox   X

2. _____ _____
   V   valentine

3. _____ _____
                  ax   X

4. _____ _____
                  six   X

5. _____ _____
   V   volcano

Say the word that names each picture. • Write *v* in front of the picture if its name begins with the same sound as *valentine*. • Write *x* after the picture if its name ends with the same sound as *six*.

McGraw-Hill School Division

334   Unit 6   Review Initial /v/v, Final /ks/x

Pupil Edition, page 334

ADDITIONAL PHONICS RESOURCES

Practice Book, *page 334*
Phonics Workbook

McGraw-Hill School
TECHNOLOGY

Phonics CD-ROM
Activities for practice with Initial and Final Letters

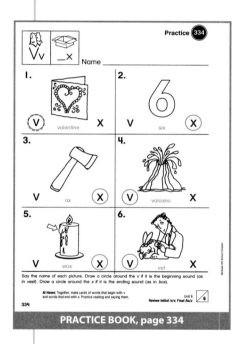

PRACTICE BOOK, page 334

Meeting Individual Needs for Phonics

EASY	ON-LEVEL	CHALLENGE	LANGUAGE SUPPORT
Write *v* and *x* on the chalkboard, and talk about how, in both cases, you are simply drawing two straight lines: in *v*, the lines meet at the bottom and in *x* they cross in the middle. Have children use craft sticks to form the letters *v* and *x*.	**Invite** children to answer riddles using words that begin with *v* or end in *x*, such as: *This is an instrument. (violin) This is another word for stir. (mix) This number comes after five. (six) This is a doctor for pets. (vet)* Have children write a *v* or *x* for every initial /v/ or final /ks/ word.	**Have** children form a circle and pass a box containing pictures of things that begin in *v* or end in *x*, such as: ax, van, vitamins, box, wax, violin. One child identifies the object pictured, and the next child makes up a sentence using the word.	**Help** ESL children distinguish the final /ks/x and /sk/sk sounds by having them repeat the following: *Ask Rex to fix the mask. Look in the box on the desk.*

334

Teacher Read Aloud

Listen

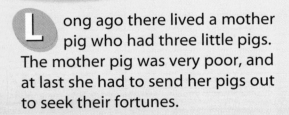

The Three Little Pigs
by Joseph Jacobs

L ong ago there lived a mother pig who had three little pigs. The mother pig was very poor, and at last she had to send her pigs out to seek their fortunes.

The first little pig that went away met a man with a bundle of straw, and he said to him, "Please, man, give me that straw so I can build me a house."

The man gave the straw to the little pig. Then the pig built a house of the straw and lived in the house.

By and by a wolf came along and knocked at the door of the little straw house.

"Little pig, little pig, let me come in!" called the wolf.

"No, not by the hair of my chinny, chin chin, I'll not let you in," answered the pig.

"Then I'll huff and I'll puff and I'll blow your house in," said the wolf.

So he huffed and he puffed and he blew the house in. Then he chased the little pig away.

The second little pig that went away met a man with a bundle of sticks, and he said to the man, "Please, man, give me your bundle of sticks so I can build me a house."

Continued on page T4

Oral Comprehension

LISTENING AND SPEAKING Ask children to name familiar fairy tales. Explain that you are going to read the fairy tale "The Three Little Pigs." Ask children to name the character who causes problems for the little pigs. Then read the story.

After you read, ask questions that focus on cause and effect, such as: *What happened when the first pig built a house of straw? Why couldn't the Wolf blow down the brick house?*

Activity Invite children to tell a variation of the story by adding a fourth pig. Have children decide what kind of house the new character will build. Provide children with construction paper and crayons. Ask them to draw what the new house will look like.

▶ **Linguistic/Spatial**

Real-Life Reading

1. Three little pigs didn't know how to spell the word *pig*.

2. Their mother told them to look up the word in a dictionary.

3. They looked under *P* because *pig* begins with *p*.

4. They found the word *pig*. Now they know it is spelled *P-I-G*.

44 45

Big Book of Real-Life Reading, pages 44–45

Objective: Use a Library/Media Center

READ THE PAGE Explain that children can get information from many sources in a library/media center. Display a picture dictionary, and explain how it is used. Point out that children can use a dictionary to look up words to find the correct spelling or meaning. Discuss the pictures on the page, and read the corresponding text.

ANSWER THE QUESTION After children discuss the pictures, have them explain each step.

• Have children write their first names and circle the initial letter.

• Let children take turns at finding the page in the dictionary that highlights the letter.

CULTURAL PERSPECTIVES

HOMES As in the story *The Three Little Pigs*, people throughout the world build their homes with very different materials. An American family might live in a wooden house. A Nigerian family might live in a house made of mud bricks that keep out the hot sun and wind. An Italian family might live in a stone house.

Discuss how climate affects the type of house.

Activity Ask children to draw a house they would like to see. Provide paper and markers.

▶ Spatial

OBJECTIVES

Children will:

- identify and read the high-frequency word *not*

MATERIALS

- word cards from the *Word Play Book*
- *The Vet Van*

TEACHING TIP

INSTRUCTIONAL Write the word *not*, and use it in a sentence. Then tell children another meaning for a word that sounds the same *(knot)*. Explain that some words sound the same, but have different spellings and meanings.

Introduce High-Frequency Words: *not*

PREPARE

Listen to Words   Tell children that they will be learning a new word: *not*. Say the following sentence: *Do not open the door*. Repeat the sentence and ask children to raise their hands when they hear the word *not*. Follow with the sentence: *Do not let the wolf in*.

TEACH

Model Reading the Word in Context   Give a word card to each child, and read the word. Reread the sentences, and have children raise their hands when they hear the word.

Identify the Word   Write the sentences above on the chalkboard. Track print and read aloud each sentence. Have children hold up their word cards when they hear the word *not*. Then ask volunteers to point to and underline the word *not* in the sentences.

Write the Word   Review how to write the letters *n, o,* and *t*. Then have children practice writing the word *not*.

PRACTICE

Complete the Pupil Edition Page   Read the directions on page 335 to children, and make sure they clearly understand what they are being asked to do. Complete the first item together. Then work through the page with children, or have them complete the page independently.

ASSESS/CLOSE

Review the Page   Review children's work, and guide children who are experiencing difficulty or need additional practice.

Name_____ | **not**

I. That is <u>not</u> my pup.

2. That is <u>not</u> my pig.

3. My pig can <u>not</u> hop.

4. My pup is <u>not</u> big.

Read the sentence. • Then draw a line under the word *not* in the sentence.

Unit 6   Introduce High-Frequency Words: *not*   **335**

Pupil Edition, page 335

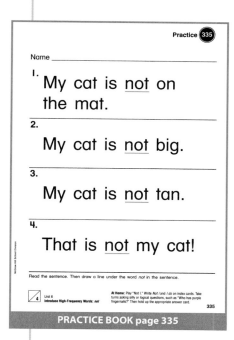

ALTERNATE TEACHING **STRATEGY**

HIGH-FREQUENCY WORDS: *not*

For a different approach to teaching the skill, see page T27.

▶ **Visual/Auditory/ Kinesthetic**

Practice 335

Name_____

I. My cat is <u>not</u> on the mat.

2. My cat is <u>not</u> big.

3. My cat is <u>not</u> tan.

4. That is <u>not</u> my cat!

Read the sentence. Then draw a line under the word *not* in the sentence.

Unit 6
Introduce High-Frequency Words: *not*

At Home: Play "Not I." Write *Not I* and *I do* on index cards. Take turns asking silly or logical questions, such as "Who has purple fingernails?" Then hold up the appropriate answer card.

335

PRACTICE BOOK page 335

Meeting Individual Needs for Vocabulary

EASY	ON-LEVEL	CHALLENGE	LANGUAGE SUPPORT
Give children letter cards for *n, o,* and *t.* Write the word *not* on the chalkboard, and have children form the word. Use the word in several sentences, and repeat.	**Write** on chalkboard sentences from "The Three Little Pigs" that include the word *not.* Have children find the word and underline it. Track print and read the sentences aloud.	**Work** with children to make a list of safety rules for the three pigs, repeating the phrase *"do not."* Have children dictate their sentences, and write them on chalkboard. Have children circle the word *not.* You may need to give an example, such as: *Do not make a house of straw.*	**Write** the word *not* and read it together with children. Use rhyming words to play a game: *This is a chair. It is not a (bear).* Write down the rhymes, and have volunteers point to the word *not.*

335

Develop Phonological Awareness

Listen

Sun Up

a poem

Tick tock. Sun up.
Rex sips from the cup.
Hot buns. Red Jam.
And a bit of ham.
Back pack. Red cap.
Back pack. Red cap.
Dad gets Rex a map.
Tick tock. Run. Run.
It is time for fun.

Objective: Focus on Rhythm

READ THE POEM Read the poem "Sun Up," emphasizing the staccato rhythm of the words tick tock.

CLAP THE RHYTHM Clap the first line of the poem. Invite children to join in. Repeat several times until children are comfortable with the rhythm of the words. Then reread the poem and have children clap the rhythm when you read lines 1,3, 5, and 7.

MOVE THE RHYTHM Invite children to sway left and right like a pendulum clock as they say "Tick tock. Tick tock." Reread the poem and have children sway and gently whisper, "Tick tock. Tick tock," as you read lines 1, 3, 5, and 7. Use the movement to help children feel the rhythm.

CLAP TO THE RHYTHM Have children clap their hands once and pat their legs once in rhythm as you reread the poem. Invite children to repeat the words from the poem that they remember.

Objective: Listen for Blending with Short *a, e, i, o, u*

LISTEN FOR THE SEGMENTED WORD
Reread the poem, segmenting the sounds in *Rex* each time you read it. After reading the poem, ask children to name the segmented word. If a clue is needed, say /r/-/e/-/x/. Have children repeat the sounds and then blend them to say *Rex*. Repeat the activity with other words in the poem.

> sun   bit   back

SUBSTITUTE NAMES Read the third to last line of the poem. Point out that Dad helps Rex by getting Rex a map. Mention that Dad helps others, too. Tell children you will give them clues to find out the names of others that Dad helps.

Say: *Dad helps Rex get a map.*
He helps /b/-/e/-/v/ find her cap.
Who else does Dad help?

Pause while children segment and then blend the sounds to say *Bev*. Repeat by substituting the segmented sounds in other names in the second sentence. Make adjustments to details in the second sentence as needed for the sentence to make sense with the new name.

> Val   Bif   Fox   Club

Read Together

From Phonemic Awareness to Phonics

Objective: Relate *a, e, i, o, u* to Short Vowel Sounds

LISTEN FOR RHYMING WORDS
Say: *Rex gets buns from the back of the tan van.* Invite children to name the rhyming words.

> tan   van

IDENTIFY THE LETTERS Say: /v/-/a/-/n/ as you write *van* on the chalkboard. Then identify the letters. Have children repeat the sounds and then the letters. Repeat with *tan*. Use colored chalk to frame the letters *an* in both words. Have children repeat after

you: /v/-/an/, /t/-/an/. Explain that the words rhyme because they have the same –*an* ending.

MAKE RHYMING WORDS Help children brainstorm rhyming words to add to *van* and *tan*.

> ban   Dan   can   fan
> man   Nan   pan   ran

OBJECTIVES

Children will:

- identify /a/a, /e/e, /i/i, /o/o, /u/u
- blend and read short *a, e, i, o, u* words
- write short *a, e, i, o, u* words
- review /v/v and /ks/x

MATERIALS

- letter cards from the *Word Building Book*

TEACHING TIP

INSTRUCTIONAL Give one short vowel card to each child, or to a small group. Ask them to build as many words as possible using their vowel as the middle letter. List their answers on chart paper under the appropriate short vowel heading.

ALTERNATE TEACHING STRATEGY

BLENDING SHORT
a, e, i, o, u

For a different approach to teaching this skill, see Unit 1, page T32; Unit 2, page T32; Unit 3, page T30; Unit 4, page T32; Unit 5, page T30.

▶ **Visual/Auditory/ Kinesthetic**

Review Blending with short *a, e, i, o, u*

TEACH

Identify *a, e, i, o, u* as Symbols for /a/, /e/, /i/, /o/, /u/

Tell children they will continue to read words with *a, e, i, o, u.*

- Display the *a, e, i, o, u* letter cards and say /a/, /e/, /i/, /o/, /u/. Have children repeat the sounds as you point to the cards.

BLENDING Model and Guide Practice

- Place the *x* card after the *i* card. Blend the sounds together and have children repeat after you.

- Place the *f* letter card before the *i* and *x* cards. Blend to read *fix.*

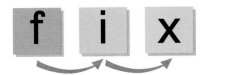 

Use the Word in Context

- Ask children to use *fix* in a sentence, perhaps telling about something they know how to repair or want to have repaired.

Repeat the Procedure

- Use the following words to continue modeling and for guided practice with short *a, e, i, o, u: van, vet, sick, leg, Max, Rex, back.*

PRACTICE

Complete the Pupil Edition Page

Read aloud the directions on page 336. Identify each picture, and complete the first item together. Then work through the page with children or have them complete the page independently.

ASSESS/CLOSE

Build Short *a, e, i, o, u* Words

Observe children as they complete page 336. Then ask them to use their letter cards to build four words that have short *a, e, i, o,* or *u* in the middle and begin with *v* or end with *x.*

Name_____

1. o x   ox

2. f o x   fox

3. v a n   van

4. b a t   bat

Blend the sounds and say the word. • Write the word. • Draw a circle around the
picture that goes with the word.

McGraw-Hill School Division

Pupil Edition, page 336

ADDITIONAL PHONICS RESOURCES

Practice Book, *page 336*
Phonics Workbook

McGraw-Hill School
TECHNOLOGY

Phonics CD-ROM
**Activities for Practice with
Blending and Segmenting**

PRACTICE BOOK page 336

Meeting Individual Needs for Phonics

EASY	ON-LEVEL	CHALLENGE	LANGUAGE SUPPORT
Show word cards: *ox, ax, fox, box, wax, fix.* Ask children to repeat after you as you blend sounds to read each word aloud. Ask how *ox* and *ax* are different from the other words. *(They only have two letters.)*	**Ask** children to write, then read aloud, the words they hear you say. Pronounce words by saying each letter sound separately. Say, for example: *fix, box, sock, vet, wed, van.*	**Give** groups of children several incomplete word cards such as: *_ox, va_, _ax, ve_, _ix, we_.* Using all letters reviewed, each group builds and records as many different CVC (including CV*ck*) words as they can.	**Ask** children to blend sounds with you to read these words you have written on the chalkboard: *fix, lick, kid, fan, van, vet, wet.* Clarify word meanings, and show pictures if possible. Talk about sounds that are similar.

336

Guided Instruction

BEFORE READING

PREVIEW AND PREDICT Take a brief **picture walk** through the book, focusing on the illustrations. Ask the children:

- *Who is this story about?*

- *What do you think will happen to Rex?*

- *Do you think the story is realistic, or is it make-believe? Why?*

SET PURPOSES Discuss with children things they may want to find out by reading this story. Ask questions such as *How can Pam help the dog?* to help the children set their own purposes.

TEACHING TIP

To put book together:

1. Tear out the story page.

2. Cut along dotted line.

3. Fold each section on fold line.

4. Assemble book.

INSTRUCTIONAL Ask children to share experiences about taking their pets to the vet. Make sure children understand what a vet does. Point out that some doctors have offices, and others travel to see their patients.

The Vet Van

Pam has a van to get a sick pet.

3

Pam is a vet.

2

Pam can go to get
Rex in the van.

4

Guided Instruction

DURING READING

☑ **Blending with Short *e, a, i, o, u***

☑ **Cause and Effect**

☑ **Concepts of Print**

☑ **High-Frequency Word: *not***

① **CONCEPTS OF PRINT** Have children look at the title page and ask them to identify the spaces between the words. Ask children to use their index fingers to cover the spaces. Invite children to count the number of words they see.

② **USE ILLUSTRATIONS** Ask children to describe what Pam is doing on page 2. (checking a cat)

③ **BLENDING WITH SHORT *e*** After you read the text on page 3, ask children which words have the short *e* sound. (get, pet)

④ **BLENDING WITH SHORT *a*** Have children make the short *a* sound. Then ask children to count the number of short *a* words they see on page 4. (3) Have children blend the letters to read these words: *P-a-m Pam, c-a-n can, v-a-n van*

LANGUAGE SUPPORT

ESL Display the word *veterinarian* on the board. Say the word and tell children that a veterinarian is an animal doctor. Then explain to children that we have a shorter way of saying this word. Erase all but the first 3 letters of the word. (vet) Ask children who speak another language to share what the word for animal doctor (vet) is in their language.

337/338B

Guided Instruction

BEFORE READING

(5) **HIGH-FREQUENCY WORDS** Ask children to look at page 5 and point to the word that begins with *n. (not)* Track print as you read it together. Then have children reread the word, tracking print.

(6) **CONCEPTS OF PRINT** Ask children to count the number of words on page 6. (7) Ask children what is the same about all these words. (They all have vowels. They all have 3 letters.)

(7) **CAUSE AND EFFECT** Explain that when something happens in a story, it can cause something else to happen. Ask children to look at page 7 and ask why they think Rex and Max are happy. (Pam has helped to fix Rex's leg.)

(8) **CONCEPTS OF PRINT** Have children frame the exclamation point on page 8 and identify it. Invite children to read the sentence in an excited voice.

INFORMAL ASSESSMENT

CAUSE AND EFFECT

HOW TO ASSESS Have children draw a picture showing why Max and Rex were happy. (Pam fixed Rex's leg.)

FOLLOW-UP Guide children through pages 6 and 7 of the story. Show them that Pam was able to fix Rex's leg *(page 6)* and that is what caused Max and Rex not to be sad (page 7).

Rex has a bad leg, and Max can not fix it.

5

Rex and Max are not sad!

7

Pam can fix the leg
for Rex.

6

Rex can go back
with Max!

8

Guided Instruction

AFTER READING

RETURN TO PREDICTIONS AND PURPOSES
Remind children of their story predictions. You may want to ask questions such as: *What happened to Rex? Was Pam able to help him?*

RETELL THE STORY Have children retell the story by acting it out. Ask volunteers to play the parts of Pam, Rex; Max, the cat; and the cat owner.

LITERARY RESPONSE To help children respond to the story, ask:

- *Why would a van be helpful to Pam?*

- *What other things does a vet do?*

Invite children to draw and write about a different visit that Pam might make to another animal.

CENTER Activity

Cross Curricular: Social Studies

WHEN I GROW UP Provide picture cards that show different occupations. Have partners identify the occupations and share what they know about them.

▶ **Logical/Intrapersonal**

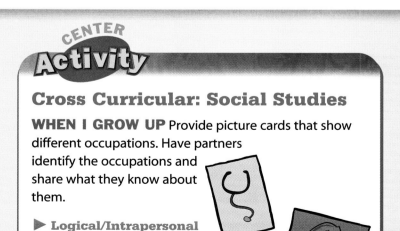

OBJECTIVES

Children will:

- recognize cause and effect to understand a story

MATERIALS

- *The Vet Van*

TEACHING TIP

INSTRUCTIONAL Clarify cause and effect if necessary by asking such simple "why" questions as: *Why do people feel happy on their birthdays?*

Review Cause and Effect

PREPARE

Think About the Story Ask children to recall the story *The Vet Van*. Ask children why Rex the dog felt better at the end of the story.

TEACH

Identify Cause and Effect Reread the story together. Then explain that when something happens in a story, it often causes something else to happen. Point out examples of this in the story. Look at page 7, and ask what will happen after the dog wears the cast.

PRACTICE

Complete the Pupil Edition Page Read the directions on page 339 to the children, and make sure they clearly understand what they are being asked to do. Identify each picture, and complete the first item together. Then work through the page with children, or have them complete the page independently.

ASSESS/CLOSE

Review the Page Review children's work, and note children who are experiencing difficulty.

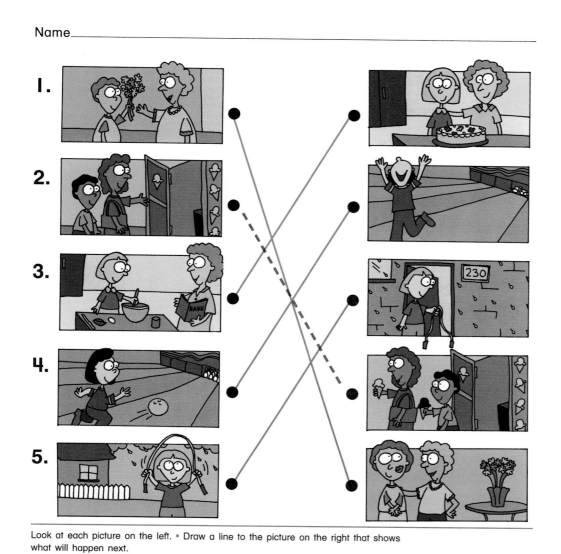

Name

1.

2.

3.

4.

5.

Look at each picture on the left. • Draw a line to the picture on the right that shows what will happen next.

Pupil Edition, page 339

ALTERNATE TEACHING
STRATEGY

CAUSE AND EFFECT

For a different approach to teaching this skill, see page T26.

▶ Visual/Auditory/ Kinesthetic

PRACTICE BOOK page 339

Meeting Individual Needs for Comprehension

EASY	ON-LEVEL	CHALLENGE	LANGUAGE SUPPORT
Ask students to remember a time when they felt happy. Make a list of the reasons they felt this way.	**Reread** page 2 of the story "The Vet Van." Ask why the cat might be visiting the vet. Discuss the cause-and-effect relationship.	**Give** each child a sheet of drawing paper and fold it in half. On the second section, have them draw a surprised self-portrait. On the first section, have them draw what made them feel surprised.	**Show** pictures of people expressing different emotions. Have children brainstorm reasons why the person in the picture might feel that way.

Develop Phonological Awareness

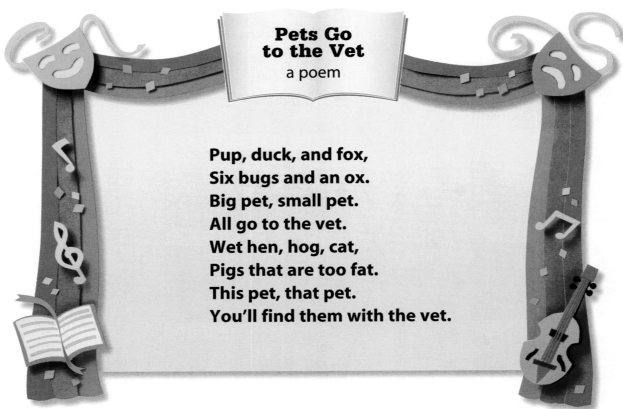

Pets Go to the Vet
a poem

Pup, duck, and fox,
Six bugs and an ox.
Big pet, small pet.
All go to the vet.
Wet hen, hog, cat,
Pigs that are too fat.
This pet, that pet.
You'll find them with the vet.

Objective: Focus on a Sequence of Sounds

READ THE POEM Read the poem "Pets Go to the Vet." Ask: *Where will you find all the pets?*

> **with the vet**

SOUNDS AT THE VET Explain that a vet is a doctor that takes care of animals. Reread the poem. Ask: *What animals will you find at the vet?*

> **pup   duck   fox   bug   ox**
> **hen   hog   cat   pig**

Mention that a vet might work in an office or travel from farm to farm. Ask: *What sounds might a vet hear?*

> **grrr   quack   meow   oink**

REPEAT A SEQUENCE Say: *Quack, quack, meow, meow.* Repeat the sequence and invite children to join in. Next say the sequence, but drop the last word. Have children complete the sequence. Continue by creating the sequence. Continue by creating other animal-sound sequences for children to repeat.

Objective: Listen for Blending with Short *a, e, i, o, u*

LISTEN FOR SEGMENTED WORDS Read the poem, segmenting the sounds in vet each time you read it. After reading the poem, have children repeat after you: /v/-/e/-/t/. Have children blend the sounds to say *vet*. Repeat the activity by segmenting the sounds in *pet* each time you read it in the poem.

WHO IS THE VET? Give children this clue.
Say: *I know a vet. It's not a him.*
In fact her name is Doctor /k/-/i/-/m/."
What is the name of the vet I know?

Pause while children repeat the segmented sound and then blend them to say *Kim*.

WHO IS AT THE VET? Tell children Dr. Kim sees lots of animals. Explain that you will give them clues to find out which animals are visiting the vet.

Say: *The vet has finished with the cow.*
Please bring your /p/-/u/-/p/ in now.
Who is the vet ready to see?

Have children repeat and then blend the segmented sound to find that the answer is *pup*. Repeat by substituting the segmented sounds in other animal names in the second sentence.

duck   fox   hen   cat

From Phonemic Awareness to Phonics

Objective: Relate *a, e, i, o, u* to Short Vowel Sounds

LISTEN TO RHYMING WORDS Reread the poem and ask children to name rhyming words. Write the words on the board. Identify the ending letters of each word.

fox-ox   pet-vet   cat-fat

THINK OF RHYMING WORDS Write the word *duck* on the chalkboard. Ask children to think of a word that rhymes with *duck*. Write it on the board and identify the ending letters. Repeat the same activity with the word *pig*.

IDENTIFY THE LETTERS Write *pet* and *vet* in a column on the chalkboard. Identify the sounds and letters in *pet*. Repeat with *vet*. Invite a volunteer to circle and identify the letters that are the same in both words. Have children say the letters *e*, and *t*, and the sounds these letters stand for: /e/-/t/, /et/. Repeat with other word pairs that rhyme.

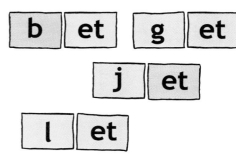

PHONICS AND DECODING

Review Blending with short a, e, i, o, u

OBJECTIVES

Children will:

- identify /a/*a*, /e/*e*, /i/*i*, /o/*o*, /u/*u*
- blend and read short *a, e, i, o, u* words
- write short *a, e, i, o, u* words
- review /v/*v*, /ks/*x*, /w/*w*, /h/*h*, /b/*b*, /g/*g*, /k/*k,ck*, /l/*l*, /p/*p*, /r/*r*, /f/*f*, /k/*c*, /t/*t*, /m/*m*, /s/*s*, /d/*d*, and /n/*n*

MATERIALS

- letter cards from the *Word Building Book*

TEACHING TIP

INSTRUCTIONAL Write the name *Max* on the chalkboard and have children blend letter sounds to read the word aloud. Show them how to stretch the /m/ sound to say *Mmmax*. Ask them to try stretching the final /ks/*x*; what final sound do they make? *(ssss)*

ALTERNATE TEACHING STRATEGY

BLENDING SHORT
a, e, i, o, u

For a different approach to teaching this skill, see Unit 1, page T32; Unit 2, page T32; Unit 3, page T30; Unit 4, page T32; Unit 5, page T30.

▶ **Visual/Auditory/ Kinesthetic**

TEACH

Identify *a, e, i, o, u* as Symbols for /a/, /e/, /i/, /o/, /u/

Tell children they will continue to read words with *a, e, i, o, u.*

- Display the *a, e, i, o, u* letter cards and say /a/, /e/, /i/, /o/, /u/. Have children repeat the sounds as you point to the cards.

BLENDING Model and Guide Practice

- Place the *x* card after the *a* card. Blend the sounds together and have children repeat after you: -ax.

$$\boxed{a}\ \boxed{x} \qquad \boxed{a\ x}$$

- Place the *w* card before the *a* and *x* cards. Blend to read *wax.*

$$\boxed{w}\ \boxed{a}\ \boxed{x} \qquad \boxed{w\ a\ x}$$

Use the Word in Context

- Have children use *wax* in a sentence, perhaps by describing what a candle or crayon looks, feels, or smells like.

Repeat the Procedure

- Use the following words to continue modeling and for guided practice with short *a, e, i, o, u: six, Rex, wet, him, hum, box, vat.*

PRACTICE

Complete the Pupil Edition Page

Read aloud the directions on page 340. Identify each picture, and complete the first item together. Work through the page, or have children complete the page independently.

ASSESS/CLOSE

Write Short *a, e, i, o, u* Words

Observe children as they complete page 340. Then give them letter cards *a, e, i, o, u* and *v, w, h, g, b* and ask children to write five words.

Name _____

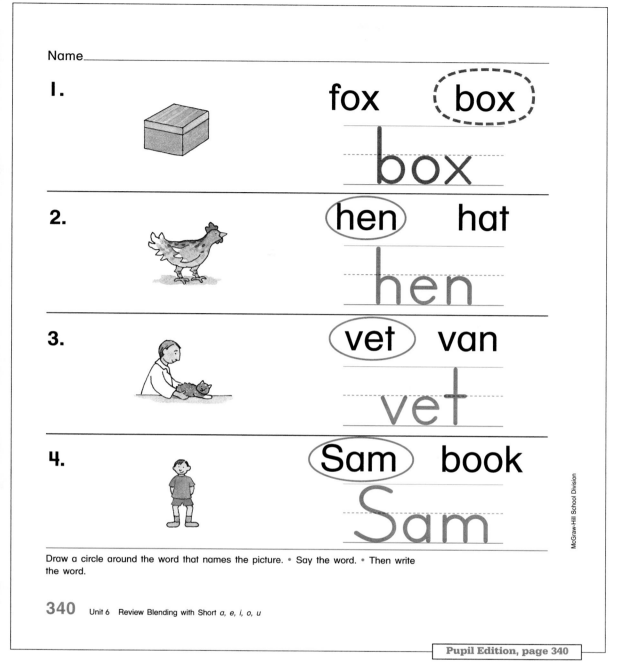

1. fox (box)

box

2. (hen) hat

hen

3. (vet) van

vet

4. (Sam) book

Sam

Draw a circle around the word that names the picture. • Say the word. • Then write the word.

McGraw-Hill School Division

340 Unit 6 Review Blending with Short *a, e, i, o, u*

Pupil Edition, page 340

ADDITIONAL PHONICS RESOURCES

Practice Book, *page 340*
Phonics Workbook

McGraw-Hill School
TECHNOLOGY

Phonics CD-ROM
Activities for Practice with
Blending and Segmenting

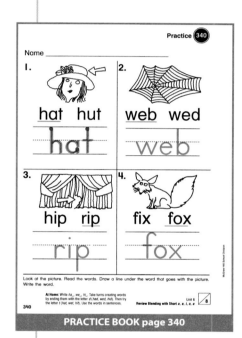

Practice 340

Name _____

1. hat hut   2. web wed

hat   web

3. hip rip   4. fix fox

rip   fox

Look at the picture. Read the words. Draw a line under the word that goes with the picture. Write the word.

At Home: Write /a__, we__, h/__. Take turns creating words by ending them with the letter d (had, wed, hid). Then try the letter t (hat, wet, hit). Use the words in sentences.

340   **Review Blending with Short *a, e, i, o, u***   Unit 6   8

PRACTICE BOOK page 340

Meeting Individual Needs for Phonics

EASY	ON-LEVEL	CHALLENGE	LANGUAGE SUPPORT
Display these word cards on the chalkboard ledge: *Rex, vet, vat, Max.* Have children repeat after you as you blend sounds to read aloud. Ask children to identify the words with initial *v* and words with final *x.* Then have them identify the letter in the middle of each word.	**Write** on the left side of the chalkboard *v, w, h, b, l;* on the right side *x, b, g, p, t;* and *a, e, i, o, u* in the middle. Have children work alone, or in small groups to see how many words they can make from these letters and list on a chart. Invite them to read their lists aloud.	**Use** all letter cards under review and have children write short *a, e, i, o, u* words on word strips. Ask them to work in a group to make up "word chains" in which each word differs by only one letter from the previous word. They may write more words to make their chains if needed.	**Give** children opportunities to blend and read words that begin with *v, w, b, f,* such as: *fat, vat, vet, wet, van, ban.* In French, *w* is often pronounced as /v/. The German *v* may be pronounced /f/ and so on.

340

Reread the Decodable Story

The Vet Van

☑ **Blend with Short Vowels**
☑ **Cause and Effect**
☑ **High-Frequency Word:** *not*
☑ **Concepts of Print**

The Vet Van

Guided Reading

SET PURPOSES Tell children that when they read the story again, they can find out more about what happened. Explain that you also want them to look for words with the initial letter *v* and the final letter *x*. Remind children that they know the word *not* and will see it again in this story.

REREAD THE BOOK As you reread the story, keep in mind any problems children experienced during the first reading. Use the following prompts to guide reading:

- **CONCEPTS OF PRINT** Ask children to look at the title of this story. Then ask them which two words begin with the same letter. (Vet, Van)

- **PHONICS** Ask which words end with *x*. (Rex, Max) Then ask why the words begin with capital letters. (They are names.)

RETURN TO PURPOSES Ask children if they found out more about what they wanted to know from the story. Have children locate the words that contain the letter *v* and the words that contain the letter *x*. Then ask children where the *v* is in the word (beginning) and where the letter *x* is found. (end)

LITERARY RESPONSE Have children draw a picture or explain how vets can help animals.

Read the  Patterned Book

That Is Not Violet!

☑ Initial *V,v*; Final *X,x*

☑ Cause and Effect

☑ High-Frequency Word: *not*

☑ Concepts of Print

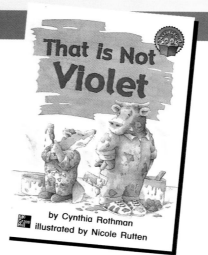

That is Not Violet

by Cynthia Rothman
illustrated by Nicole Rutten

Guided Reading

PREVIEW AND PREDICT Read the title and the author's and the illustrator's name. Ask who writes the words and who draws the illustrations. Take a **picture walk** through pages 2-4, noting the setting of the story and the characters. Have children make a prediction about what will happen in the story.

SET PURPOSES Have children decide what they want to find out from the story. Tell children you will read the story to find out what colors the animals make. Tell them that the story contains words with the letters *v* and *x*.

READ THE BOOK Use the following prompts while the children are reading or after they have read independently. Remind them to run their fingers under each word as they read.

Pages 2-3: Model: *Let's use what we know to read the second word. What sound does* x *make? Let's blend the sounds:* m-i-x *mix. What other word ends with* x? (ox) *Phonics and Decoding*

Pages 4-5: Point to the word that begins with *n*. *Let's read the word together:* not. *High-Frequency Words*

Pages 6-7: *Look at page 6. How many sentences are on this page?* (2) *How many words are in the first sentence?* (7) *How many words are in the second sentence?* (6) *Concepts of Print*

Page 8: *What happened when the animals mixed red and blue?* (They made violet.) *Cause and Effect*

RETURN TO PREDICTIONS AND PURPOSES Ask children if they found out what they needed to know from the story. See if their predictions were correct.

LITERARY RESPONSE The following questions will help focus children's responses:

• *What colors did the animals make?*

• *What is your favorite color? Write about it and draw a picture.*

CENTER Activity

Cross Curricular: Art

DEGREES OF COLOR Make color squares by cutting apart squares from paint sample sheets. Use five or six squares from the same color family. Place each color family in an envelope. Children align the squares from the darkest to the lightest.

▶ Logical//Spatial

OBJECTIVES

Children will:

- identify and read the high-frequency word *not*

....

MATERIALS

- word cards from the *Word Play Book*
- *The Vet Van*

TEACHING TIP

INSTRUCTIONAL Guide children to notice the word *no* in the word *not*. Talk about how the *o* makes a different sound in each word. Have children practice repeating *no* and *not*.

Review not, was, is, do, we, are, with

PREPARE

Listen to Words   Tell children that they will review the word *not*. Read the following sentence, and have children raise hands when they hear the word *not*: *The cat is not sick.*

TEACH

Model Reading the Word in Context   Reread the decodable book. Ask children to listen for the word *not*.

Identify the Word   Tell children to first look at their word cards, and then to look for the word in the story. Read the sentences, tracking print, and ask children to come up and point to the word *not*. Have volunteers put a stick-on dot below the word.

Review High-Frequency Words   Hold up word cards for the following: *the, a, my, that, and, I, is, said, we, are, you, have, to, me, go, do, for, he, she, has, with, was.* Have children read the words together.

PRACTICE

Complete the Pupil Edition Page   Read the directions on page 341 to children, and make sure they clearly understand what they are being asked to do. Complete the first item together. Then work through the page with children or have them complete the page independently.

ASSESS/CLOSE

Review the Page   Review children's work, and guide children who are experiencing difficulty or need additional practice.

Name_____

1.

Do (not) pet the pup with the red cap.

2.

The pup (was) not sick, but the ox is sick.

3.

We (are) not to pet the ox.

Read each sentence. **1.** Draw a circle around the word *not*. Draw a line under the word *do*. Draw two lines under the word *with*. **2.** Draw a circle around the word *was*. Draw a line under the word *is*. **3.** Draw a circle around the word *are*. Draw a line under the word *we*.

Unit 6   Review *not, was, is, do, we, are, with*   **341**

Pupil Edition, page 341

ALTERNATE TEACHING STRATEGY
....
HIGH-FREQUENCY WORDS: *not*
For a different approach to teaching the skill, see page T27.

▶ **Visual/Auditory/ Kinesthetic**

Practice **341**

Name_____

1. "Is the pup with you?" said Mom.

2. The pup was not with Kim and Tom.

3. "We do not have the pup," said Kim.

4. "Dad and Ben are with the pup," said Tom.

Read each sentence. **1.** Draw a line under the words *is* and *with*. **2.** Draw a line under the words *was* and *not*. **3.** Draw a line under the words *we* and *do*. **4.** Draw a line under the word *are*.

At Home: Write each of the seven Review Words on two sets of paper strips. Place the strips facedown and take turns finding matching pairs.

Unit 6 **Review *not, was, is, do, we, are, with***   **341**

PRACTICE BOOK page 341

Meeting Individual Needs for Vocabulary

EASY	ON-LEVEL	CHALLENGE	LANGUAGE SUPPORT
Write the word *not* on the chalkboard. Then give each child letter cards for *n, o,* and *t*. Have children arrange the letters to spell *not*, and then use the word in a sentence.	**Talk** about the animals in *The Vet Van*. Then give each child a word card for *not*, and have children complete sentences as they hold up the word: *A____ is not a cat.*	**Write** the words *not* and *have*. Guide children to read them aloud. Then ask a volunteer to choose a color. Have classmates complete sentences, such as: *I do (not) like it. I (have) a cat.* Have children continue the lesson with other colors.	**Write** the word *not* and guide children to blend the sounds. Then have children use the word to talk about the day: *It is not sunny today. We are not going to the library today.*

341

GRAMMAR/SPELLING
CONNECTIONS
Model subject-verb agreement, complete sentences, and correct tense so that students may gain increasing control of grammar when speaking and writing.

Interactive Writing

Create a Class Book

Prewrite

LOOK AT THE STORY PATTERN Reread the story *White Rabbit's Color Book*. Talk about the pattern of the story: the Rabbit takes a dip in different colors, changes color, and then washes off. Make a list of the colors in the book. Then continue the list with children's favorite colors.

Draft

MAKE A CLASS BOOK Explain that children are going to work together to make a class book about colors.

- Begin by having each child choose a favorite color that the rabbit could be. Help them to complete the sentences: *The rabbit is not white. He is as ___ as a ___*. You may wish to give several examples before children begin.

- As children write left-to-right across the page, they will most likely need to begin a new line for the second sentence. Remind them to begin the second sentence below the first one.

- Each child illustrates his or her page.

Publish

CREATE THE BOOK Bind the pages together to make a book. Volunteers may create a book cover.

The rabbit is not white. He is as red as a fire engine.

Presentation Ideas

 READ THE STORY Have children take turns reading their parts of the story to the rest of the class.

▶ Listening/Speaking

READ WITH A PARTNER Have partners read the book together. Children can take turns, or read several pages and then change roles.

▶ Listening/Speaking

COMMUNICATION TIPS

- **Speaking** When children read, remind them to speak clearly and in a voice that everyone can hear. Help children as necessary.

TECHNOLOGY TIP

Help children use a paint software program to make a color picture.

LANGUAGE SUPPORT

ESL Help children review color words by asking questions about color, using pictures from magazines and picture books.

Meeting Individual Needs for Writing

EASY	ON-LEVEL	CHALLENGE
Write a Color Word Have children write the names of their favorite colors. Then children draw pictures of things that are those colors.	**Guess a Riddle** Describe something in the classroom, focusing on color and shape. Children write what you are describing. Then compare the guesses.	**Write a Description** Show pictures and describe different types of rabbits. Then have children complete this sentence, describing a rabbit: *The rabbit is as (soft) as a ___.*

Jen and Yip

The variety of literature in this lesson will offer children several opportunities to read and listen to stories about making decisions.

**Decodable Story,
pages 349–350 of the
Pupil Edition**

Listening
Library
Audiocassette

by Cynthia Rothman
illustrated by John Hovell

**Patterned Book,
page 353B**

Little Red Hen

**Teacher Read Aloud,
page 347A**

WRITTEN BY JUDY NAYER
ILLUSTRATED BY SUSAN SWAN

**ABC Big Book,
pages 343A–343B**

Listening
Library
Audiocassette

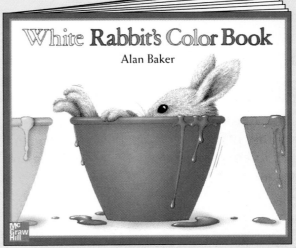

White **Rabbit's Color Book**
Alan Baker

**Literature Big Book,
pages 345A–345B**

Listening
Library
Audiocassette

**Pupil Edition,
pages 342–353**

**Big Book of Real-Life Reading,
page 46**

**Big Book of Phonics Rhymes and
Poems, pages 28, 43, 61**

 Listening
Library
Audiocassette

ADDITIONAL RESOURCES

**Practice Book,
pages 342–353**

- **Phonics Kit**
- **Language Support Book**
- **Alternate Teaching Strategies,** pp T32–T37

McGraw-Hill School
TECHNOLOGY

Phonics CD-ROM Provides extra phonics support.

interNET CONNECTION Research & Inquiry Ideas.

Visit www.mhschool.com

Jen and Yip

READING AND LANGUAGE ARTS

- **Phonological Awareness**
- **Phonics** *initial /kw/ qu, /j/j, /y/y, /z/z*
- **Comprehension**
- **Vocabulary**
- **Beginning Reading Concepts**
- **Listening, Speaking, Viewing, Representing**

- **Cross Curriculum**

- **Writing**

DAY 1

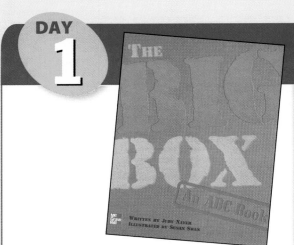

Focus on Reading Skills

Develop Phonological Awareness, 342G-342H
"Quentin Quiggly" *Big Book of Phonics Rhymes and Poems,* 43

 Introduce Initial /kw/*qu,* 342I-342
Practice Book, 342
Phonics/Phonemic Awareness
Practice Book

 **Phonics CD-ROM**

Read the Literature

Read *The Big Box: An ABC Book* **Big Book,** 343A-343B
Shared Reading

Build Skills

☑ Categories, 343C-343
Practice Book, 343

 **Activity** Language Arts, 343B

 Writing Prompt: Write about an imaginary adventure on the boat.

 Journal Writing, 343B
Letter Formation, 342I

DAY 2

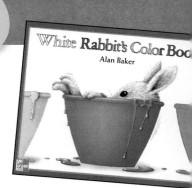

White Rabbit's Color Book
Alan Baker

Focus on Reading Skills

Develop Phonological Awareness, 344A-344B
"Jenny and Jeffrey" *Big Book of Phonics Rhymes and Poems,* 28

 **Introduce Initial /j/j,** 344C-344
Practice Book, 344
Phonics/Phonemic Awareness
Practice Book

Phonics CD-ROM

Read the Literature

Read *White Rabbit's Color Book* **Big Book,** 345A-345B
Shared Reading

Build Skills

☑ Make Inferences, 345C-345
Practice Book, 345

 **Activity** Art, 345B

 Writing Prompt: What is your favorite color? Write about it.

 Journal Writing, 345B
Letter Formation, 344C

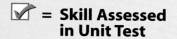 = **Skill Assessed in Unit Test**

DAY 3

Little Red Hen

Focus on Reading Skills

Develop Phonological Awareness, 346A-346B

"The Yak" and "Zachary Zoo" *Big Book of Phonics Rhymes and Poems,* 61-62

 **Introduce Initial /y/y, /z/z,** 346C-346
Practice Book, 346
Phonics/Phonemic Awareness
Practice Book

Phonics CD-ROM

Read the Literature

Read "Little Red Hen" Teacher Read Aloud, 347A-347B
Shared Reading
Read the Big Book of Real-Life Reading, 46
☑ Library

Build Skills

☑ High-Frequency Words: *of,* 347C-347
Practice Book, 347

 Drama, 347B

 Writing Prompt: Have you ever cooked something with a grown-up? Write about what it was like.

DAY 4

Jen and Yip

Focus on Reading Skills

Develop Phonological Awareness, 348A-348B

"Jog, Hop, and Run"
Review Blending with Short *a, e, i, o, u,* 348C-348
Practice Book, 108
Phonics/Phonemic Awareness
Practice Book

Phonics CD-ROM

Read the Literature

Read "Jen and Yip" Decodable Story, 349/350A-349/350D

☑ Initial /kw/*qu,* /j/j, /y/y, /z/z; Blending
☑ Make Inferences
☑ High-Frequency Words: *of*
☑ Concepts of Print

Build Skills

☑ Make Inferences, 351A-351
Practice Book, 351

 Math, 349/350D

 Writing Prompt: Write about a different ending for this story.

Letter Formation,
Practice Book, 349-350

DAY 5

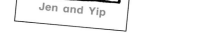
Jen and Yip

Six Yellow Ducks
by Cynthia Rothman
illustrated by John Hovell

Focus on Reading Skills

Develop Phonological Awareness, 352A-352B

"Jog, Hop, and Run"
Review Blending with Short *a, e, i, o, u,* 352C-352
Practice Book, 352
Phonics/Phonemic Awareness
Practice Book

Phonics CD-ROM

Read the Literature

Reread "Jen and Yip" Decodable Story, 353A
Read "Six Yellow Ducks" Patterned Book, 353B
Guided Reading
☑ Initial /kw/*qu,* /j/j, /y/y, /z/z; Blending
☑ Make Inferences
☑ High-Frequency Words: *of*
☑ Concepts of Print

Build Skills

☑ High-Frequency Words: *of, that, my, not,* 353C-353
Practice Book, 353

 Math, 353B

 Writing Prompt: Write about a time when you and a friend had a difficult time making your minds up about something.

Interactive Writing, 354A-354B

Develop Phonological Awareness

Listen

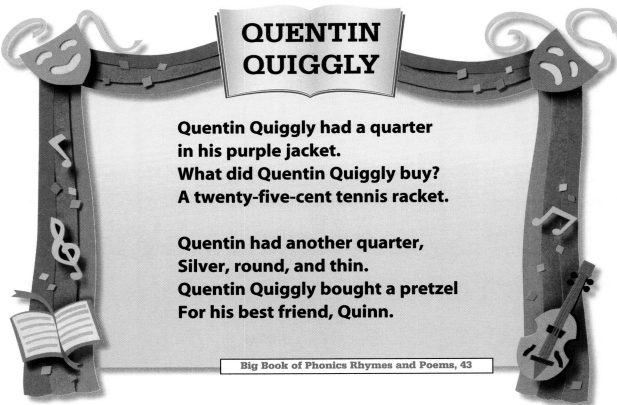

QUENTIN QUIGGLY

Quentin Quiggly had a quarter
in his purple jacket.
What did Quentin Quiggly buy?
A twenty-five-cent tennis racket.

Quentin had another quarter,
Silver, round, and thin.
Quentin Quiggly bought a pretzel
For his best friend, Quinn.

Big Book of Phonics Rhymes and Poems, 43

Objective: Identify Long and Short Words

LISTEN TO THE POEM

- Read the poem "Quentin Quiggly" aloud.
- Point out that some words are longer than others.

LISTEN FOR SYLLABLES

- Point to and then say the words *thin* and *Quiggly*. Have children clap the syllables with you. Then help children determine that there are two syllables in *Quiggly* and one in *thin*.
- Then ask children to identify the longer word.

LISTEN FOR THE LONGER WORD

- Have children listen to pairs of words. Then have them clap the syllables and identify the longer word of each pair.

  Quentin/did, cent/racket, bought/another

Objective: Listen for /kw/

USE THE POEM

- Read the title of the poem, identifying the initial sound in the name. Have children repeat the /kw/ sound after you.

LISTEN FOR THE SOUND

- Tell the children the following story. Have them shrug their shoulders when they hear words that begin with /kw/.

> It was quiet outside. Then I heard a quick quacking sound. That silly duck thinks that she is queen of the barnyard!

REPEAT THE WORDS

- Say the names in the poem. Emphasize the /kw/ sound, and have children repeat the names after you.

Read Together

From Phonemic Awareness to Phonics

Objective: Identify /kw/Qu,*qu*

IDENTIFY THE LETTERS FOR THE SOUND

- Explain to children that the letters *Qu,qu* stand for the /kw/ sound.

- Display the Big Book of Phonics Rhymes and Poems, page 43. Point to the letters and identify them. Have children repeat the /kw/ sound as you point to the letters.

REREAD THE POEM

- Reread the poem. When you are finished, have children repeat each word that begins with /kw/.

THINK OF MORE WORDS

- Ask children to point to each *Qu* and *qu* in the poem. Show an index card with *Qu, qu* for each word. Have children think of more words that begin with the /kw/ sound. Add an index card for each.

Quentin Quiggly

Quentin Quiggly had a quarter
In his purple jacket.
What did Quentin Quiggly buy?
A twenty-five-cent tennis racket.

Quentin had another quarter,
Silver, round, and thin.
Quentin Quiggly bought a pretzel
For his best friend, Quinn.

Big Book of Phonics Rhymes and Poems, 43

OBJECTIVES

Children will:

- identify the letters *Qu, qu*
- identify /kw/ *Qu, qu*
- form the letters *Qu, qu*

MATERIALS

- letter cards from the Word Play Book

TEACHING TIP

INSTRUCTIONAL Point out that the letter *q* is always followed by the letter *u*. Have children look for examples of words that begin with *qu* in classroom picture books, picture dictionaries and alphabet charts.

ALTERNATE TEACHING STRATEGY

FINAL */kw/qu*

For a different approach to teaching this skill, see page T32.

▶ **Visual/Auditory/Kinesthetic**

Introduce Initial /kw/qu

TEACH

Identify /kw/ Qu, qu   Tell children they will learn to write the sound /kw/ with the letters *Qu, qu*. Write the letters on the chalkboard, and ask children to say the sound /kw/. Show pictures of *queen, quilt*. Help children identify what they see, using words that begin with *qu*. Invite children to think of other words that have the /kw/ sound.

Form Qu, qu   Display letters *Qu, qu,* and talk about how the *q*s are alike and how they are different. Compare uppercase *q* to uppercase *o* and lowercase *q* to lowercase *g*. With your back to the children, trace *Qu, qu* in the air. Ask children to do the same. Have them trace their letter cards; then have them write *Qu* and *qu* four times on drawing paper folded into fourths.

PRACTICE

Complete the Pupil Edition Page   Read the directions on page 342 to the children, and make sure they clearly understand what they are being asked to do. Identify each picture, and complete the first item together. Then work through the page with children, or have them complete the page independently.

ASSESS/CLOSE

Identify and Use Qu, qu   Write the following sentences on the chalkboard. Point to each word as you read it aloud, and ask children to clap when they recognize a word that begins with the letters qu: The duck was quiet. *Then it began to quack. The queen saw the duck. The queen walked quickly.*

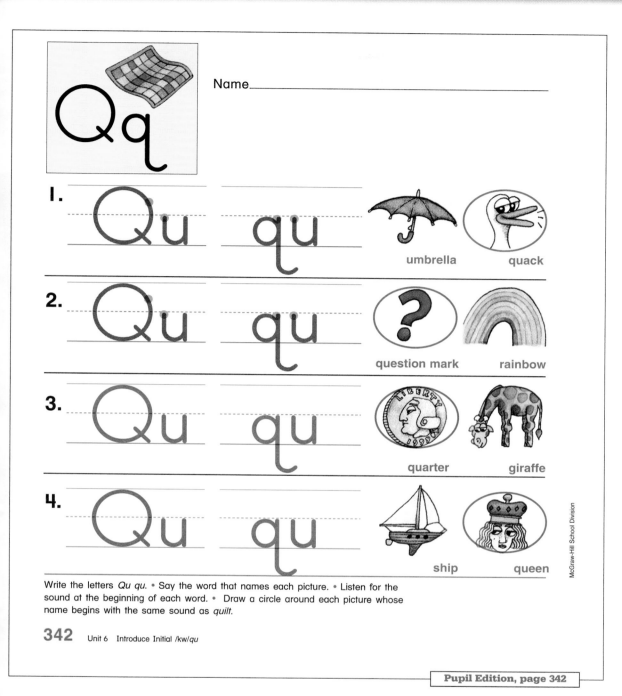

Name_____

1. Qu　qu　

umbrella　quack

2. Qu　qu

question mark　rainbow

3. Qu　qu

quarter　giraffe

4. Qu　qu

ship　queen

McGraw-Hill School Division

Write the letters *Qu qu*. • Say the word that names each picture. • Listen for the sound at the beginning of each word. • Draw a circle around each picture whose name begins with the same sound as *quilt*.

342 Unit 6 Introduce Initial /kw/*qu*

Pupil Edition, page 342

ADDITIONAL PHONICS RESOURCES

Practice Book, *page 342*
Phonics Workbook

McGraw-Hill School
TECHNOLOGY

Phonics **CD-ROM**
Activities for practice with Initial Letters

Practice 242

Name_____

Run to Pat.

Run to Pat.

Mud is fun!

Mud is fun!

Trace the words in the sentence. Then write the words.

At Home: Make sure that the child is holding his/her pencil comfortably and correctly.

242

Unit 4
Handwriting Review 4

PRACTICE BOOK page 342

Meeting Individual Needs for Phonics

EASY	ON-LEVEL	CHALLENGE	LANGUAGE SUPPORT
Give children letter strips that show a row of Q and q without the "tails." Display letter cards Q, q, and have children complete the row of q's. Then ask children to write Qu and qu on drawing paper folded into four sections.	**Ask** children to rhyme the following words with words that begin with *qu: seen, built, tick, fit, pack*. Have them write the letters qu on index cards each time they identify an initial *qu* word that rhymes.	**Invite** children to answer the following riddles, using words that begin with qu: A woman ruler. (queen) Another word for fast. (quick) The opposite of noisy. (quiet) A fancy bed cover. (quilt) Stop. (quit)	In some languages, such as Spanish and French, the letters *qu* are pronounced /k/. Reinforce Children's understanding of /kw/*qu* by making signs to use frequently during classroom activities, such as *quiet, questions*, and *quickly*. Write the *qu* in a different color.

342

OBJECTIVES

Children will:

- recognize rhyming words
- recognize words with initial *qu*
- recognize capital and lowercase letters

LANGUAGE SUPPORT

ESL Help children use color words and positional words as they describe pictures in the story. Ask questions that require specific answers.

Read the Big Book

Before Reading

Develop Oral Language   Read "The Alphabet Name Game" with children on page 5 in the Big Book of Phonics Rhymes and Chimes. Have children use their first names and do the actions to the song.

Remind children that they have read a story about some friends who find a box. Ask children what some of the ideas for the box were.

Set Purposes   Explain that as children reread the story, they will look for rhyming words. They will also think of the order of the letters in the alphabet.

"We can make a giant **umbrella**," said Rob.
24

"We can make a **van**," said Ann.
25

The Big Box, pages 24-25

During Reading

Read Together

- Before you begin to read, point to the first word in the sentence. Explain that this is where you will begin to read. Continue to track print as you read the story. *Tracking Print*

- After you read pages 2-3, ask which two letters will come next. Then turn the page and confirm. Continue as you read the story. *Phonics*

- After you read page 4, ask children to think of words that rhyme with boat. Repeat with the words *fire, game, lake, and nest.* *Phonemic Awareness*

- Say the /kw/ sound and have children say it with you. After you read page 20, have children say the word that begins with that sound. *Phonics*

"We can make an **elevator**," said Sam.

8

The Big Box, page 8

After Reading

Literary Response

JOURNAL WRITING Help children to write a rhyme, using a word from the story. Then have them illustrate the rhyme. Give suggestions, such as:

- *Did a goat row a boat?*

- *Can you rake a lake?*

ORAL RESPONSE Ask volunteers to share rhymes.

ABC Activity

Say names of characters in the story. Children say the letter that begins the name.

CENTER Activity

Cross Curricular: Language Arts

BEFORE AND AFTER Place uppercase letters in a box. One child takes a letter out of the box. A partner finds the letter that comes just before and just after. Then children write the letter. Have partners reverse roles and continue.

OBJECTIVES

Children will:

- sort and classify objects

MATERIALS

- *White Rabbit's Color Book*
- crayons

TEACHING TIP

INSTRUCTIONAL

Display the cover of the Big Book *White Rabbit's Color Book*, and ask volunteers to point to and name the uppercase letters. Then have them point to the author's and the illustrator's names, and point out that names begin with uppercase letters.

Review Categories

PREPARE

Review Colors
Hold up a red crayon. Ask children to name the color and find items in the classroom that are the same color. Continue with blue, yellow, green, and orange.

TEACH

Describe Categories
Display the Big Book *White Rabbit's Color Book*, and have volunteers retell the story. Ask children to name the color of the rabbit at the beginning of the story. Have them name other things that are white and make a picture or a word list of several of these items. Then continue with different colors in the story.

PRACTICE

Make Groups
Read the directions on page 343 to the children, and make sure they clearly understand what they are asked to do. *Identify each picture, and complete the first item.* Then work through the page with children, or have them complete the page independently.

ASSESS/CLOSE

Review the Page
Check children's work on the Pupil Edition page. Note areas where children need extra help.

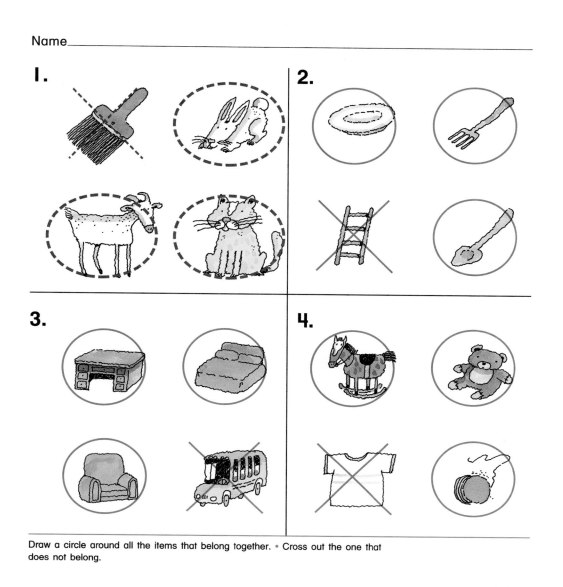

Name

1.

2.

3.

4.

Draw a circle around all the items that belong together. • Cross out the one that does not belong.

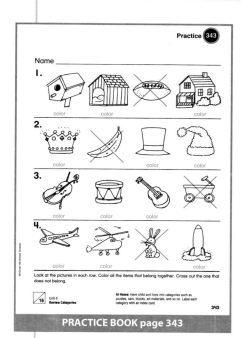

Pupil Edition, page 343

ALTERNATE TEACHING STRATEGY

For a different approach to teaching this skill, see page T33.

► Visual/Auditory/ Kinesthetic

PRACTICE BOOK page 343

Meeting Individual Needs for Beginning Reading Concepts

EASY	ON-LEVEL	CHALLENGE	LANGUAGE SUPPORT
Give children small squares of red, blue, green, and yellow construction paper. Have them find objects in the classroom that are these colors. Make a group picture or a word list for each color category.	**Give** pairs of children a box of buttons. Have children sort by color. Then have them sort by shape and size. Discuss how the categories change the groupings.	**Make** a display of 10 familiar picture books. Ask children to think of categories for these books, such as: reality or fantasy; animals or people; drawings or photographs. Then children sort the books into their categories.	**Help** children make a Color Book. Use construction paper for each page: red, green, blue, yellow, brown, orange, black. Children draw pictures of items that can be the color of the page.

Develop Phonological Awareness

Listen

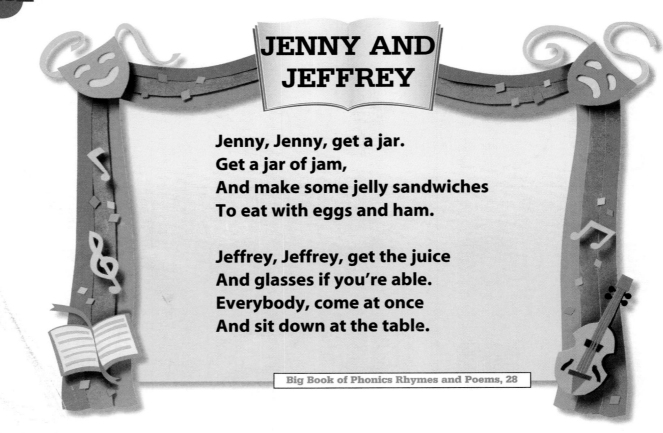

JENNY AND JEFFREY

Jenny, Jenny, get a jar.
Get a jar of jam,
And make some jelly sandwiches
To eat with eggs and ham.

Jeffrey, Jeffrey, get the juice
And glasses if you're able.
Everybody, come at once
And sit down at the table.

Big Book of Phonics Rhymes and Poems, 28

Objective: Identify and Make Rhymes

LISTEN TO THE POEM

- Read the first verse of the poem "Jenny and Jeffrey" aloud to the children. Ask children to listen and say the word that rhymes with *jam*.

> jam   ham

- Read the second verse and ask children to identify the two words that rhyme. As you read, emphasize the words *able* and *table*.

PLAY A GAME

- Play the game "Pack a Silly Picnic." Invite children to think of words that rhyme with *jam*. They pretend to have a picnic basket and "pack" any word that rhymes: *am, blam, clam, ham, lamb, Sam, slam, yam*. Accept nonsense words.

EXTEND THE LEARNING

- Continue the game. Invite children to think of their own words to rhyme to continue the game.

Objective: Listen for /j/

LISTEN TO THE POEM

- Say the title of the poem "Jenny and Jeffrey." Emphasize the initial /j/ sound and point out that both names begin with the same sound. Have children repeat the sound.

- Reread the poem, and ask what Jenny was supposed to get. Emphasize the /j/ sound.

JUMP FOR /J/

- Have children stand in a circle. Say the following list of words: *jar, Jim, cup, juice, put, jam, sit, Jack, dog, Joyce.* Children jump in place each time they hear a word that begins with /j/.

Read Together

From Phonemic Awareness to Phonics

Objective: Identify /j/J,j

RELATE THE LETTER TO THE SOUND

- Explain to children that the letters *J,j* stand for the sound /j/. Have children repeat the sound after you.

- Display page 28 in the Big Book of Phonics Rhymes and Poems. Point to the letters in the corner and identify them as *J,j.* Say the /j/ sound and have children say the sound with you.

REREAD THE POEM

- Read the poem again as you point to each word. Emphasize words with the initial sound of /j/.

- Have children repeat the words that begin with *J* or *j.*

NAMES WITH J

- Invite volunteers to find the names that begin with *J* in the poem. Say the name each time a child identifies it.

- Then ask children to think of other names that begin with /j/.

- Write a *J* on the blackboard for each *J* name.

Jack Joe Jim Jen Jessie Joanna

Jj

Jenny and Jeffrey

Jenny, Jenny, get a jar.
Get a jar of jam.
And make some jelly sandwiches
To eat with eggs and ham.

Jeffrey, Jeffrey, get the juice
And glasses if you're able.
Everybody come at once
And sit down at the table.

28

Big Book of Phonics Rhymes and Poems, 28

344B

Children will:
- identify the letters *J, j*
- identify /j/ *J, j*
- form the letters *J, j*

MATERIALS
- letter cards from the Word Play Book

TEACHING TIP

INSTRUCTIONAL Draw upper, lower, and medial guidelines on the chalkboard, and write *J* and *j*. Ask children to talk about how both forms have similar straight lines that curve at the bottom, but that the forms begin and end at different places. Point out the similarity of the letter *j*'s top horizontal line (*J*) or dot (*j*) with capital and lowercase *I, i*.

ALTERNATE TEACHING STRATEGY

···

FINAL /j/

For a different approach to teaching this skill, see page T34.

▶ **Visual/Auditory/ Kinesthetic**

Introduce Initial /j/j

TEACH

Identify /j/ J, j Tell children they will learn to write the sound /j/ with the letters *J, j*. Write the letters, and have children say the sound with you. Ask them to say the sound /j/, and write on the chalkboard *Jim has jam. Jeb has a jug.* Read the sentences as you point to each word. Have children hold up their *j* letter cards when they hear a word that begins with /j/. Ask children to suggest other names that begin with *J*, such as *Jan, Jeb, Jack, John, Judy, Jess* and write the names on the chalkboard. Have children underline the J in each name.

Form J, j Display letters *J, j* and, with your back to the children, trace them in the air. Ask children to do the same. Then have them write *J* on two index cards. Call on children to say a person's name that begins with /j/ and to hold up their *J*. Ask them to write four *j*'s on the reverse sides of the index cards.

PRACTICE

Complete the Pupil Edition Page Read the directions on page 344 to the children, and make sure they clearly understand what they are asked to do. Identify each picture, and complete the first item together. Then work through the page with children, or have them complete the page independently.

ASSESS/CLOSE

Identify and Use J, j Say the following list of words, and have children show their *J* or *j* cards when they hear a word that begins with /j/: *jungle, bush, just, January, joy.*

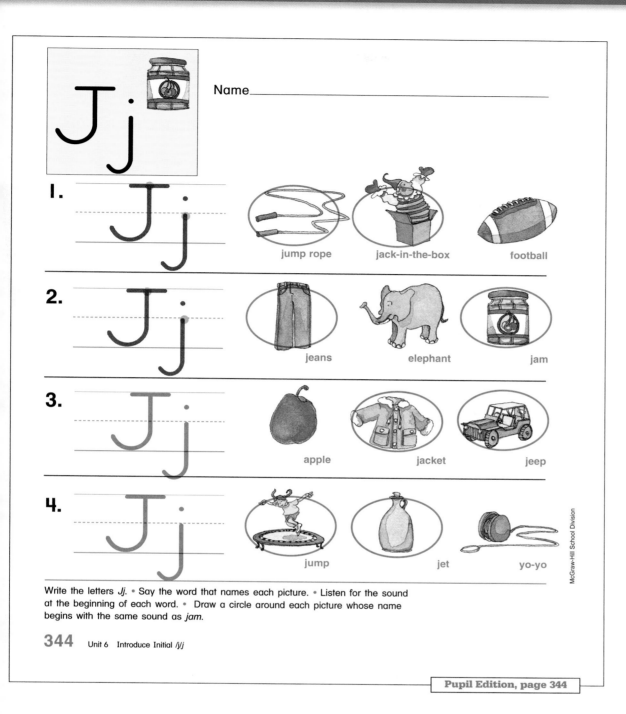

Name _____

1. J j

jump rope   jack-in-the-box   football

2. J j

jeans   elephant   jam

3. J j

apple   jacket   jeep

4. J j

jump   jet   yo-yo

Write the letters *Jj*. • Say the word that names each picture. • Listen for the sound at the beginning of each word. • Draw a circle around each picture whose name begins with the same sound as *jam*.

McGraw-Hill School Division

344   Unit 6   Introduce Initial /j/j

Pupil Edition, page 344

ADDITIONAL PHONICS RESOURCES

Practice Book *page 344*
Phonics Workbook

McGraw-Hill School
TECHNOLOGY

Phonics CD-ROM
Activities for practice with Initial Letters

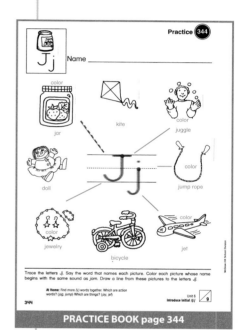

PRACTICE BOOK page 344

Meeting Individual Needs for Phonics

EASY	ON-LEVEL	CHALLENGE	LANGUAGE SUPPORT
Read children the nursery rhyme "Jack Be Nimble." Have them identify initial /j/ words by a little *jump* in their seats. Have children place self-stick notes on the initial *j* words in the rhyme; then ask them to write *J* or *j* on each note to show the form that word uses.	**Place** a large *jar* on the table, and invite children to draw things that begin with *j*, such as: *jug, jay, joke, jaguar, Japan, jelly-fish* on index cards. Invite children to use picture dictionaries to find items. Children write J or j for each item.	**Have** children complete sentences using initial *j* words, such as: *Lions and tigers live in the ____. (jungle) The bottom part of your face is called your ___. (jaw) If it gets chilly, put on a ___. (jacket)* Invite children to make up new incomplete sentences. Children write j for each word.	**Model** actions for: *jog, joke, join, jump, juggle, jiggle.* Discuss the meaning of each word, and repeat the word several times. Ask children to act out words in a group. Each person has a chance to act out one of the words, while the others guess and say the word.

344

OBJECTIVES

- recognize words with initial *j*
- make inferences

TEACHING TIP

Use the color chart to play a game of "I Spy." Have children describe something in the classroom. Instead of saying the color, children say the colors that were mixed to create the color of the object.

Read the Big Book

Before Reading

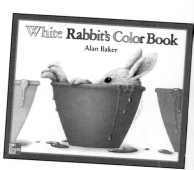

Develop Oral Language

Teach children the following finger play:

LITTLE BROWN RABBIT

A little brown rabbit popped out of the ground,
(Index and middle finger pop up.)
Wiggled his whiskers and looked all around.
(Wiggle rabbit-ear fingers.)
Another wee rabbit who lived in the grass
(Left rabbit ears pop up.)
Popped his head out and watched him pass.
(Right hand crosses over left hand.)
Then both wee rabbits turned themselves around
(Uncross hands.)
And ran off home to their holes in the ground.
(Hands hop behind back.)

Ask children to share what they know about rabbits, and remind children about White Rabbit and his adventure with mixing paint.

Set Purposes

Model: We read about White Rabbit and saw how he created different colors. When we read this time, let's think about words he used to describe the colors.

White Rabbit's Color Book, pp. 14-15

During Reading

Read Together

- Before you begin to read, point to the first word in the first sentence. Explain that this is where you will begin to read. Continue to track print as you read the story. *Tracking Print*

- After children read page 12, talk about the description of red: sizzling hot red. As you continue through the story, talk about the color descriptions. *Develop Vocabulary*

- After you read page 12, explain that the author doesn't always use words to tell what the characters are feeling. Ask children: *How do you think the rabbit is feeling? What clues helped you to decide this? Make Inferences*

- Say the sound /j/, and have children repeat it after you. Then read the last sentence of the book on page 24. Have children say the word that begins with /j/. *(just) Phonics and Decoding*

Hooray! Brown Rabbit. Lovely warm brown.
Blue, yellow, and red together make brown.
And brown's just right for me.

24

White Rabbit's Color Book, p.24

After Reading

Retell the Story   Cut out pairs of rabbit ears to match Rabbit's colors in the story. Children use the rabbit ears to retell the story. Then ask whether the story was realistic or a fantasy. Encourage children to name other fantasy stories about rabbits.

Literary Response   **JOURNAL WRITING** Ask children to draw a colorful picture. Then help them to write descriptions of the colors they used. You may wish to refer to the descriptions in the book to help.

ORAL RESPONSE Have children describe their drawing to the class.

INFORMAL ASSESSMENT

MAKE INFERENCES
HOW TO ASSESS Have children choose a page in the story and paint out how the rabbit is feeling.

FOLLOW UP Point out how the rabbit's expression helps you to find out how he is feeling.

CENTER Activity

Cross Curricular: Science

COLORINGS THAT PROTECT
Explain to children that the colors and the markings of animals can help them in their environment. Provide books that show pictures of animals, such as insects that are the color of leaves and bark, deer that are the colors of the forest, and frogs that are the color of ponds and lakes. Have children draw and label pictures of animals and their colors and markings.

▶ **Spatial/Logical**

OBJECTIVES

Children will:

- make inferences to understand a story

....

MATERIALS

- *White Rabbit's Color Book*

TEACHING TIP

INSTRUCTIONAL Ask children how they can tell how people are feeling. Point out that people use words, expressions, and body gestures to get information.

Review **Make Inferences**

PREPARE

Think About the Story

Have children recall the story *White Rabbit's Color Book*. Ask children why they think Rabbit kept changing colors. How do they think Rabbit felt each time her color changed?

TEACH

Use Illustrations To Make Inferences

Reread the story, stopping after page 12. Suggest children use Rabbit's expression to imagine how she feels. Ask why she might feel that way. Continue through the story having children use clues from the illustrations and their own experience to infer Rabbit's reactions.

PRACTICE

Complete the Pupil Edition Page

Read the directions on page 345 to the children, and make sure they clearly understand what they are being asked to do. Identify each picture, and complete the first item together. Then work through the page with children or have them complete the page independently.

ASSESS/CLOSE

Review the Page

Review children's work, and note children who are experiencing difficulty.

Name _____

1.    

2.    

3.    

Look at the picture on the left. • Draw a circle around the face that shows how the person in the picture is feeling.

Unit 6 Review Make Inferences   345

Pupil Edition, page 345

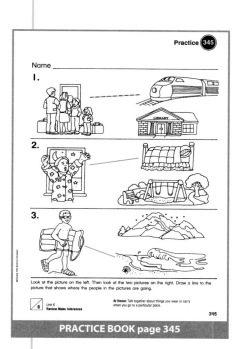

ALTERNATE TEACHING STRATEGY

MAKE INFERENCES
For a different approach to teaching this skill, see page T29.

▶ Visual/Auditory/Kinesthetic

PRACTICE BOOK page 345

Meeting Individual Needs for Comprehension

EASY	ON-LEVEL	CHALLENGE	LANGUAGE SUPPORT
Invite children to draw a picture that shows how they feel when they wake up in the morning. Discuss the pictures, noting the different emotions that the pictures show.	**Take** photos of children or use magazine photos. Then display the photos, and have children describe how children in photos might have been feeling by looking at their expressions.	**Play** charades, and have children act out different situations that you suggest. Others guess the emotion that they might be feeling in the situation. For instance: a birthday party or a surprise visitor.	**Choose** books from your classroom library and invite children to choose an illustration. Talk about how the characters might be feeling by looking at the picture. What are some reasons they might be feeling that way?

Develop Phonological Awareness

Listen

THE YAK
ZACHARY ZOO

Yickity-yackity, yickity-yak,
The yak has a scriffily,
scraffily back;
Some yaks are brown yaks
and some yaks are black,
Yickity-yackity, yickity-yak.
Jack Prelutsky

Zachary Zebulun Zebedee Zoo
Is a long name for a boy
    aged two.
When Zack grows up, he hopes
    that he
Will be called just plain Zachary.

Big Book of Phonics Rhymes and Poems, 61-62

Objective: Create a Chant

EXTEND THE POEM

- Read the poem "The Yak." Then reread the first line several times. Invite children to join in with you when they are ready.
- Ask a volunteer to substitute another letter for the initial *y*, such as *b*.

bickity-backity,　bickity-bak

- Have children repeat the new line several times.
- Repeat with other letters.

CONTINUE THE CHANT

- When children are ready, use different letters and try the chant with two lines.

lickity-lackity,　lickity-lak,　pickity-packity,　pickity-pak

Objective: Listen for Initial /z/

SEGMENTING

- Reread the title and poem. Say the word *Zachary*. Emphasize the /z/ sound and have children repeat it after you.
- Say the following list of words. Children say *z-z-z-z* if the word begins with /z/.
- Read the poem again. Have children repeat the words that begin with *Z* or *z*.

Read Together

From Phonemic Awareness to Phonics

Objective: Identify /y/Y,y and /z/Z,z

IDENTIFY THE LETTER FOR THE SOUND

- Explain that the letters *Y* and *y* stand for the sound /y/. Say the sound and have children say it with you.

- Display the Big Book of Phonics Rhymes and Poems, page 61. Point to the letters in the corner as you identify them. Say the sound with the children.

REREAD THE POEM

- Read the poem again, emphasizing the initial /y/ words as you point to each word.

IDENTIFY THE LETTER FOR THE SOUND

- Explain that the letters *Z, z* sound like /z/. Have children repeat the sound.

- Display the Big Book of Phonics Rhymes and Poems, page 62. Identify the letters *Z, z* in the corner of the page and say the letter names. Have children repeat the /z/ sound.

REREAD THE POEM

- Read the poem again, emphasizing the initial /z/ names as you point to each word.

The Yak

Yickity-yackity, yickity-yak,
the yak has a scriffily,
scraffily back;
some yaks are brown yaks
and some yaks are black,
yickity-yackity, yickity-yak.

Jack Prelutsky

Big Book of Phonics Rhymes and Poems, 61

Introduce Initial /y/ y and /z/ z

OBJECTIVES

Children will:

- identify the letters *Y, y, Z, z*
- identify /y/ *Y, y,* /z/ *Z, z*
- form the letters *Y, y, Z, z*

MATERIALS

- letter cards from the Word Play Book

TEACHING TIP

INSTRUCTIONAL Discuss with children how the letters *y* and *z* are similar and different. Elicit that both lowercase letters are formed with straight lines, but that *z* is formed with three straight lines while *y* is formed with two straight lines. Then have children compare the capital forms of both letters.

ALTERNATE TEACHING STRATEGY

INITIAL /y/y, /z/z

For a different approach to teaching this skill, see pages T35, T36.

▶ **Visual/Auditory/ Kinesthetic**

TEACH

Identify /y/ Y, y and /z/ Z, z   Tell children they will learn to write the sound /y/ with the letters *Y, y.* Ask them to say the sound /y/ and write *Y, y* on the chalkboard. Then write the word *yes* and have children repeat it as you read the word aloud. Call on several children and ask, *Are you five or six years old?* Emphasize the initial /y/ in *you* and *years.* Ask children to answer in a complete sentence: *Yes, I am six years old.* Then tell children they will learn to write the sound /z/ with the letters *Z, z.* Ask them to say the sound /z/ and write *Z, z* on the chalkboard. Then ask the following question: *Did you see the zebra at the zoo?* Ask children to hold up the *z* card when they hear a word that begins with /z/.

Form Y, y   Display letters *Y, y* and point out how similar they are, as well as noting their differences. With your back to the children, trace the letters in the air. Ask children to do the same. Then have them trace their letter cards. Follow the same procedure with *Z, z.* Then give each child two large index cards. Have them write *Z* and *z* on each side of one card and *Y* and *y* on each side of the other card. Then read and display the following word cards and ask children to hold up the appropriate card: *yet, Zack, zip, yum, yam, zig-zag, Yip.*

PRACTICE

Complete the Pupil Edition Page   Read the directions on page 346 to the children, and make sure they clearly understand what they are being asked to do. Identify each picture, and complete the first item together. Then work through the page with children, or have them complete the page independently.

ASSESS/CLOSE

Identify and Use Y, y   Write the following sentence on the chalkboard, and read it aloud as you track print with your hand: *Your yellow jacket has a zipper.* Have children hold up their *y* cards when they recognize a word that begins with /y/ *y* and their *z* cards when they recognize a word that begins with /z/ *z.*

 **Yy** **Zz**

Name_____

I.

fan   yarn   yolk

2.

yawn   guitar   yellow

3.

zebra   bicycle   zero

4.

zoo   zigzag   sun

Write the letters *Yy*. • Say the word that names each picture. • Listen for the sound at the beginning of each word. • Draw a circle around each picture whose name begins with the same sound as *yo-yo*. • Do the same with the letters *Zz*. • Draw a circle around each picture whose name begins with the same sound as *zipper*.

346   Unit 6   Introduce Initial /y/y and /z/z

McGraw-Hill School Division

Pupil Edition, page 346

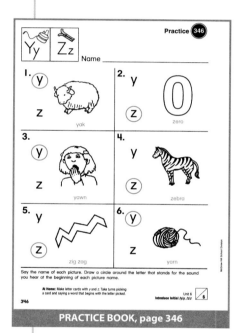

PRACTICE BOOK, page 346

Meeting Individual Needs for Phonics

EASY	ON-LEVEL	CHALLENGE	LANGUAGE SUPPORT
Give each child the letter cards for *Y, y, Z, z*. Write three of the letters on the chalkboard, and ask children to hold up the card that has the missing letter and form. Repeat with other arrangements. Ask children to think of one word that begins with *y* and one word that begins with *z*.	**Write** the following sentence on the chalkboard: *Can you zip up the bag for Zack?* Read it aloud as you track print with your hand. Give children letter cards for *Y, y, Z, z*. Ask them to place the cards to show the same arrangements of *y*'s and *z*'s. Repeat with other sentences or series of words.	**Children** can play "I've Got Something In My Backpack That Starts with *y*." Have children sit in a circle, and ask them to think of an object—any kind of object—whose name begins with *Y, y*. Continue the game with objects whose names begin with /z/z.	**Provide** opportunities for children to learn initial *y* and *z* words that are commonly used. Read aloud a picture book, perhaps about a zoo, and ask children to hold up *y* and *z* letter card when they hear words that begin /y/ and /z/.

346

Teacher Read Aloud

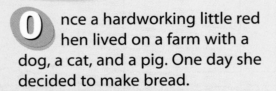

Listen

The Little Red Hen
a fable

Once a hardworking little red hen lived on a farm with a dog, a cat, and a pig. One day she decided to make bread.

"Who will help me cut the wheat to make my bread?" she asked.

"Not I," said the dog.

"Not I," yawned the cat.

"Not I," grunted the pig.

"Then I will do it myself," said the little red hen.

When she had cut the wheat, the little red hen asked, "Who will help me take the wheat to the miller for grinding?"

"Not I," growled the dog.

"Not I," hissed the cat.

"Not I," snorted the pig.

"Then I will do it myself," said the little red hen.

When the wheat had been ground into flour, the little red hen asked, "Who will help me make the flour into bread dough?"

"Not I," sighed the dog.

"Not I," whined the cat.

"Not I," sniffed the pig.

Continued on page T%

Oral Comprehension

LISTENING AND SPEAKING Ask children if they ever watched or helped someone make a loaf of bread. Discuss the ingredients and the process. You may wish to explain that flour comes from wheat and that they will hear a fable about a Little Red Hen who bakes some bread. Explain that a fable is a story with animal characters and usually teaches a lesson.

After you read the story, ask: *How do you think the Little Red Hen felt when her friends wouldn't help her? What lesson did the animals learn?*

Activity Provide clay and water in plastic bowls. Tell children they are going to make bread. Encourage them to mix the dough well and form the bread into any shape they want. Explain that they can make it heart-shaped, circular, square, rectangular, star-shaped, or any other form they can imagine. Have them display their results.

▶ **Spatial**

Real-Life Reading

READ A BOOK TODAY!

PICTURE BOOKS

LISTENING AREA

LIBRARIAN

Little Red Hen is at the library.
She wants a book.
Can you show her around?

46

Big Book of Real-Life Reading, page 46

Objective: Library/Media Center

READ THE PAGE Ask children if they have visited a library or a media center. Invite children to describe experiences they have had there. Then ask who the Little Red Hen was, and have them recount the story. Explain that the Little Red Hen is going to the library. Read the text and discuss the pictures. Have children point out the bookshelves, the computer areas, the tables and the chairs, and the listening area.

ANSWER THE QUESTION Have children point to and identify areas and to decide where they might find fairy tales. Ask: *How could the librarian help? What will the Little Red Hen need before she checks out a book?*

Cross Curricular: Drama

ROLE-PLAY AT THE LIBRARY
Invite children to role-play being the librarian and the Little Red Hen. Have the librarian take the Hen on a tour and point out areas of the library and media center. Provide some fairy tales for the little Red Hen to check out and take home.

▶ **Interpersonal/Linguistic**

Introduce High-Frequency Words: *of*

TESTED
OBJECTIVES

Children will:

- identify and read the high-frequency word: *of*

MATERIALS

- word cards from the *Word Building Book*

TEACHING TIP

INSTRUCTIONAL

Some children may be ready to write words, and others may need additional help. Children can trace letters, and others may benefit from dashed letter paper.

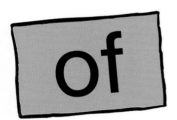

PREPARE

Listen to Words
Explain to the children that they will be learning a new word: *of*. Say the following sentence: *Hen had a loaf of bread*. Say the sentence again, and ask children to raise a hand when they hear the word *of*. Repeat with the sentence: *Hen has a cup of tea*.

TEACH

Model Reading the Word in Context
Give a word card to each child, and read the word. Reread the sentences, and have children raise their hands when they hear the word.

Identify the Word
Write the sentences above on the chalkboard. Track print and read each sentence. Children hold up their word cards when they hear the word *of*. Then ask volunteers to point to and underline the word *of* in the sentences.

Write the Word
Review how to write the letters *o* and *f*. Then have children practice writing and tracing the word.

PRACTICE

Complete the Pupil Edition Page
Read the directions on page 347 to the children, and make sure they clearly understand what they are being asked to do. Complete the first item together. Then work through the page with children or have them complete the page independently.

ASSESS/CLOSE

Review the Page
Review children's work, and note children who are experiencing difficulty or need additional practice.

Name_____

| of |

1.

Jim had a pot <u>of</u> jam.

2.

Kim had a tin <u>of</u> ham.

3.

I had a mix <u>of</u> ham and yam.

4.

We had a lot <u>of</u> fun.

Read the sentence. • Then draw a line under the word *of* in the sentence.

Pupil Edition, page 347

ALTERNATE TEACHING
STRATEGY

HIGH-FREQUENCY
WORDS: *of*

For a different approach to
teaching this skill, see
page T27.

▶ Visual/Auditory/
Kinesthetic

Practice 347

Name_____

1.

I have a box <u>of</u> wax.

2.

You have a pot <u>of</u> jam.

3.

He has a pack <u>of</u> gum.

4.

She has a tin <u>of</u> ham.

Read the sentence. Then draw a line under the word *of* in the sentence.

Unit 6
Introduce High-Frequency Words: *of*

At Home: Have the child think of things that come in a
box. Then have the child draw a picture of one thing and
help him or her label it: *I have a box of ___.*

347

PRACTICE BOOK, page 347

Meeting Individual Needs

EASY	ON-LEVEL	CHALLENGE	LANGUAGE SUPPORT
Give children several letter cards, including the letters *o* and *f*. Have children find the letters to form *of*. Then they use the word in a sentence.	**Make** bingo cards with high-frequency words, including the word *of*. Say words, and have children put counters on matching words. The first child to make a row wins the round.	**Make** two word cards with all previously learned high-frequency words. Have children play concentration and find the matching words. The person who finds *of* gets an extra turn.	**Write** the word *of*, and have children trace the word. Then say the sentence: *I'd like a cup of milk.* Then have children repeat the sentence substituting something they would like to drink. (*I'd like a cup of _____.*)

347

Develop Phonological Awareness

Listen

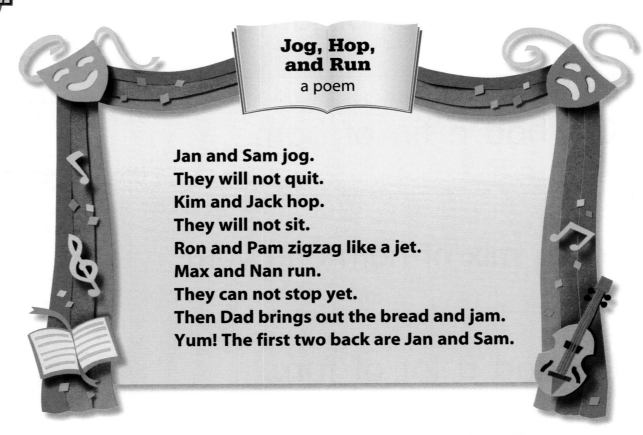

Jog, Hop, and Run
a poem

Jan and Sam jog.
They will not quit.
Kim and Jack hop.
They will not sit.
Ron and Pam zigzag like a jet.
Max and Nan run.
They can not stop yet.
Then Dad brings out the bread and jam.
Yum! The first two back are Jan and Sam.

Objective: Listen to Follow Directions

READ THE POEM Read the poem "Jog, Hop, and Run." Ask: *What actions are named in the poem?*

> jog   hop   zigzag   run

PANTOMIME ACTIONS Read the first line of the poem and invite a volunteer to pantomime jogging in place. Repeat with other action words in the poem. Challenge volunteers to name and pantomime other actions the people in the poem might do.

> skip   swim   roll   bend

SUBSTITUTE NAMES Reread the poem but substitute children's names. Tell children when they hear their

names in the poem they should do that action in their places until the poem ends.

Repeat several times until all children have had an opportunity to respond to their names.

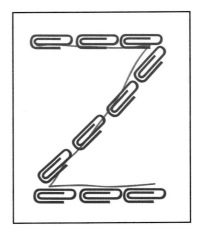

Objective: Listen for Blending with Short *a, e, i, o, u*

LISTEN FOR BLENDING Read the two lines of the poem segmenting, and then blending, the sounds to say: /kw/-/i/-/t/, /kw/-/it/, *quit*. After reading the lines, have children repeat the sounds and then blend them to say *quit*. Repeat the activity with other words in the poem.

> **jog   yet   zigzag**

RIDDLES ANYONE? Provide additional practice blending short vowel sounds with *qu, j, y,* and *z*, by inviting children to solve riddles. Say: *I am the sound a duck makes. What am I?* Kw/-/a/-/k/.

Pause while children repeat and then blend the sounds to find the answer to the riddle: *quack.* Repeat with other words that provide practice blending short vowel sounds with *qu, j, y,* and *z*.

> **yes   zip   quick**

CLUES: I am the opposite of the word no.
I am a way to close your jacket.
I am another word that means fast.

From Phonemic Awareness to Phonics

Objective: Relate *a, e, i, o, u* to Short Vowel Sounds

LISTEN TO RHYMING WORDS
Read the poem and ask children to name rhyming words

> **quit-sit   jet-yet   jam-Sam**

IDENTIFY THE LETTERS Say: /kw/-/i/-/t/ as you write quit on chart paper. Identify the letters in quit. Remind children that qu stands for /kw/ sound. Repeat with *sit.* Ask a volunteer to circle the letters that are the same in both words. Explain that the words rhyme because they have the same /it/ ending.

MAKE RHYMING WORDS
Invite children to name words that rhyme with *quit* and *sit.*

> **bit   fit   hit   kit**
> **lit   pit   wit**

As you add a new word to the list such as *bit*, emphasize /b/ as you write *b* and then emphasize /it/ as you write and highlight *it.* Have children say /b/-/it/ and then blend the sounds to say *bit.*

quit   kit
sit   lit
bit   pit
fit   wit
hit

Review Blending with short *a, e, i, o, u*

OBJECTIVES

Children will:

- identify /a/*a*, /e/*e*, /i/*i*, /o/*o*, /u/*u*
- blend and read short *a, e, i, o, u* words
- write short *a, e, i, o, u* words
- review /kw/ *qu*, /j/*j*, /y/ *y*, /z/ *z*

MATERIALS

- letter cards from the *Word Building Book*

TEACHING TIP

INSTRUCTIONAL Write the words *quit, jam, yip, zip, yam* on the chalkboard. Ask a volunteer to draw circles around two words that rhyme with *ham*. (jam, yam) Then ask another volunteer to underline two words that rhyme with *rip*. (yip, zip) Have children blend the sounds to read the word *quit*. Ask them to use their letter cards and build words that rhyme with *quit*.

ALTERNATE TEACHING STRATEGY

BLENDING SHORT *a, e, i, o, u*

For a different approach to teaching this skill, see Unit 1, page T32; Unit 2, page T32; Unit 3, page T30; Unit 4, page T32; Unit 5, page T30.

▶ **Visual/Auditory/ Kinesthetic**

Identify *a, e, i, o, u* as Symbols for /a/, /e/, /i/, /o/, /u/

Tell children they will read words with *a, e, i, o, u.*

- Display the *a, e, i, o, u* letter cards and say /a/, /e/, /i/, /o/, /u/. Have children repeat the sounds as you point to the cards.

BLENDING Model and Guide Practice

- Place an *i* card after the *z* card. Blend the sounds together and have children repeat after you.

- Place a *p* letter card after the *z, i* cards. Blend to read *zip.*

Use the Word in Context

- Have children use *zip* in a sentence, perhaps talking about putting on coats and getting ready to go outside on a cold winter day.

Repeat the Procedure

- Use the following words to continue modeling and for guided practice with short *a, e, i, o, u*: yum, Jim, job, quit, quick, Zeb, Zip.

PRACTICE

Complete the Pupil Edition Page

Read aloud the directions on page 348. Identify each picture and complete the first item together. Then work through the page with children, or have them complete the page independently.

ASSESS/CLOSE

Build Short *a, e, i, o, u* Words

Observe children as they complete page 348. Then write on the chalkboard _*ed*, _*ack*, _*im*, _*en*. Display letter cards *j, qu, y* and *z*. Have children build words that are names. (Jed, Jack, Jim, Jen, Zack)

Name

1. j a m   jam

2. y a m   yam

3. z i p   zip

4. qu a ck   quack

Blend the sounds and say the word. • Write the word. • Draw a circle around the picture that goes with the word.

McGraw-Hill School Division

348   Unit 6   Review Blending with Short *a, e, i, o, u*

Pupil Edition, page 348

ADDITIONAL PHONICS RESOURCES

Practice Book, *page 348*

Phonics Workbook

McGraw-Hill School

TECHNOLOGY

Phonics CD-ROM

Activities for practice with Blending and Segmenting

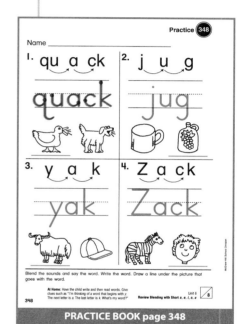

Practice 348

Name

1. qu a ck quack

2. j u g jug

3. y a k yak

4. Z a ck Zack

Blend the sounds and say the word. Write the word. Draw a line under the picture that goes with the word.

At Home: Have the child write and then read words. Give clues such as "I'm thinking of a word that begins with *y*. The next letter is *a*. The last letter is *k*. What's my word?"

348   Review Blending with Short *z, e, i, o, u*   Unit 6

PRACTICE BOOK page 348

Meeting Individual Needs for Phonics

EASY	ON-LEVEL	CHALLENGE	LANGUAGE SUPPORT
Put two cards for each letter *j, qu, y* and *z* in a jar. Let a volunteer pick a letter out of the jar and say a word that begins with that letter sound. Write each word on an index card. Have children sort the cards into four groups. Ask how the words in each group are alike.	**Say** *Did Zeb zip his coat?* Ask children which two words have the same beginning sound. (Zeb, Zip). Repeat with *Jen did a good job* (Jen, job); *That duck is quick to quack* (quick, quack).	**Brainstorm** some *z* and *y* words with the children and write them on the chalkboard. Begin a story about Zak the Yak. Call on volunteers to add sentences to the story using as many of the *z* and *y* words as they can. Ask volunteers to circle the *z* and *y* words in the story.	**Some** children may have trouble discriminating between capital *Z* and capital *S*. Have them work in parts to practice tracing letter cards for the two letters. Encourage them to talk about the differences.

348

Guided Instruction

BEFORE READING

PREVIEW AND PREDICT Take a brief **picture walk** through the book, focusing on the illustrations. Ask the children:

- Who is this story about? Where does it take place?

- Do you think the story is realistic, or is it make-believe? Why?

SET PURPOSES Talk to children about what they would like to find out as they read the story. Suggest a question about what Jen and Yip might do.

TEACHING TIP

To put book together:

1. Tear out the story page.

2. Cut along dotted line.

3. Fold each section on fold line.

4. Assemble book.

INSTRUCTIONAL Show a picture of a duck and ask children to describe what it looks like. Ask children to share what they know about ducks, including where they live and what they eat.

Jen and Yip

Yip is the duck in the pen.

3

McGraw-Hill School Division

Jen has a pen with
a duck and a hen.

2

McGraw-Hill School Division

Jen can jog to the top
of a rock.

4

Guided Instruction

DURING READING

☑ **Initial *j, y, qu, z***

☑ **Compare and Contrast**

☑ **Concepts of Print**

☑ **High-Frequency Word: *of***

1 **CONCEPTS OF PRINT** Point to the space between the words *Jen* and *and*. Then point to the space between *and* and *Yip* on the title page. Remind students that a space is left between words so that it is easier to see and read the words.

2 **COMPARE AND CONTRAST** Ask children to point to the duck and the hen on page 2. Talk about how they are alike and how they are different.

3 **CONCEPTS OF PRINT** Ask children which word on page 3 has a capital letter and why. (Name; first word in sentence)

4 **HIGH-FREQUENCY WORDS** Ask children to point to the word on page 4 that begins with *o*. Track print and read it together: *of*.

LANGUAGE SUPPORT

ESL Demonstrate *zig-zag* for children who may not understand this word. Place a large paper *Z* on the floor and walk along it. Take up the paper and zig-zag along an imaginary *Z*. Encourage children to have fun walking this way.

Guided Instruction

DURING READING

5 **PHONICS** After you read page 5, ask children to find the word that begins with *Y*. Direct them to blend sounds to read the name. (Yip) Ask children to find the word that begins with *J*. Ask them to blend sounds again to read this name. (Jen)

6 **PHONICS** After you read page 6, have children find the word that begins with *z* and read it together. Discuss how Jen and Yip are moving in the path. (in a zig-zag pattern)

7 **PHONICS** Have children find the word on page 7 that begins with *qu*. Remind children that *ck* makes the /k/ sound. Read the word together. (quick)

8 **MAKE INFERENCES** After you read page 8, discuss what it means for Yip to be a *quick quack*.

INFORMAL ASSESSMENT

HIGH-FREQUENCY WORD: *of*

HOW TO ASSESS Give children several rebus phrases that include the word *of*, such as: *top of the table*, using a simple sketch for *the table*. Ask children to read the phrases.

FOLLOW-UP If children have trouble, refer them to page 4, point out the word and ask them to tell you other things that Jen could jog to the top of. Write their responses, underlining the word each time they use it.

Yip can go for a jog with Jen.

5

Jen is quick.

7

Jen can zig-zag
with Yip.

6

Yip is a quick quack!

8

Guided Instruction

AFTER READING

RETURN TO PREDICTIONS AND PURPOSES
Ask children to check their predictions about the story. Ask if they found out what Jen and Yip did.

RETELL THE STORY Have children retell the story. Children can take turns telling parts of the story. They may refer to the story to make sure that the sequence is correct.

LITERARY RESPONSE To help children respond to the story, ask:

- *Why is Yip an unusual duck?*

- *Would you like to have a duck as a pet? Why or why not?*

Invite children to draw and write about something else that Jen and Yip might do.

CENTER
Activity

Cross Curricular: Math

Draw zig-zag lines on large sheets of drawing paper. Children measure the lines using paper clips or connecting cubes. Have them record their measurements.

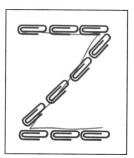

▶ **Logical/Mathematical**

Children will:

- make inferences to understand a story

MATERIALS

- *Jen and Yip*

TEACHING TIP

INSTRUCTIONAL Talk about ways that children get exercise. Discuss activities that children do in the gym and on the playground. Discuss why exercise is important to children and adults.

Review Make Inferences

PREPARE

Revisit the Story

Ask children to recall the story *Jen and Yip*. Ask children how they know that Yip is a quick quack. Encourage volunteers to give their own ideas.

TEACH

Use Clues from the Story

Reread the story, and ask if children think Yip enjoys jogging with Jen. Discuss clues that children use to help them decide. Point out that text and illustrations give clues about how characters are feeling and what they are thinking. Ask how Jen might feel as she jogs with Yip. Elicit children's own interpretations.

PRACTICE

Complete the Pupil Edition Page

Read the directions on page 351 to the children, and make sure they clearly understand what they are asked to do. Identify each picture, and complete the first item together. Then work through the page with children or have them complete the page independently.

ASSESS/CLOSE

Review the Page

Review children's work, and note children who are experiencing difficulty. You may wish to pair children of different abilities and have them work together on this page.

Name _____

1.

2.

3.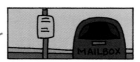

Look at the picture on the left. • Then look at the two pictures on the right. • Draw a line to the picture that shows where the person is going.

Unit 6 Review Make Inferences   **351**

ALTERNATE TEACHING STRATEGY

MAKE INFERENCES

For a different approach to teaching this skill, see page T29.

▶ **Visual/Auditory/Kinesthetic**

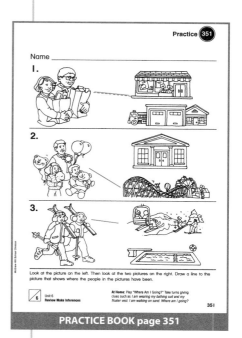

PRACTICE BOOK page 351

Meeting Individual Needs for Comprehension

EASY	ON-LEVEL	CHALLENGE	LANGUAGE SUPPORT
Ask children to choose a page in the book. Talk about the text and the pictures, and ask how the characters might be feeling. Ask them what clues they found on that page to help them figure that out.	**Talk** about Jen, and ask children what they know about Jen from the story. Make a list, such as: *likes animals, likes exercise,* and so on. Point out that children are using clues from the story to find out about the character so they can understand the story better.	**Ask** children to think of something else that Jen might like to do with Yip. Children may draw a picture, and write or dictate text. Have children share the illustrations, and talk about what they know about Jen from the illustration and text.	**Show** a picture from a magazine with people doing an activity. Ask children how the people might be feeling. Help them with the vocabulary needed to discuss feelings. Use pantomimes, facial expressions, and gestures.

351

Develop Phonological Awareness

Listen

Jog, Hop, and Run
a poem

Jan and Sam jog.
They will not quit.
Kim and Jack hop.
They will not sit.
Ron and Pam zigzag like a jet.
Max and Nan run.
They can not stop yet.
Then Dad brings out the bread and jam.
Yum! The first two back are Jan and Sam.

Objective: Listen for Sense

READ THE POEM Read the poem "Jog, Hop, and Run" several times until children are familiar with the words.

IDENTIFY NONSENSE WORDS Read the first line of the poem, but substitute hog and jog. Ask: *What word does not make sense?*

> hog

Point out that hog and jog sound alike. Discuss why hog does not make sense in the sentence.

REREAD THE POEM Repeat by substituting rhyming nonsense words for other words in the poem.

> top for hop
> wig-wag for zigzag
> fit for sit
> bun for run

Have children clap each time they hear a nonsense word.

Objective: Listen for Blending with
Short *a, e, I, o, u*

LISTEN FOR SEGMENTED WORDS As you read the poem, segment the sounds for *Jan* each time you say it. After reading the poem, ask children to repeat the segmented sounds with you as you say: /j/-a-/-/n. Then have children blend the sounds to say *Jan*. Repeat with other words in the poem.

> jet   quilt   jog   yum   zig-zag

JUMPING JACKS   Point out that the children in the poem are very active. Model how to do jumping jacks and invite children to join in. After practicing jumping jacks, have children stand very still and listen as you segment the sounds in a word.

Say: /kw/-/i/-/k/. Ask: What's my word? Tell children when they know the word, they can do jumping jacks in place until you say stop. Remind children to repeat the sounds and then blend the sounds to find out the word.

After children say the word quick, repeat the activity with other words that blend short vowels and *qu, j, y,* and *z* sounds.

> yam   yes   zip   jot   jug

Read Together

From Phonemic Awareness to Phonics

Objective: Relate *a, e, i, o, u*
to Short Vowel Sounds

LISTEN TO RHYMING WORDS Say: *The jet hasn't left yet.* Invite children to name the rhyming words.

> jet   yet

IDENTIFY THE LETTERS Say /j/-/e/-/t/ as you write jet on chart paper. Then identify the letters. Have children repeat the sounds. Repeat with *yet.* Circle the letters *et* in both words. Have children repeat after you: /j/ /et/, /y/ /et/. Explain that these words rhyme because they have the same /et/ ending.

FIND RHYMING WORDS Write the following words on index cards: *quit, fit, zap, tap, yet, bet, jot, pot, jug, tug, quiz, jog, zip.* Set out four cards: two that rhyme and two that do not.

Ask children to find the words with the same ending letters: for example, zap and tap. As you read the words, segment and blend the sounds. Say: /z/-/ap/, zap. Repeat with tap.

OBJECTIVES

Children will:

- identify /a/*a*, /e/*e*, /i/*i*, /o/*o*, /u/*u*
- blend and read short *a, e, i, o, u* words
- write short *a, e, i, o, u* words
- review /kw/*qu*, /j/*j*, /y/*y*, /z/*z*

·····································

MATERIALS

- letter cards from the *Word Building Book*

TEACHING **TIP**

INSTRUCTIONAL Write the word *zigzag* on the chalkboard and hold your hand over *zag* as you blend sounds to read *zig*. Have children repeat after you. Hold your hand over *zig* and continue as before with *zag*. Compare the two syllables with children.

ALTERNATE TEACHING STRATEGY

····································

BLENDING SHORT
a, e, i, o, u

For a different approach to teaching this skill, see Unit 1, page T32; Unit 2, page T32; Unit 3, page T30; Unit 4, page T32; Unit 5, page T30.

▶ **Visual/Auditory/ Kinesthetic**

Review Blending with short *a, e, i, o, u*

TEACH

Identify *a, e, i, o, u* as Symbols for /a/, /e/, /i/, /o/, /u/

Tell children they will continue to read words with *a, e, i, o, u*.

- Display the *a, e, i, o, u* letter cards and say /a/, /e/, /i/, /o/, /u/. Have children repeat the sounds as you point to the cards.

BLENDING Model and Guide Practice

- Place an *i* card after the *qu* card. Blend the sounds together and have children repeat after you.

- Place a *t* letter card after the *qu* and *i* cards. Blend the sounds in the word to read *quit*. Have children repeat after you.

Use the Word in Context

- Have children use *quit* in a sentence, perhaps talking about some activity they don't like to stop doing.

Repeat the Procedure

- Use the following words to continue modeling and for guided practice with short *a, e, i, o, u*: *zip, jet, Jen, jog, quick, quack, zigzag*.

PRACTICE

Complete the Pupil Edition Page

Read aloud the directions on page 352. Identify each picture, and complete the first item together. Then work through the page with children or have them complete the page independently.

ASSESS/CLOSE

Build Short *a, e, i, o, u* Words

Observe children as they complete page 352. Then write on the chalkboard _*ack,*_*et,*_*ip,*_*og,*_*ug*. Have children use letter cards and *qu, j, y, z* to build words, using the letter *j* twice. (*quack, yet, zip, jog, jug*)

Name_____

1. jet   job
   (jet)
   jet

2. quit   (quack)
   quack

3. yam   (jam)
   jam

4. jog   (zip)
   zip

Draw a circle around the word that names the picture. • Say the word. • Then write the word.

352   Unit 6   Review Blending with Short *a, e, i, o, u*

McGraw-Hill School Division

Pupil Edition, page 352

ADDITIONAL PHONICS RESOURCES

Practice Book, *page 352*
Phonics Workbook

McGraw-Hill School
TECHNOLOGY

Phonics CD-ROM
Activities for Practice with Blending and Segmenting

Practice 352

Name_____

1. pen   quick
   pen

2. ox   wax
   ox

3. yam   ham
   ham

4. ax   jug
   ax

Look at the picture. Read the words. Draw a line under the word that goes with the picture. Write the word.

At Home: Make cards for *a, e, i, o, u* and hide them in a room. Have the child look for them. When one is found, you say a word that uses the selected letter (e.g., *cat, net, pig, pot, sun*). When all five cards are found, switch roles.

352   **Review Blending with Short *a, e, i, o, u***   Unit 6

PRACTICE BOOK page 352

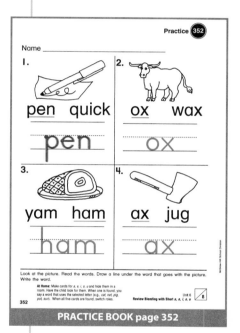

Meeting Individual Needs for Phonics

EASY	ON-LEVEL	CHALLENGE	LANGUAGE SUPPORT
Give children word cards *quick, quit, jet, Jen, yuck, yum* and ask them to sort to show three groups. Encourage them to tell how each word in the group is alike and how each word in the group is different.	**Show** pictures of objects such as: *jet, jug, jam, yam, zip, zigzag.* Ask children to identify the pictures using words that begin with *j, y,* or *z.* Then help them to write the words and blend sounds to read them aloud together.	**Invite** children to make up a story using some of the following words: *quick, jet, job, jog, yet, yuck, yum, zip, zap, zigzag.* Help them by asking questions and giving hints that will keep them focused on storytelling and make it easier to integrate their list of words.	**Give** children additional opportunities to practice initial *j* words. Write on the chalkboard: *Jan, Jen, Jon, Jim, Jack, Jeb, Jed, Jud.* Ask children to say the sound in the middle, then have them repeat as you blend sounds to read the names aloud.

352

Reread the Decodable Story

Jen and Yip

☑ Initial *qu, j, y, z*
☑ Make Inferences
☑ High-Frequency Word: *of*
☑ Concepts of Print

Jen and Yip

Guided Reading

SET PURPOSES Tell children that when they read the story again, they can find out more about what happened. Explain that you also want them to look for words with the initial *qu, j, y,* and *z*. Remind them that they know the word *of* and will see it again in this story.

REREAD THE BOOK As you guide children through the story, address specific problems they may have had during the first read. Use the following prompts to guide the lesson:

• **CONCEPTS OF PRINT** Have children point to the words that begin with a capital letter. Remind them that sentences always begin with a capital letter, as do names for a specific person or place.

• **MAKE INFERENCES** Ask children to use illustrations to figure out who is quicker, Jen or Yip. (Jen) Ask how they know. (Jen is in front of Yip)

RETURN TO PURPOSES Ask children if they found out more about what happened in the story. Ask children if they found words that begin with *qu, j, y,* and *z*. Ask if anyone saw the word *of* in the story.

LITERARY RESPONSE Ask children to draw a picture of an exercise that they like to do. Discuss different forms of exercising: playing sports, swimming, gymnastics, and so on.

• Ask children to describe and demonstrate a favorite exercise.

• Ask children why they think exercising is important.

TEACHING TIP

ZMANAGEMENT You may wish to reread the story with a small group of children who had difficulties during the first reading. Remind children to use picture clues to help them understand the story better.

ASSESSMENT

PHONICS: initial *qu*
HOW TO ASSESS
Display the letters *qu* and have children identify them. Make the /kw/ sound together. Have children find words in the story that begin with these letters.

FOLLOW UP If children have difficulty, write these words on the chalkboard and have children underline *qu: quit, quiet, quick.*

Read the Patterned Book

Six Yellow Ducks

- ☑ **Initial** *qu, j, y, z*
- ☑ **Make Inferences**
- ☑ **High-Frequency Word:** *of*
- ☑ **Concepts of Print**

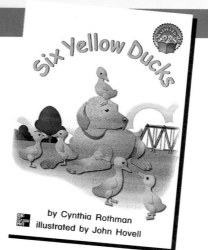

Six Yellow Ducks

by Cynthia Rothman
illustrated by John Hovell

Guided Reading

PREVIEW AND PREDICT Read the title and the author's and the illustrator's name. Ask who writes the words and who draws the illustrations. Take a **picture walk** through pages 2-4, noting the setting of the story, the season, and the characters. Ask whether the story seems to be real or a fantasy.

SET PURPOSES Have children decide what they want to find out from the story. Tell them you will read to find out what happens to the ducks.

READ THE BOOK Use the following prompts while the children are reading or after they have read independently. Remind them to run their fingers under each word as they read.

PAGES 2-3: Model: *Point to the last word. Each letter makes its own sound. Let's blend the sounds to say the word:* z-i-p zip. *Blending*

PAGES 4-5: Point to the second word. *Let's read it together:* of. *High-Frequency Words*

PAGES 6-7: *Why do you think the ducks are tired? (from playing) Make Inferences*

PAGE 8: *Look at the last word. Why is it in uppercase letters? (It should be read in a loud voice.) Concepts of Print*

RETURN TO PREDICTIONS AND PURPOSES Ask children if they found out what they needed to know from the story. See if their predictions were correct.

LITERARY RESPONSE The following questions will help focus children's responses:

- What did the ducks like to do?

- Write and draw about something else that the ducks could do.

LANGUAGE SUPPORT

ESL Review counting 1 through 6 with the children. Then read the story again, encouraging children to read with you when they can.

CENTER Activity

Cross Curricular: Math

CONCENTRATION
Make concentration cards from index cards with numbers and number words 1-10. Children make a grid with the cards and then turn over pairs of cards to make matches.

▶ **Logical/ Mathematical**

OBJECTIVES

Children will:

- identify and read the high-frequency word *of*

....

MATERIALS

- **word cards from the Word Play Book**
- *Jen and Yip*

TEACHING TIP

INSTRUCTIONAL Ask children to say how many letters are in the word *of*. Then show word cards for other two-letter high-frequency words *(is, my, we, to, me, go, do, he)*, and make a list on the chalkboard.

Review *of, not, that, my*

PREPARE

Listen to Words   Tell children that they will review the word *of*. Read the following sentence, and have children raise hands when they hear the word *of*: *Drink a glass of milk.*

TEACH

Model Reading the Word in Context   Reread the decodable book. Ask children to listen for the word *of*.

Identify the Word   Tell children to first look at their word cards, and then to look for the word in the story. Read the book, tracking print, and ask children to come up and point to the word *of*. Have volunteers put a stick-on dot below the word.

Review High-Frequency Words   Hold up word cards for the following: *the, a, my, that, and, I, is, said, we, are, you, have, to, me, go, do, for, he, she, has, with, was, not.*
Have children read the words together.

PRACTICE

Complete the Pupil Edition Page   Read the directions on page 353 to children, and make sure they clearly understand what they are being asked to do. Complete the first item together. Then work through the page with children or have them complete the page independently.

ASSESS/CLOSE

Review the Page   Review children's work, and guide children who are experiencing difficulty or need additional practice.

Name_____

1.

Yes, we do have a lot of fun.

_____

2.

Rob can not pick up that sack.

_____

3.

The bug is on the top of my net.

Read each sentence. **1.** Draw a line under the word *of.* **2.** Draw a line under the words *not* and *that.* **3.** Draw a line under the word *my.*

Unit 6   Review *of, not, that, my*   353

Pupil Edition, page 353

ALTERNATE TEACHING
STRATEGY
....
**HIGH-FREQUENCY
WORDS:** *of*

For a different approach to
teaching the skill,
see page T27.

▶ **Visual/Auditory/
Kinesthetic**

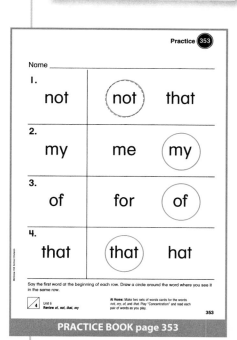

PRACTICE BOOK page 353

Meeting Individual Needs for Vocabulary

EASY	ON-LEVEL	CHALLENGE	LANGUAGE SUPPORT
Give children four letter cards with the letter *o* and four letter cards with the letter *f*. Have children put the letters together to spell *of*. Ask children how many times they can spell the word.	**Write** on the chalkboard: *Drink a glass of ___.* Highlight the word *of*. Then have children suggest different words to complete the sentence. Write children's words, and read the sentences with them as you track print.	**Play** the game "I Have a Bag of ___." Have children sit in a circle. Begin by prompting one child to complete the phrase with a word beginning with /a/. Continue through the alphabet, guiding children when necessary.	**Reread** a classroom picture book, and stop when you read the words *of* and *that*. Have children repeat the sentences with you and point to the words.

353

GRAMMAR/SPELLING CONNECTIONS

Model subject-verb agreement, complete sentences, and correct tense so that students may gain increasing control of grammar when speaking and writing.

Interactive Writing

Write a Poem

Prewrite

LOOK AT THE STORY PATTERN Revisit *White Rabbit's Color Book*, and talk about the pattern of the text. Then make a list of the color words in the book, and talk about the descriptive language: *icy cold blue, warm yellow*.

Draft

WRITE A CLASS POEM Discuss each of the colors listed, and ask children how each color makes the children feel. Make a list of their responses. Then explain that children will write a poem that tells how the colors make them feel. Point out that poems do not have to rhyme. If possible, read some examples.

- Begin by making a class decision if the poem should rhyme or not rhyme. Then work together to decide which colors to include in the poem.

- Have children complete phrases such as:

  (Blue) makes me feel (cold).

  (Yellow) feels like (the sun).

- Combine the phrases to create the poem.

Publish

CREATE THE POEM Reread the poem, and see if children decide as a group to make any changes. Then have volunteers help you write the poem on chart paper.

Blue makes me feel cold.

Yellow feels like the sun.

Gray makes me feel sleepy.

Orange feels like fun.

Presentation Ideas

MAKE A MURAL Have children work together to make a mural that illustrates the poem. Have children work with partners or small groups, and decide which part they want to illustrate. Provide crayons, markers, or paints.

▶ **Representing/Viewing**

DO A CHORAL READING Read the poem as a class, having children join in on words they can read or remember. Track print as everyone reads together. You may wish to have a volunteer point to sections of the mural as children read.

▶ **Speaking/Representing**

Meeting Individual Needs for Writing

EASY	ON-LEVEL	CHALLENGE
Write an Emotion Show children a crayon, and ask how the color makes them feel. Help them write the word that describes the emotion.	**Write a List** Show children a color. Have them write a picture/word list of as many items that they can think of that are that color. Remind children to sound out words as they write their lists. Compare the lists.	**Write a Rhyme** Help children write rhymes based on color words. Give some examples: *I really like the color red.* *It's the color of the cap on my head.*

Zack and Jan

Children will read and listen to a variety of stories about different kinds of choices that people make.

Zack and Jan

**Listening
Library
Audiocassette**

**Decodable Story,
pages 361–362 of the
Pupil Edition**

**Hen Had
Her Ham**

by Meish Goldish
illustrated by Andy San Diego

**Patterned Books,
page 317B**

Annie's Pet
by Barbara Brenner

**Teacher Read Aloud,
page 311A**

WRITTEN BY JUDY NAYER
ILLUSTRATED BY SUSAN SWAN

**Listening
Library
Audiocassette**

**ABC Big Book,
pages 355A–355B**

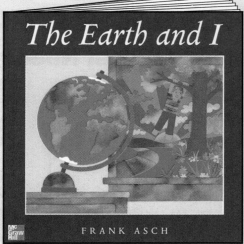
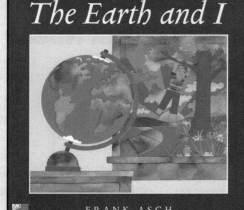

The Earth and I

FRANK ASCH

**Listening
Library
Audiocassette**

**Literature Big Book,
pages 357A–357B**

**Pupil Edition,
pages 354–365**

**Big Book of Real-Life Reading,
page 40**

**Big Book of Phonics Rhymes and
Poems, pages 23, 43, 56, 59, 61, 62**

 Listening
Library
Audiocassette

ADDITIONAL RESOURCES

**Practice Book,
pages 354–365**

- **Phonics Kit**
- **Language Support Book**
- **Alternate Teaching Strategies,** pp T24–T37

McGraw-Hill School
TECHNOLOGY

Phonics CD-ROM Provides
extra phonics support.

interNET CONNECTION Research & Inquiry Ideas.

Visit www.mhschool.com

Zack and Jan

READING AND LANGUAGE ARTS

- **Phonological Awareness**
- **Phonics** *review*
- **Comprehension**
- **Vocabulary**
- **Beginning Reading Concepts**
- **Listening, Speaking, Viewing, Representing**

DAY 1

Written by Judy Nayer
Illustrated by Susan Swan

Focus on Reading Skills

Develop Phonological Awareness, 354G-354H
"Vickie's Velvet Vest," "I Am Six," and "Happy Henry" *Big Book of Phonics Rhymes and Poems,* 23, 56, 59

 **Review Blending with *a, e, i, o, u,*** 354I-354
Practice Book, 354
Phonics/Phonemic Awareness Practice Book

Phonics CD-ROM

Read the Literature

Read *The Big Box: An ABC Book* Big Book, 355A-355B
Shared Reading

Build Skills

☑ Shapes and Categories, 355C-355
Practice Book, 355

DAY 2

The Earth and I

FRANK ASCH

Focus on Reading Skills

Develop Phonological Awareness, 356A-356B
"Quentin Quiggly," "The Yak," "Zachary Zoo" *Big Book of Phonics Rhymes and Poems,* 43, 61-62

Review Blending with *a, e, i, o, u,* 356C-356
Practice Book, 356
Phonics/Phonemic Awareness Practice Book

Phonics CD-ROM

Read the Literature

Read *The Earth and I* Big Book, 357A-357B
Shared Reading

Build Skills

☑ Cause and Effect, 357C-357
Practice Book, 357

- **Cross Curriculum**

Activity Language Arts, 355B

Activity Music, 357B

- **Writing**

 Writing Prompt: What kind of home would you make out of the box?

 Journal Writing, 355B
Letter Formation, 355B

 Writing Prompt: Have you ever made a really important decision? Write about and draw a picture.

 Journal Writing, 357B

  = **Skill Assessed in Unit Test**

DAY 3

Annie's Pet

Focus on Reading Skills

Develop Phonological Awareness, 358A-358B

"Very Musical" and "Happy Henry" *Big Book of Phonics Rhymes and Poems, 23, 55*

 **Review Blending with *a, e, i, o, u,* 358C-358**
Practice Book, 358
Phonics/Phonemic Awareness Practice Book

 **CD-ROM**

Read the Literature

Read "Annie's Pet" Teacher Read Aloud, 359A-359B
Shared Reading
Read the Big Book of Real-Life Reading, 32-33
☑ Maps

Build Skills

☑ High-Frequency Words: *with, was, not, of,* 359C-359
Practice Book, 359

 **Art,** 359B

 Writing Prompt: What do you think Annie did after she bought her puppy? Write a story about what she did with her puppy next.

DAY 4

Zack and Jan

Focus on Reading Skills

Develop Phonological Awareness, 360A-360B

"A Big, Red Box"

 **Review Blending with Short *a, e, i, o, u,* 360C-360**
Practice Book, 360
Phonics/Phonemic Awareness Practice Book

 CD-ROM

Read the Literature

Read "Zack and Jan" Decodable Story, 361/362A-361/362D

☑ Review *h, w, v, x, qu, j, y, z;* Blending
☑ Make Inferences
☑ High-Frequency Words: *with, was, not, of*
☑ Concepts of Print

Build Skills

☑ Make Inferences, 363A-363
Practice Book, 363

 Social Studies, 361/362D

 Writing Prompt: How do you feel when someone does something nice for you?

Letter Formation,
Practice Book, 361-362

DAY 5

Zack and Jan

Focus on Reading Skills

Develop Phonological Awareness, 364A-364B

"A Big, Red box"

 **Review Blending with Short *a, e, i, o, u,* 364C-364**
Practice Book, 364
Phonics/Phonemic Awareness Practice Book

CD-ROM

Read the Literature

Reread "Zack and Jan" Decodable Story, 365A
Read "Hen Had Her Ham" Patterned Book, 305B
Guided Reading
☑ Review *h, w, v, x, qu, j, y, z;* Blending
☑ Make Inferences
☑ High-Frequency Words: *with, was, not, of*
☑ Concepts of Print

Build Skills

☑ High-Frequency Words: *with, was, not, of,* 365C-365
Practice Book, 365

Language Arts, 365B

 Writing Prompt: Tell about a choice you make every day. Write your thoughts.

Interactive Writing, 366A-366B

Develop Phonological Awareness

Listen

Vickie's Velvet Vest
a poem

I Am Six
a poem

Vickie has a velvet vest
That's very, very pretty.
Vickie wears her velvet vest
To go into the city.

Vickie went to visit
Aunt Vera and Uncle Joe.
They had a very good dinner
And saw a funny show.

Six, six, I am six.
I am six today.
I will open up this box
From grandma far away.

Six, six, I am six.
I am six today.
Look what's inside
grandma's box.
A game for me to play!

Big Book of Phonics Rhymes and Poems, pages 56, 59

Objective: Focus on Syllables

LISTEN TO THE POEM Read the poem "Vickie's Velvet Vest." Then say the words *Vickie* and *vest*. Point out that each word begins with the /v/ sound. Clap and count the syllables. Determine the number of syllables in each word. Then have the children count the syllables with you.

COUNTING BLOCKS FOR SYLLABLES Place two blocks in front of you to represent the word *Vic-kie* and one block for

vest. Ask children to tell you which word is longer. Compare the syllables of other *v* words.

velvet/very   Vera/visit

CONTINUE WITH *x*, *x* WORDS
• Read the poem "I Am Six." Then compare the *x* words and the number of syllables in each word.

Objective: Listen for Initial /h/

SEGMENTING

- Review the first line of the poem "Vickie's Velvet Vest." Say the word *has*. Ask the children to identify the initial sound. Then have children segment the initial sound.

> **h-as**

- Do the same for the word *her*.

BRAINSTORM WORDS

- Have children brainstorm words that begin with the /h/ sound. After the child says a word, he/she should say it without the /h/ sound.
- Repeat the activity until all children have had a chance.

> **happy/appy hall/all**
> **hamburger/amburger hint/int**

GUESS THE WORD

- Tell children you are going to play a game called "Guess the Word." You will say a word without the initial sound and children will have to guess what word it is.

> **appy/happy enry/Henry en/hen**
> **amburger/hamburger and/hand**

Read Together

From Phonemic Awareness to Phonics

Objective: Identify /w/W,w

IDENTIFY THE CONSONANT

Tell children that the letter *w* stands for the sound /w/. Display the Big Book of Phonics Rhymes and Poems, p. 58, and point to the letters in the corner. Explain that the letter is *w* and say the /w/ sound. Have children trace a *w* in the air.

READ THE POEM As you read "Willie Walrus," point to each word. Emphasize the words with /w/.

FIND THE LETTERS

Have children identify *w* in words as you read the poem, line by line.

ORDER LINES IN POEM

- Write each line of the poem on a sentence strip. Mix up the lines and display them to the class.

- Then point to the first line in the poem and ask a volunteer to find the sentence strip that has the same words.

- Repeat this procedure for the remaining lines.

- Have children reread the poem with you.

Ww

Wally Walrus

Wally Walrus is oh so wide,
He waddles around from side to side.

Wally Walrus is wild and brave,
As he rides an ocean wave.

Wally Walrus loves playing in water.
You can see him with his
wife and daughter.

58

Big Book of Phonics Rhymes and Poems, p. 58

Review Blending with short *a, e, i, o, u*

OBJECTIVES

Children will:

- identify /a/a, /e/e, /i/i, /o/o, /u/u
- blend and read short *a, e, i, o, u* words
- write short *a, e, i, o, u* words
- review /v/v, /ks/x, /w/w, /h/h

MATERIALS

- letter cards from the *Word Building Book*

TEACHING TIP

INSTRUCTIONAL Review the letters /v/ and /w/. Make the sound of each letter and ask children to repeat it. On the chalkboard write the following words and have children sort by initial letter: *wed, wag, van, win, vet, wig, vat, wet.* Invite children to blend sounds and read the words aloud with you.

ALTERNATE TEACHING STRATEGY

BLENDING SHORT *a, e, i, o, u*

For a different approach to teaching this skill, see Unit 1, page T32; Unit 2, page T32; Unit 3, page T30; Unit 4, page T32; Unit 5, page T30.

▶ **Visual/Auditory/ Kinesthetic**

TEACH

Identify *a, e, i, o, u* as Symbols for /a/, /e/, /i/, /o/, /u/

Tell children they will continue to read words with *a, e, i, o, u.*

- Display the *a, e, i, o, u* letter cards and say /a/, /e/, /i/, /o/, /u/. Have children repeat the sounds as you point to each card.

BLENDING Model and Guide Practice

- Place an *x* card after the *o* card. Blend the sounds together and have children repeat after you.

- Place a *b* letter card before the *o, x* cards. Blend to read *box.*

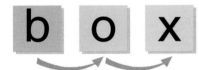 

Use the Word in Context

- Have children pass around a box of objects. Direct each child to take out an object and say, *I took a (crayon) out of the box.*

Repeat the Procedure

- Use the following words to continue modeling and for guided practice with short *a, e, i, o, u: had, ham, van, vet, web, wax, win.*

PRACTICE

Complete the Pupil Edition Page

Read aloud the directions on page 354. Identify each picture, and complete the first item together. Then work through the page with the children, or have them complete the page independently.

ASSESS/CLOSE

Build Short *a, e, i, o, u* Words

Observe children as they complete page 354. Then display letter cards *w, h, v, x* and *a, e, i, o, u.* Ask children to use these and other letter cards to build five words, using each vowel once in the middle.

Name _____

1. v a n   van

2. h o p   hop

3. m i x   mix

4. w e t   wet

Blend the sounds and say the word. • Write the word. • Draw a circle around the picture that goes with the word.

McGraw-Hill School Division

Pupil Edition, page 354

ADDITIONAL PHONICS RESOURCES

Practice Book, *page 354*
Phonics Workbook

McGraw-Hill School
TECHNOLOGY

Phonics CD-ROM
Activities for Practice with Blending and Segmenting

Practice **354**

Name _____

1. b u g   bug

2. j e t   jet

3. J a c k   Jack

4. f o x   fox

Blend the sounds and say the word. Write the word. Draw a line under the picture that goes with the word.

At Home: Write *_ick.* Take turns writing under it words that end with *ick* (*kick, lick, nick, Nick, pick, quick, Rick, sick, tick, wick*).

Review Blending with Short *a, e, i, o, u*   Unit 6   8

354

PRACTICE BOOK page 354

Meeting Individual Needs for Phonics

EASY	ON-LEVEL	CHALLENGE	LANGUAGE SUPPORT
Ask children to blend and read aloud the following words: *hug, hog, fix, wax, wag, wig, fox, hit, vet, vat.* Invite them to use word cards to sort the words as many ways as they can, such as: *words that begin with h, f, w, v; words that end with g, x, t;* or *by words with medial a, e, i, o, u.*	**Show** word cards *wet, hen, vet, hog.* Tell this story: *On a wet, rainy day, Hilda the hen and Vic the vet came to see Harry the hog.* Ask children to blend and read the cards, and add to the story using *w, h, v, x* words.	**Give** children these word cards in random order: *can, you, fix, the, van, I, can, fix, it, at, six.* Ask them to arrange the cards to show two sentences, a question and an answer. Afterwards, write the sentences on the board. Help with capitalization and punctuation.	**Give** children the following word cards and ask them to hold up the card, then blend and read aloud the words you pronounce. For example: *fox, wax, six, hop, had, hip, web, wed, wet, van, vat, vet.* Review all word meanings, showing pictures when possible, and repeat the activity.

354

OBJECTIVES

Children will:

- match letter cards with letters in the story
- use letters to recognize key words in the story

Read the Big Book

Before Reading

Develop Oral Language Read "The Alphabet Chant" with the children on pages 6-7 in the Big Book of Phonics Rhymes and Chimes. Remind children of the story about the box. Ask children what they would like to do with the box.

Set Purposes Explain that children will use letters to name key words. They will also match letter cards with the letters in the book. Distribute two or three uppercase and lowercase letters to each child. As you read the story, children holding the letter in the story stand up and name the letter. Tell children that they will also think about how the characters are feeling during the story.

"We can paint **yellow** things on the box," said Matt.

28

"We can make a **zebra** with black and white stripes," said Ann.

29

The Big Box, pages 28-29

During Reading

Read Together

- As you point to the letter, have children holding the letter cards stand up and identify them. Run your finger under each word in the story as you read. Have children repeat the words after you. *Concepts of Print*

- After you read page 2, ask a volunteer to frame the quotation marks. Remind children that these marks tell us that a character is speaking. *Concepts of Print*

- After you read page 18, ask children to describe how the children in the story are working together. *Use Illustrations*

- After you read pages 30-31, ask children to think about how the children in the story might be feeling. *Make Inferences*

"We can make a **house**," said Gina.

The Big Box, page 11

After Reading

Literary Response

JOURNAL WRITING Ask children to draw a picture, and write about a time when they worked together with a friend.

ORAL RESPONSE Ask questions such as:

- *How did you work together?*

- *What did you make?*

- *What materials did you use?*

ABC Activity Say a key word from the story. Children say and point to the initial letter.

CENTER Activity

Cross Curricular: Language Arts

NUMBER THE LETTER Provide an alphabet strip and number cards 1-26. One volunteer takes a number. The partner counts and finds that letter. Children take turns.

OBJECTIVES

Children will:
- identify shapes
- classify objects

MATERIALS
- *The Earth and I*

TEACHING TIP

INSTRUCTIONAL

Ask children to sort a set of pattern blocks by color. Discuss other ways children could have sorted to get these same groups. *(by shape, by size)*

Review Shapes and Categories

PREPARE

Plan a Game

Have children sit in a circle. Say: *"I'm thinking of something small and white. You hit it with a bat. What is it?"* Continue the guessing game, incorporating shapes and colors. Then ask volunteers to give clues.

TEACH

Recognize Shapes and Classify

Display *The Earth and I*. Take a picture and walk through the book, and ask children to identify objects shaped like circles, triangles, squares, and rectangles. Make a picture or a word list. Then work together to make a chart that shows how to classify the items in various ways.

PRACTICE

Complete the Pupil Edition Page

Read the directions on page 355 to the children, and make sure they clearly understand what they are asked to do. *Identify each picture, and complete the first item.* Then work through the page with the children, or have them complete the page independently.

ASSESS/CLOSE

Review the Page

Check children's work on the Pupil Edition page. Note areas where children need extra help.

Name _____

Draw a circle around the animals. • Draw a triangle around the clothing. • Draw a square around the toys.

Unit 6 Review Shapes and Categories   355

Pupil Edition, page 355

PRACTICE BOOK page 355

Meeting Individual Needs for Beginning Reading Concepts

EASY	ON-LEVEL	CHALLENGE	LANGUAGE SUPPORT
Name a familiar category, such as food or furniture. Reread a familiar classroom picture book. Have children name items in the story that belong in the classification category.	**Name** a category, such as dogs. Have children think of different ways to classify dogs, such as by size, color, or breed. Have them draw pictures to show each category.	**Place** pipe cleaners in a large envelope. Have children guess the name of a shape as it is slowly pulled out of the envelope.	**Give** children ample opportunities to sort shapes before asking them to identify the shapes. Use terms such as round, sides, and corners to describe the shape.

Develop Phonological Awareness

Listen

Quentin Quiggly
a poem

The Yak
a poem

Quentin Quiggly had a quarter
In his purple jacket.
What did Quentin Quiggly buy?
A twenty-five-cent tennis
    racket.

Quentin had another quarter,
Silver, round, and thin.
Quentin Quiggly bought a
    pretzel
For his best friend, Quinn.

Yickety-yackity, yickity-yak,
The yak has a scriffily,
    scraffily back;
Some yaks are brown yaks
    and some yaks are black,
Yickity-yackity, yickity-yak.

Jack Prelutsky

Big Book of Phonics Rhymes and Poems, pp. 43, 61

Objective: Blend Words

READ THE POEM

Read aloud the poem "Quentin Quiggly." Have children tell who the poem is about. Ask, "What sound do you hear at the beginning of Quentin? Quiggly? Let's say this sound together." Reread the poem and have children identify other words that begin with the same sound. Repeat this activity for the /j/ sound.

> quarter   Quinn   jacket

BLEND WITH SHORT VOWELS

Review the short vowel sounds with the class. Then ask children to listen to the sounds you say and blend them into a word. For example: k-w-i-t (quit). Say each sound slowly and then progress to saying the sounds quickly. Have children repeat the blending with you.

PLAY A LISTENING GAME

Tell children you will say the sounds of a word from the poem. Have them try to guess the word and say it.

Objective: Listen to Blended Words

INTRODUCE THE POEM
Tell children you are going to review a funny poem. Then read the title "The Yak." Ask children who the poem will be about. Say, "What sound does *yak* begin with? Let's say the sound together." Repeat the word *yak* several times. Then read the poem to the class.

BLEND WORDS Review the short vowel sounds. Then ask children to listen to the sounds you say and blend them into a word. For example:

- y-a-k (yak)   y-e-t (yet)   y-u-k (yuk)
- b-a-k (back)   b-e-d (bed)   b-i-t (bit)
- b-o-k-s (box)

DRAW IT Have children listen as you segment words. Explain that they should blend the sounds to find out what the word is, then draw a picture of it. Words to use might include:

h-a-t

m-o-p

p-i-g

t-u-b

Read Together

From Phonemic Awareness to Phonics

Objective: Blend Words with /z/ Z, z

IDENTIFY THE LETTER Tell children that the letter *z* stands for the sound /z/. Draw children's attention to the phonics rhyme on page 62 and point out the letter in the upper left corner. Say the sound /z/ and have children repeat the sound. Talk about how the tongue is behind the teeth when making this sound.

READ THE POEM Read aloud the poem, pointing to each word. Exaggerate the words that begin with /z/. Have children identify the letter *z* in words in the poem.

BLEND THE NICKNAMES. Tell children that Zachary Zebulun Zebedee Zoo has two nicknames. Ask children to figure out what they are as you segment the sounds:

z-a-k (Zach)   z-e-b (Zeb)

Have children blend the sounds to say the nicknames.

Zachary Zoo

Zachary Zebulun Zebedee Zoo
is a long name
for a boy aged two.

When Zack grows up,
he hopes that he
Will be called
just plain Zachary.

Big Book of Phonics Rhymes and Poems, p.62

Review Blending with short *a, e, i, o, u*

OBJECTIVES

Children will:

- identify /a/*a*, /e/*e*, /i/*i*, /o/*o*, /u/*u*
- blend and read short *a, e, i, o, u* words
- write short *a, e, i, o, u* words
- review /kw/*qu*, /j/*j*, /y/*y*, /z/*z*

MATERIALS

- letter cards and word cards from the *Word Building Book*

TEACHING TIP

INSTRUCTIONAL When working with words that begin with *g*, be careful not to include any words that begin with the /j/ sound such as *gerbil, giant, George,* or *Geoff.* If children suggest any of these words, briefly explain that sometimes *g* makes another sound, which they will learn at another time.

ALTERNATE TEACHING STRATEGY

BLENDING SHORT *a, e, i, o, u*

For a different approach to teaching this skill, see Unit 1, page T32; Unit 2, page T32; Unit 3, page T30; Unit 4, page T32; Unit 5, page T30.

▶ **Visual/Auditory/ Kinesthetic**

TEACH

Identify *a, e, i, o, u* as Symbols for /a/, /e/, /i/, /o/, /u/

Tell children they will continue to read words with *a, e, i, o, u.*

- Display the *a, e, i, o, u* letter cards and say /a/, /e/, /i/, /o/, /u/. Have children repeat the sounds /a/, /e/, /i/, /o/, /u/ after you as you point to the *a, e, i, o, u* cards.

BLENDING Model and Guide Practice

- Place an *a* card after the *j* card. Blend the sounds together and have children repeat after you.

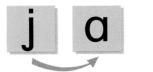 

- Place an *m* letter card after the *j a* cards. Blend to read *jam.*

Use the Word in Context

- Have children use *jam* in a sentence, perhaps talking about what they like to eat on bread or toast.

Repeat the Procedure

- Use the following words to continue modeling and for guided practice with short *a, e, i, o, u: yum, yam, yuck, quick, Jan, Zack, zip.*

PRACTICE

Complete the Pupil Edition Page

Read the directions on page 356 to children, and make sure they clearly understand what they are being asked to do. Identify each picture, and complete the first item. Then work through the page with the children, or have them complete the page independently.

ASSESS/CLOSE

Write Short *a, e, i, o, u* Words

Observe children as they complete page 356. Have children use letter cards and *qu, j, y, z* as many times as they can to build, then write five words that use *a, e, i, o,* or *u* in the middle.

Name

1. j a m   jam

2. y u m   yum

3. z i p   zip

4. qu i ck   quick

Blend the sounds and say the word. • Write the word. • Draw a circle around the picture that goes with the word.

McGraw-Hill School Division

356   Unit 6   Review Blending with Short *a, e, i, o, u*

Pupil Edition, page 356

ADDITIONAL PHONICS RESOURCES

Practice Book, *page 356*
Phonics Workbook

McGraw-Hill School
TECHNOLOGY

Phonics CD-ROM
Activities for Practice with
Blending and Segmenting

Name   Practice 356

1. m o p   2. z i p

   mop   zip

3. j a m   4. s u n

   jam   sun

Blend the sounds and say the word. Write the word. Draw a line under the picture that goes with the word.

At Name: Write *zip*. Ask the child to change *zip* to *zap*.
Write *mop*. Ask the child to change *mop* to *map, jam* to
Jim, and *fix* to *fox*. Use each word in a sentence.

356   Review Blending with Short *a, e, i, o, u*   Unit 6
                                                          6

PRACTICE BOOK page 356

Meeting Individual Needs for Phonics

EASY	ON-LEVEL	CHALLENGE	LANGUAGE SUPPORT
Give children the following word cards: *job, jog, jig.* Have them repeat as you blend sounds to read words aloud. Ask how the first and second words are alike, then repeat the question about the second and third words. Continue the activity with *zig, zip, yip.*	**Have** children complete sentences with initial *qu, j, y, z* words, such as: *Work until the (job) is done. A sweet potato is a lot like a (yam). Is she back (yet)? She is a (quick) runner. Before you roll up your sleeping bag, (zip) it up. Do you like strawberry (jam)?*	**Write** the following words on the chalkboard and help children blend sounds to read them aloud: *quiz, Jack, Zack, yap, Jim, jug.* Children have decoded words similar to all of these new words. After decoding, ask children to use each word in a sentence.	**Write** these words on the chalkboard: *jig, jog, yip, yum.* Have children blend sounds to read each aloud. Provide context for these words by using them in sentences and using pantomime and sound effects. Have children act out the words as you point to them in random order.

356

OBJECTIVES

Children will:

- review words with initial /h/h
- review words with initial /w/w
- identify cause and effect
- make inferences

MATERIALS

- Literature Big Book *The Earth and I*

TEACHING TIP

INSTRUCTIONAL Have available a collection of library books and other easy references on pollution for the learning center. Invite a representative from a local recycling center to visit the class if possible. You may also wish to plan a field trip to a recycling center.

Read the Big Book

Before Reading

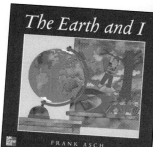

Develop Oral Language

OBSERVE THE WORLD If weather permits, take the children outdoors and have them look up and down and all around their word. If it is not possible to go outside, simply have children look out a window. Then lead them in the finger play found on pages 321A–321B.

REVISIT THE LITERATURE Have children recall the title of the Big Book in which a boy sang to Earth. Ask children to summarize *The Earth and I*.

Set Purposes

Let children set their own purposes for reading *The Earth and I*. For example, they may wish to read to determine which parts of the story are real and which parts are fantasy.

I tell her what's on my mind.

4

She listens to every word.

5

The Earth and I, pages 4-5

During Reading

Read Together

- As you read *The Earth and I*, pause each time before the memorable phrase, "The Earth and I are friends." Have children join you in saying the words.

- As you read, move your finger left to right and word for word, down the page (return sweep). *Concepts of Print*

- Throughout the reading, ask children to say words that have initial /h/h or /w/w. *Phonemic Awareness*

- Remind children that when one thing happens, it can make something else happen. Have children examine the polluted Earth on pages 22–23. Ask: *What might have happened to make Earth so dirty? Cause and Effect*

- Have children talk about all the things the boy did for Earth. Ask: *How do you think Earth felt about the boy? Make Inferences*

The Earth and I are friends.

The Earth and I, page 1

After Reading

Return to Purposes

Ask children to tell what happened first, next, and so on in *The Earth and I*. Revisit the Big Book as needed.

Retell the Story

Invite children to retell the story. Use illustrations from the book as necessary.

Literary Response

JOURNAL WRITING Have children write about or draw their favorite parts of the story.

ORAL RESPONSE Have children share their journal entries with the class.

CENTER Activity

Cross Curricular: Music

EARTH SONGS Talk about the litter and pollution shown in *The Earth and I*. Children will:

- list ideas for caring for Earth, such as picking up litter.

- use their ideas to compose a few lines that can be sung to a familiar tune.

▶ **Linguistic/Musical**

RESEARCH AND INQUIRY Ask children what else they would like to learn about cleaning up litter and pollution in their community.

 interNET CONNECTION Help children log on to the Publisher's Web site where they can access links to various sites about clean-up efforts. **www.mhschool.com/reading**

OBJECTIVES

Children will:

- use cause and effect to understand a story

....

MATERIALS

- *The Earth and I*

TEACHING TIP

MANAGEMENT If children experience difficulty completing the worksheets individually, you might have them work with a partner.

PREPARE

Recall the Story   Recall with children the story *The Earth and I*. Then ask them to remember how the boy feels when Earth is sad.

TEACH

Understanding Cause and Effect   Reread pages 4–5 of the story and ask children what happens when the boy tells Earth what's on his mind. Remind children that when one thing happens in a story, it can cause something else to happen. Guide children in finding other examples by asking questions such as: *What happens when it rains? What happens when Earth is happy?*

PRACTICE

Complete the Pupil Edition Page   Read the directions on page 357 to children, and make sure they clearly understand what they are asked to do. Identify each picture, and complete the first item together. Then work through the page with children or have them complete the page independently.

ASSESS/CLOSE

Review the Page   Review children's work and note children who need additional help.

Name_____

1.

2.

3.

4.

5.

Look at each picture on the left. • Draw a line to the picture on the right that shows what will happen next.

Unit 6   Review Cause and Effect   **357**

Pupil Edition, page 357

ALTERNATE TEACHING STRATEGY
....
CAUSE AND EFFECT
For a different approach to teaching this skill, see page T26.

▶ **Visual/Auditory/ Kinesthetic**

Practice **357**

Name_____

1.

2.

3.

Look at the first picture in each row. Circle the picture that shows why it happened.

Unit 6
Review Cause and Effect

At Home: Talk about something that happened. Ask the child why it happened. Guide his or her answer where necessary.

357

PRACTICE BOOK page 357

Meeting Individual Needs for Comprehension

EASY	ON-LEVEL	CHALLENGE	LANGUAGE SUPPORT
Display the page in *The Earth and I* where it rains. Ask children what the boy does when it rains. Encourage children to think of other things that happen as a result of rain. If necessary, give prompts such as: *Where do you play when it rains? What do you wear in the rain?*	**Have** children fold a piece of paper in half. On one side have them draw a picture of what happens when a friend is sad; on the other side they should show what happens when a friend is happy. Have children complete the sentence frame: *When my friend is sad (happy), …*	**Provide** old magazines and have children cut out pictures to make collages showing what happens when they, too, are friends with Earth. Encourage children to dictate sentences about the effect of their friendship with Earth.	**Use** the text in *The Earth and I* to review verbs. Have children repeat these verbs after you and act out their meaning: *dance, listen, walk, play, help, grow, sing.*

357

Develop Phonological Awareness

Listen

Very Musical
a poem

Happy Henry
a poem

Victor plays the violin.
He holds it underneath his chin.
His sister's name is Violet.
She plays a long, black clarinet.

Uncle Vern has a beautiful voice.
The cello is their mother's choice.
Dad plays the vibraphone...and
   so,
The family made a video.

Henry is a happy horse.
Henry likes to smile, of course.
Henry has a happy grin,
From ear to ear and mane to
   chin.
Happy Henry! Ho, ho, ho!
He's a happy horse to know.

Big Book of Phonics Rhymes and Poems, pages 54–55 and 23

Objective: Listen for Syllables

READ THE POEM Read the poem "Very Musical." Tap each syllable with an unsharpened pencil as you say: *mu-si-cal*. Point out that each tap represents one syllable. Ask: *How many times did I tap?* (3)

TAP A TUNE Have children tap the syllables as you say: *vi-o-lin*. Talk about how many syllables there are in *violin*.

Repeat the activity by tapping the syllables for each instrument named in the poem.

clarinet cello vibraphone

NAME OTHER INSTRUMENTS Invite children to name other musical instruments. Have them tap the number of syllables in each name. Then have one child pantomine playing an instrument. Other children tap the syllables as they state their guesses.

drums piano saxophone triangle

Objective: Listen and Blend Sounds

BLEND TWO SOUNDS Read the poem "Very Musical." Then reread the second line. Say the word *it*, pausing between each sound. Help children determine that the word *it* has two sounds. Have children repeat the sounds several times, gradually blending them together.

> /i/ - /t/

BLEND THREE SOUNDS Read the poem "Happy Henry." Ask: *Is Henry a horse?* After children respond, say the word *yes*, pausing between each sound. Help children determine that the word *yes* has three sounds. Have children repeat the sounds several times, gradually blending them together.

> /y/ - /e/ - /s/

SHOW THE SOUNDS Give each child several small blocks. Have children set out one block for each sound they hear in the segmented words you say aloud. Have children move the blocks closer together as they blend the sounds.

> jam bit hug rat fit win ax
> quack zip lid van cat kit

Read Together

From Phonemic Awareness to Phonics

Objective: Associate Sounds with Letters

IDENTIFY LETTERS AND SOUNDS Display pages 54–55 in the *Big Book of Phonics Rhymes and Poems*. Point to the letters, identify them, and say the sounds they stand for. Have children say the letters and sounds.

REREAD THE POEM Reread the poem. Point to each word, blending these as you present them: *it, his, is, has, dad*.

FIND WORDS Write the words *it, his, is, has*, and *dad* on index cards. Have children match these word cards with words in the poems.

Vv

Very Musical

Victor plays the violin.
He holds it underneath his chin.

His sister's name is Violet.
She plays a long, black clarinet.

Uncle Vern has a beautiful voice.
The cello is their mother's choice.

Dad plays the vibraphone ... and so,
The family made a video.

Big Book of Phonics Rhymes and Poems, pp. 54–55

358B

OBJECTIVES

Children will:

- identify /a/*a*, /e/*e*, /i/*i*, /o/*o*, /u/*u*
- blend and read short *a, e, i, o, u* words
- write short *a, e, i, o, u* words
- review /v/*v*, /ks/*x*, /w/*w*, /h/*h*, /kw/*qu*, /j/*j*, /y/*y*, /z/*z*, /b/*b*, /g/*g*, /k/*k*, *ck*, /l/*l*, /p/*p*, /r/*r*, /f/*f*, /k/*c*, /t/*t*, /m/*m*, /s/*s*, /d/*d*, and /n/*n*

....

MATERIALS

- letter cards from the *Word Building Book*

TEACHING TIP

INSTRUCTIONAL Review words which children have blended that can be used as either objects or action words; for example: *can, lock,* and *rock.* Ask volunteers to use each word in a sentence, once as an action word and once as an object.

ALTERNATE TEACHING STRATEGY

....

BLENDING SHORT
a, e, i, o, u

For a different approach to teaching this skill, see Unit 1, page T32; Unit 2, page T32; Unit 3, page T30; Unit 4, page T32, Unit 5, page T30.

▶ **Visual/Auditory/ Kinesthetic**

Review Blending with short *a, e, i, o, u*

TEACH

Identify *a, e, i, o, u* as Symbols for /a/, /e/, /i/, /o/, /u/

Tell children they will continue to read words with *a, e, i, o, u.*

- Display the *a, e, i, o, u* letter cards and say /a/, /e/, /i/, /o/, /u/. Have children repeat the sounds /a/, /e/, /i/, /o/, /u/ after you as you point to the *a, e, i, o, u* cards.

BLENDING Model and Guide Practice

- Place an *n* card after the *a* card. Blend the sounds together and have children repeat after you.

- Place a *c* letter card before the *a, n* cards. Blend to read *can.*

Use the Word in Context

- Have children use *can* in a sentence. Ask them to talk about things they can do now that they could not do at the beginning of the year.

Repeat the Procedure

- Use the following words to continue modeling and for guided practice with short *a, e, i, o, u: big, yet, tin, not, box, map, pat.*

PRACTICE

Complete the Pupil Edition Page

Read aloud the directions on page 358. Identify each picture, and complete the first item together. Then work through the page with children, or have them complete the page independently.

ASSESS/CLOSE

Write *a, e, i, o, u* Words

Observe children as they complete page 358. Then have children write two words each for short *a, e, i, o, u* in the middle.

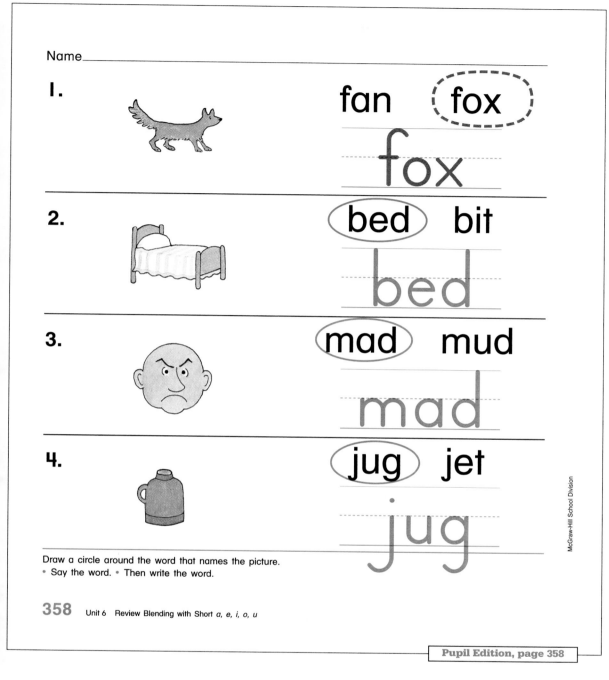

Name _____

1. fan (fox)

   fox

2. (bed) bit

   bed

3. (mad) mud

   mad

4. (jug) jet

   jug

Draw a circle around the word that names the picture.
• Say the word. • Then write the word.

McGraw-Hill School Division

Pupil Edition, page 358

ADDITIONAL PHONICS RESOURCES

Practice Book, *page 358*
Phonics Workbook

McGraw-Hill School
TECHNOLOGY

Phonics CD-ROM
Activities for Practice with Blending and Segmenting

PRACTICE BOOK page 358

Meeting Individual Needs for Phonics

EASY	ON-LEVEL	CHALLENGE	LANGUAGE SUPPORT
On the chalkboard write: *luck, box, van, wet, sip, quack, yum, get, kid, lot.* Show letter cards *a, e, i, o, u* and *l, k, ck, g, b, h, w, n, t, p, m, d, v, x, qu, y,* and *z.* Ask children to read the words and identify the letters that make up each word.	**Say** this sentence: *Bob had fun with his pet cat.* Ask children to identify the word that has the short o sound. Write it on the chalkboard. *(Bob)* Repeat the sentence asking them to identify words for a different short vowel sound each time.	**Have** partners work together to make up a simple riddle whose answer has the sound /a/, /e/, /i/, /o/, /u/. Ask them to tell their riddle to another pair of children who has to figure out the answer. You may also want children to dictate their riddle to you and to draw a picture of the answer.	**Show** these word cards one at a time: *pack, peck, pick, tick, tock, tuck, sick, sock, sack, dock, deck, duck.* Have children repeat each word as you read it aloud. Clarify word meanings. Ask children to first sort for initial sound and then for medial vowel sound.

358

Teacher Read Aloud

Listen

Annie's Pet
by Barbara Brenner

A nnie has 5 dollars to buy a pet, but each time she stops, she ends up with 1 dollar less. Can she get a pet for 0 dollars?

On her birthday, Annie went to the zoo with her parents. That's where she got a great idea. "I have five birthday dollars," she said to her family. "I'm going to buy an animal."

Annie didn't know what kind of animal she wanted. But she knew what she didn't want.

"I don't want a bear," she said. "Bears are too hairy. I don't want a snake. You can't take a snake for a walk."

"Try not to buy too big an animal," said her father.

"You don't want too small an animal," said her mother.

"Get a wild animal," said her brother.

"I don't want a wild animal," said Annie. "I want a pet."

So the very next day, Annie and her mom went off to find the perfect pet for Annie.

They walked down the street until they came to a house.

Continued on page T3

Oral Comprehension

LISTENING AND SPEAKING Review "Annie's Pet" with children. Go over the story sequence, and help them to recall where Annie and her mom went in their search for the perfect pet.

Ask children what they think appealed to Annie about each thing she bought with her birthday money. Do you that think she was too excited about buying a pet to keep track of her money?

 **Activity** Have children act out scenes from "Annie's Pet." You can have small groups of children re-enact what happened as Annie stopped at the toy store, gift shop, shopping mall, the snack shop, and at GIVE A PET A HOME. They can also create hand-made props representing the things that Annie buys.

▶ **Kinesthetic**

Real-Life Reading

1. Annie wanted to know more about dogs.

2. She had a great idea.

3. She went to the library.

4. The librarian helped her find a book about dogs.

40   41

Big Book of Real-Life Reading, pages 40-41

Objective: Use a Library/Media Center

REVIEW THE PAGE Ask children to think about wild animals they would like to discover more about in a library. Have children name the animals, and elicit their ideas on what they would like to learn about them.

FOLLOW-UP ACTIVITY Provide age-appropriate books and magazines featuring animals. Ask children to name the different animal actions they see in the books, such as feeding their young, running, flying. Have children make drawings showing one animal in different actions. They can caption their drawings with a word or two.

CENTER
Activity

Cross-Curricular: Art

Discuss with children the difference Ask children to name a wild animal they would most like to have as a pet. Have them:

- make a list telling why they would like to keep the animal as a pet
- discuss how they would take care of the animal

- model a sculpture of the animal, from self-hardening clay

▶ **Interpersonal/Kinesthetic**

OBJECTIVES

Children will:

- review high-frequency words *with, was, not, of*

....

MATERIALS

- word cards from the Word Play Book
- *Zack and Jan*

TEACHING TIP

MANAGEMENT Some children may be able to follow text better if they place an index card under each line.

Review *with, was, not, of*

PREPARE

Listen to Words Tell children that they will be reviewing the words *with, was, not*, and *of*. Read each of the following sentences aloud and ask children to listen carefully:

1. Annie shopped <u>with</u> her mother.

2. Annie <u>was</u> <u>not</u> sure what her pet would be.

3. Annie ran out <u>of</u> money.

Read the sentences a second time and ask children to raise their hands when they hear one of the high-frequency words.

TEACH

Model Reading the Word in Context Distribute word cards containing the high-frequency words to each child. Hold up each word card and pronounce the word. Tell children to listen for each word as you reread the sentences. Have children hold up their cards when they hear the words.

Identify the Words Write the three sentences on the chalkboard. Reread the sentences tracking the print as you read. Have children hold up the correct word card when they hear a high-frequency word. Call on volunteers to come up and circle the words in the sentences.

Write the Words Have children write the words *not* and *of*.

PRACTICE

Complete the Pupil Edition Page Read the directions on page 359 to the children, and make sure they clearly understand what they are asked to do. Complete the first item together. Then work through the page with children or have them complete the page independently.

ASSESS/CLOSE

Review the Page Review children's pages and note any children who need additional support.

Name_____

1.

of   was   not   (with)

2.

was   (of)   with   not

3.

not   with   (was)   of

4.

with   of   (not)   was

Read the four words in each row. **1.** Draw a circle around the word *with*. **2.** Draw a
circle around the word *of*. **3.** Draw a circle around the word *was*. **4.** Draw a circle
around the word *not*.

Unit 6   Review *with, was, not, of*   359

Pupil Edition, page 359

**ALTERNATE TEACHING
STRATEGY**

**HIGH-FREQUENCY
WORDS:** *with*

For a different approach to
teaching this skill,
see page T27.

▶ **Visual/Auditory/
Kinesthetic**

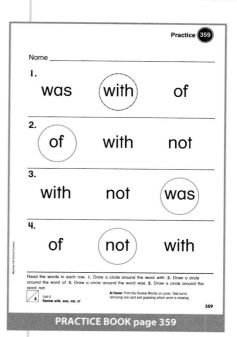

Practice 359

Name _____

1.

was   (with)   of

2.

(of)   with   not

3.

with   not   (was)

4.

of   (not)   with

Read the words in each row. **1.** Draw a circle around the word *with*. **2.** Draw a circle
around the word *of*. **3.** Draw a circle around the word *was*. **2.** Draw a circle around the
word *not*.

At Home: Print the Review Words on cards. Take turns
removing one card and guessing which word is missing

4 Unit 6
Review *with, was, not, of*

359

PRACTICE BOOK page 359

Meeting Individual Needs for Vocabulary

EASY	ON-LEVEL	CHALLENGE	LANGUAGE SUPPORT
Review the high-frequency words with children. Then reread the story "Annie's Pet" to them. Have children hold up their word cards from the Word Play book each time they hear one of the high-frequency words.	**Have** children draw pictures to illustrate the story. Then ask children to dictate sentences about their pictures using at least one of the words they have been learning. Read children's sentences aloud and ask the class to identify the high-frequency words.	**Have** children play a game using the word cards for all the high-frequency words they have learned. Hold up a card and call on a player to pronounce the word. Call on another player to use the word in a sentence. Continue until all the words have been used at least once.	**Give** children practice in using the verb *was* with *not*. Have children repeat the following sentence after you. Then talk about what the sentences with *not* mean: *The boy was good. The boy was not good.* *The sun was out. The sun was not out.*

359

Develop Phonological Awareness

Listen

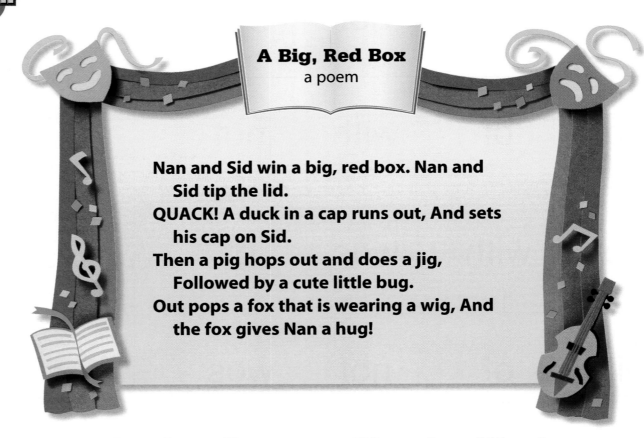

A Big, Red Box
a poem

Nan and Sid win a big, red box. Nan and
  Sid tip the lid.
QUACK! A duck in a cap runs out, And sets
  his cap on Sid.
Then a pig hops out and does a jig,
  Followed by a cute little bug.
Out pops a fox that is wearing a wig, And
  the fox gives Nan a hug!

Objective: Focus on Rhyming Words

READ THE POEM Read the poem "A Big, Red Box"
several times. As you read, emphasize the rhyming
words.

IDENTIFY THE RHYMING WORDS Ask children to
identify the rhyming words as you reread the first four
lines. Then do the same for the last four lines.

> lid   Sid   bug   hug

PLAY A RHYMING GAME Have children sit in a
circle. Hold a ball or beanbag for children to see. To
begin the game, say: *In the box, there's a pig.* Then pass
the beanbag to the child at your right. The child should
repeat the sentence, *In the box, there's a _____,* and fill in a
rhyming word. Continue until all children have had a
turn.

> pig   wig   fig

REPEAT WITH OTHER WORDS Continue playing
the game with other rhyming words. Accept nonsense
words that rhyme but encourage children to use real
words.

> bug   hug   rug   jug

Objective: Listen for Blending with Short *a, e, i, o, u*

LISTEN FOR THE SEGMENTED WORD As you read the poem, segment the sounds in *Quack* by saying: /kw/-/a/-/k/. After reading the poem, ask children to repeat the segmented sounds with you as you say: /kw/-/a/-/k/. Then have children blend the sounds to say *quack*. Repeat with the word *jig*.

WHAT IS IN THE BOX? Provide a big red box covered in red paper. Beforehand write the words below on index cards to be placed in the box.

> yam zap jet quiz job jug

Ask for a volunteer to come stand by the box.

Say: *Reach in but do not look! You must not see.*
Take one card and give it to me.
Soon you'll know what the word must be.
Listen! /j/-/e/-/t/. What's my word?

Have children repeat the sounds and then blend the sounds to discover the word from the box is *jet*.

Repeat the activity by inviting a new volunteer to listen and pull a card from the box.

Read Together

From Phonemic Awareness to Phonics

Objective: Relate *a, e, i, o, u* to Short Vowel Sounds

LISTEN TO RHYMING WORDS
Say: *The big pig did a jig in a wig.* Ask children to name the rhyming words.

> big pig jig wig

IDENTIFY THE LETTERS
Identify the letters in each word as you write *big, pig, jig,* and *wig* in a column on the chalkboard. Use a long strip of paper to cover the initial letter in each word. Underline *ig* in each word. Identify the letters, *i,* and *g,* and the sound these letters stand for: /ig/.

MAKE RHYMING WORDS
Write these words on index cards: *jog, hog, yam, ham, zip, rip, quack, jug, zap*. Set out four index cards: two that rhyme and two that do not.

Ask children to find the words with the same ending letters, for example, *jog* and *hog*. As children read the words, ask them to segment and then blend the sounds by saying: /j/-/o/-/g/ *jog*. Repeat with *hog*.

Repeat with other combinations of cards.

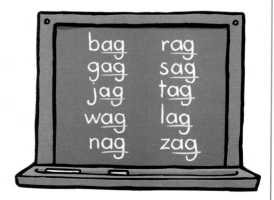

360B

OBJECTIVES

Children will:

- identify /a/*a*, /e/*e*, /i/*i*, /o/*o*, /u/*u*

- blend and read short *a, e, i, o, u* words

- write short *a, e, i, o, u* words

- review /v/*v*, /ks/*x*, /w/*w*, /h/*h*, /kw/*qu*, /j/*j*, /y/*y*, /z/*z*, /b/*b*, /g/*g*, /k/*k,ck*, l/*l*, /p/*p*, /r/*r*, /f/*f*, /k/*c*, /t/*t*, m/*m* /s/*s* /d/*d*, and /n/*n*

MATERIALS

- letter cards from the *Word Building Book*

TEACHING TIP

INSTRUCTIONAL Display the following word cards and ask children to blend sounds to read them aloud; then ask them to sort the cards to show words that rhyme: *jam, zip, fox, yum, yam, hip, box, hum.* Point out that rhyming words have the same sounds in the middle and at the end of the word.

ALTERNATE TEACHING STRATEGY

BLENDING SHORT
a, e, i, o, u

For a different approach to teaching this skill, see Unit 1, page T32; Unit 2, page T32; Unit 3, page T30; Unit 4, page T32; Unit 5, page T30.

▶ **Visual/Auditory/ Kinesthetic**

Review Blending with short *a, e, i, o, u*

TEACH

Identify *a, e, i, o, u* as Symbols for /a/, /e/, /i/, /o/, /u/

Tell children they will continue to read words with *a, e, i, o, u.*

- Display the *a, e, i, o, u* letter cards and say /a/, /e/, /i/, /o/, /u/. Have children repeat the sounds as you point to the cards.

BLENDING Model and Guide Practice

- Place a *ck* card after the *a* card. Blend the sounds together and have children repeat after you.

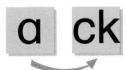 

- Place a *Z* letter card before the *a, ck* cards. Blend to read *Zack.*

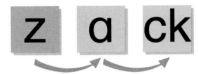 

Use the Word in Context

- Have children use *Zack* in a sentence. Ask them to pretend that Zack is a special friend.

Repeat the Procedure

- Use the following words to continue modeling and guided practice with short *a, e, i, o, u: Jan, Rex, Rob, Ben, Kim, Bud, Mick.*

PRACTICE

Complete the Pupil Edition Page

Read aloud the directions on page 360. Identify each picture, and complete the first item together. Work through the page with them, or have children complete the page independently.

ASSESS/CLOSE

Write Short *a, e, i, o, u* Words

Observe children as they complete page 360. Then ask children to write two first names that have short *a, e, i, o,* or *u* in the middle. Remind children to write initial capital letters.

Name_____

1. hat hen
   hat

2. rod rock
   rock

3. win web
   web

4. van vet
   van

McGraw-Hill School Division

Draw a circle around the word that names the picture. • Say the word.
• Then write the word.

Pupil Edition, page 360

ADDITIONAL PHONICS RESOURCES

Practice Book, *page 360*
Phonics Workbook

McGraw-Hill School
TECHNOLOGY

 CD-ROM
Activities for Practice with
Blending and Segmenting

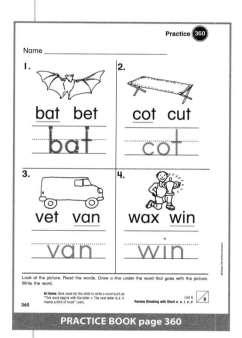

Practice 360

Name_____

1. bat bet
   bat

2. cot cut
   cot

3. vet van
   van

4. wax win
   win

Look at the picture. Read the words. Draw a line under the word that goes with the picture.
Write the word.

At Home: Give clues for the child to write a word such as "This word begins with the letter v. The next letter is a. It means a kind of truck" (van).

360

Review Blending with Short *a, e, i, o, u*   Unit 6
8

PRACTICE BOOK page 360

Meeting Individual Needs for Phonics

EASY	ON-LEVEL	CHALLENGE	LANGUAGE SUPPORT
Create word cards for the following names: *Dick, Ted, Ron, Dot, Bud, Meg, Pat, Nick, Pam.* Ask children to blend sounds to read each name aloud. Then have them sort the names by short vowel sound /a/, /e/, /i/, /o/, and /u/. Ask children to think of other names with a short vowel sound in the middle.	**Show** word cards with short vowel words, such as the following: *fan, get, zip, hot, sun.* Ask children to blend sounds to read the words; then invite them to make up a story using all the words. Ask them to choose five more cards and continue the story or make up another story.	**Give** one set of short *a, e, i, o, u* word cards to each of several pairs or groups of children. Each group must make up riddles to ask the rest of the class whose goal is to guess and write the words.	**Write** the following sentence on the chalkboard and read it slowly: *Sam, the pup, did not run to Meg.* Ask children to find the word that has the short *a* sound in the middle, say it, and draw a line under it. *(Sam)* Follow the same procedure for the words with short *e, i, o,* and *u* sounds.

360

Guided Instruction

BEFORE READING

PREVIEW AND PREDICT Take a brief **picture walk** through the book, focusing on the illustrations.

- Who is this story about? Where does it take place?

- Do you think the story is realistic or make-believe? Why?

SET PURPOSES Discuss with children what they may want to find out about as they read the story. Ask questions to prompt discussion, such as: *What do you think the man and woman will do with the food? Where do you think they are going?*

TEACHING TIP

To put book together:

1. Tear out the story page.

2. Cut along dotted line.

3. Fold each section on fold line.

4. Assemble book.

INSTRUCTIONAL Show pictures and photographs of Arizona, and locate the state on a map.

Zack and Jan

Jan had a pot of jam in a big box.

3

McGraw-Hill School Division

Zack had a tin of ham.

2

McGraw-Hill School Division

The box with the jam and ham is for Mom.

4

Guided Instruction

DURING READING

☑ **Letters** *h, w, v, x, qu, j, y, z*

☑ **Make Inferences**

☑ **Concepts of Print**

☑ **High-Frequency Words:** *with, was, not, of*

① **CONCEPTS OF PRINT** Model how to run your finger from left to right under each word as you read the title page. Remind children that tracking print may help them.

② **PHONICS: Letter** *z* Have children point to the word with *z* on page 2. Read the name *Zack* aloud. Ask children which other words have the short *a* sound. (had, ham)

③ **CONCEPTS OF PRINT** Ask children how many words are in the sentence on page 3. (10) Then ask which word only has one letter. (a)

④ **HIGH-FREQUENCY WORDS:** *with* Ask children to look at page 4 and to point to the word that begins with *w*. Track print and read it together: *with*.

LANGUAGE SUPPORT

ESL Bring in a jar of jam labeled "jam." Explain what jam is and have children repeat the word. Have children from other cultures describe a similar food that is enjoyed in their cultures.

Guided Instruction

DURING READING

⑤ PHONICS Letter *v* Ask children to find the word that begins with the letter *v* on page 5. Blend the sounds and read it together: *v a n van*. Then find other words in the sentence with the short *a* sound. (can, Jan)

⑥ MAKE INFERENCES Read the sentence on page 6 and discuss how you think Jan and Zack are feeling, and why. Have children focus on the illustration as well as the text.

⑦ CONCEPTS OF PRINT Have children find the quotation marks on page 7. Ask what these tell about the sentence. (Someone is speaking.) Ask who is speaking. (Zack or Jan)

⑧ MAKE INFERENCES After reading page 8, ask children how all of the characters might be feeling, and why. Encourage class discussion.

INFORMAL ASSESSMENT

MAKE INFERENCES

HOW TO ASSESS Ask children what clues they use to tell how the people in the story are feeling.

FOLLOW UP Explain to children that they can look at picture clues to discover how people are feeling. Ask children to look at the picture clues on page 8. Allow a variety of responses.

"We can go in my van," said Jan.

5

Jan and Zack gave the box to Mom.

7

The van was not quick.

6

"Yum, yum!" said Mom.

8

Guided Instruction

RETURN TO PREDICTIONS AND PURPOSES
Ask children to check if their predictions about the story were correct. Discuss whether their questions were answered. You may want to ask: *Where did Zack and Jan go?*

RETELL THE STORY Have children work together to recreate the story scenes on paper. Then ask children to retell the story using their drawings for reference.

LITERARY RESPONSE To help children respond to the story, ask:

● *What did Zack and Jan give to Mom?*

Invite children to draw and write about a present they would like to give to someone in their family.

CENTER
Activity

Cross Curricular: Social Studies

Provide books with pictures and photos about the desert. Have children make a mural showing desert animals, plants, and terrain. Children may find pictures in magazines or may draw pictures.

▶ **Spatial/Interpersonal**

OBJECTIVES

Children will:

- make inferences to understand a story

MATERIALS

- *Zack and Jan*

TEACHING TIP

INSTRUCTIONAL Give children opportunities to make inferences during the day. Ask questions such as: *How do you think we would feel if we didn't go to lunch today? How do you think we would feel if it started to rain?*

Review Make Inferences

> **PREPARE**

Recall the Story
Ask children to recall the story *Zack and Jan*. Ask how Zack and Jan felt about giving Mom the present.

> **TEACH**

Look for Clues in the Story
Reread the story, then ask children to take a closer look at the van on page 6. Ask them to think about why the van is not quick. (It might be old. The road is rough so Jan might drive slowly.) Point out that text and illustrations give clues about the story. Explain that you can understand a story better when you look for clues and use what you already know.

> **PRACTICE**

Complete the Pupil Edition Page
Read the directions on page 363 to the children, and make sure they clearly understand what they are asked to do. Identify each picture, and complete the first item together. Then work through the page with children, or have them complete the page independently.

> **ASSESS/CLOSE**

Review the Page
Review children's work, and note children who are experiencing difficulty.

Name _____

1.

2.

3.

Look at the picture on the left. • Then look at the two pictures on the right. • Draw a line to the picture that shows where the person is going.

Unit 6 Review Make Inferences **363**

Pupil Edition, page 363

ALTERNATE TEACHING STRATEGY

....

MAKE INFERENCES
For a different approach to teaching this skill, see page T29.

▶ **Visual/Auditory/ Kinesthetic**

PRACTICE BOOK page 363

Meeting Individual Needs for Comprehension

EASY	ON-LEVEL	CHALLENGE	LANGUAGE SUPPORT
Discuss how Mom felt after getting the ham and jam. Ask how they can tell she feels that way. Talk about how children feel when they receive a present. Have them role-play the situation, and explain that receiving a present usually makes us feel happy or pleased.	**Reread** page 6, and talk about how Zack and Jan are wearing seat belts. Ask what happens when people wear seat belts, and why they wear them. Continue the discussion, focusing on safety items such as bike helmets, car seats, knee pads, and so on.	**Ask** children to list what they can figure out from the pictures and from what they already know. Ask questions such as: *Do you think it is a cold day or a warm day? How can you tell?* (It must be warm because Zack and Jan are wearing warm-weather clothes.)	**Choose** some classroom objects and role-play giving and receiving the item as a present. Give children an opportunity to say the phrases *Thank you* and *You're welcome.*

363

Develop Phonological Awareness

Listen

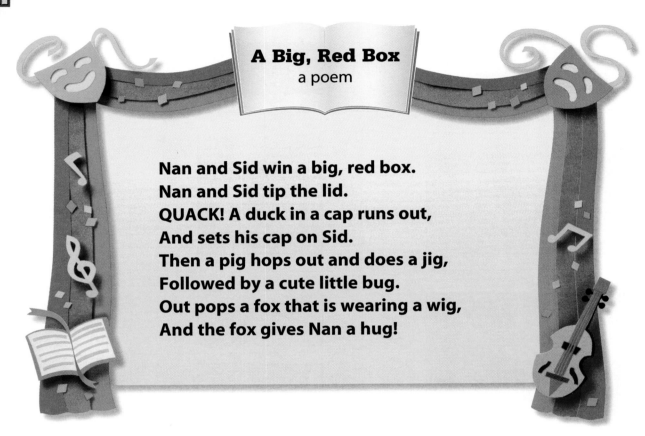

A Big, Red Box
a poem

Nan and Sid win a big, red box.
Nan and Sid tip the lid.
QUACK! A duck in a cap runs out,
And sets his cap on Sid.
Then a pig hops out and does a jig,
Followed by a cute little bug.
Out pops a fox that is wearing a wig,
And the fox gives Nan a hug!

Objective: Focus on Content

READ THE POEM Read the Poem "A Big, Red Box" several times. Ask questions to help children focus on the content.

> **What did Nan and Sid win? (a big, red box)**
> **What did they do with the box? (open the lid)**
> **What did duck have on his head? (a cap)**

DISCUSS DETAILS Have children close their eyes and picture what you say. First say *Box*. Give children time to picture the box, then say: *Big, red box*. Talk about how the details *big* and *red* help them picture the box. Repeat with *bug* and then *cute little bug*.

ADD DETAILS Say a key word from the poem such as *duck* and invite children to add words that tell more about the duck such as *fluffy, funny, yellow*. Repeat with other words from the poem.

> cap   pig   fox   wig

Objective: Listen for Blending with Short *a, e, i, o, u*

LISTEN FOR BLENDING Read the title of the poem by segmenting and then blending the sounds in each word. Have children repeat the sounds and then blend them to say the title of the poem.

Continue reading the poem segmenting and then blending the sounds in one word in each line. After reading the poem, invite children to name which word in each line you said as segmented and then blended sounds. If children do not remember a word, say the segmented sounds for the word and have them blend the sounds to identify the word.

> **Nan   Sid   duck   sets**
> **hops   bug   wig   hug**

WHAT'S MY WORD? Write these words on index cards: *quack, jig, zip, van, cap, lid, win, fox, tip,* and *Kim.* Shuffle the cards and select one. Say /f/-/o/-/x/. Have

children repeat the sounds and then blend them to say *fox.* Invite a volunteer to use the word in a sentence. Repeat the activity by selecting another card. After the words on all cards have been identified, continue by using words that rhyme with words on the cards. Say the segmented sounds in the word and have children blend the sounds to identify the word.

> **fig   dip   can   lap   bid**
> **tin   box   hip   rim**

Read Together

From Phonemic Awareness to Phonics

Objective: Relate *a, e, i, o, u* to Short Vowel Sounds

LISTEN TO RHYMING WORDS Read the poem. Have children identify words in the poem that rhyme.

> | | |
> |---|---|
> | box – fox | Sid – lid |
> | jig – wig | bug – hug |
> | pig – jig | pops – hops |

IDENTIFY THE LETTERS Write *Sid* and *lid* in a column on chart paper. Highlight *–id* in each word. Identify the letters, *i,* and *d,* and the sound these letters stand for: /id/.

Have children repeat the sounds. Repeat with other rhyme pairs from the poem.

MAKE RHYMING WORDS Help children brainstorm rhyming words to add to *Sid* and *lid.*

> **bid   did   hid   kid   rid**

As you write a new word such as *bid,* emphasize /b/ as you write *b* and then emphasize /id/ as you write and highlight *–id.* Have children say /b/-/id/.

Sid
lid
bid
did
hid
kid
rid

OBJECTIVES

Children will:

- identify /a/*a*, /e/*e*, /i/*i*, /o/*o*, /u/*u*
- blend and read short *a, e, i, o, u* words
- write short *a, e, i, o, u* words
- review /v/*v*, /ks/*x*, /w/*w*, /h/*h*, /kw/*qu*, /j/*j*, /y/*y*, /z/*z*, /b/*b*, /g/*g*, /k/*k*, *ck*, /l/*l*, /p/*p*, /r/*r*, /f/*f*, /k/*c*, /t/*t*, /m/*m*, /s/*s*, /d/*d*, and /n/*n*

....

MATERIALS

- letter cards from the *Word Building Book*

TEACHING TIP

INSTRUCTIONAL Invite children to repeat after you as you point to each letter in the alphabet and say the sound it symbolizes. Then let children take turns being the one to point to the letters.

ALTERNATE TEACHING STRATEGY

....

BLENDING SHORT *a, e, i, o, u*

For a different approach to teaching this skill, see Unit 1, page T32; Unit 2, page T32; Unit 3, page T30; Unit 4, page T32; Unit 5, page T30.

▶ **Visual/Auditory/ Kinesthetic**

Review Blending with short *a, e, i, o, u*

Identify *a, e, i, o, u* as Symbols for /a/, /e/, /i/, /o/, /u/

Tell children they will continue to read words with *a, e, i, o, u.*

- Display the *a, e, i, o, u* letter cards and say /a/, /e/, /i/, /o/, /u/. Have children repeat the sounds as you point to each card.

BLENDING Model and Guide Practice

- Place an *x* card after the *i* card. Blend the sounds together and have children repeat after you.

- Place an *s* letter card before the *i, x* cards. Blend to read *six.*

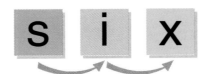

Use the Word in Context

- Have children use *six* in a sentence. Ask them to talk about their birthdays and when they were or will be *six.*

Repeat the Procedure

- Use the following words to continue modeling and for guided practice with short *a, e, i, o, u: quick, duck, yum, hum, hug, dug, mix.*

PRACTICE

Complete the Pupil Edition Page

Read aloud the directions on page 364. Identify each picture, and complete the first item together. Work through the page with children, or have them complete the page independently.

ASSESS/CLOSE

Write Short *a, e, i, o, u* Words

Observe children as they complete page 364. Then display letter cards *v, w, qu, j, y, z* and *a, e, i, o, u.* Ask children to use these and other letter cards to build five words, using each vowel once in the middle.

Name_____

1. ten （six）

   six

2. bug （bag）

   bag

3. （duck） dot

   duck

4. map （men）

   men

Draw a circle around the word that names the picture. • Say the word.
• Then write the word.

McGraw-Hill School Division

364 Unit 6 Review Blending with Short *a, e, i, o, u*

Pupil Edition, page 364

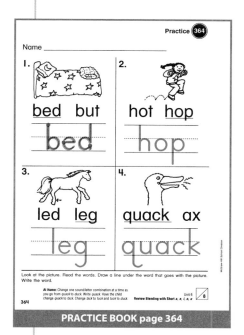

Practice 364

Name_____

1. bed but   2. hot hop

   bed   hop

3. led leg   4. quack ax

   leg   quack

Look at the picture. Read the words. Draw a line under the word that goes with the picture. Write the word.

At Name: Change one sound/letter combination at a time as you go from *quack* to *duck.* Write *quack.* Have the child change *quack* to *duck.* Change *back* to *tack* and *tuck* to *duck.*

Unit 6   8

364   Review Blending with Short *a, e, i, o, u*

PRACTICE BOOK page 364

Meeting Individual Needs for Phonics

EASY	ON-LEVEL	CHALLENGE	LANGUAGE SUPPORT
Give children the following word cards: *am, an, at, ax, in, it, on, ox, up.* Invite children to choose a letter card to use as the first letter of a new word. Ask them to see how many new words they can make, for example: *fan, fat, fin, fit,* and *fox.*	**Say** incomplete sentences such as: *Rain is ___.* Display several similar word cards: *vet, wet, yet.* Children select one silently and write it down. Ask volunteers to read their answers, and remind children that sometimes there is more than one right answer.	**Ask** children in groups to sort from all their word cards those which fit a certain category, such as action words, animals, or objects. Try asking a group to sort for kinds of containers. *(can, tin, pack, sack, kit, cup, tub, bag, bin, box, vat)*	**Show** ESL children these word cards: *cat, pup, hen, fox, duck, pig, dog, bug, rat, kid, bat, hog, ox.* Blend sounds to read aloud together. Display pictures of the animals and discuss them; then invite children to pantomime as you point to the animal names.

Reread the Decodable Story

Zack and Jan

- ☑ **Letters** *h, w, v, x, qu, j, y, z*
- ☑ **Make Inferences**
- ☑ **High-Frequency Word:** *with, was, not, of*
- ☑ **Use Illustrations**

Zack and Jan

Guided Reading

SET PURPOSES Tell children that when they read the story again, they can find out more about what happened. Explain that you also want them to look for words with the letters *h, w, v, x, qu, j, y, z*.

REREAD THE BOOK As you reread the story, keep in mind any problems children experienced during the first reading. Use the following prompts to guide reading:

- **MAKE INFERENCES** Ask children how Zack and Jan are probably related. (answers may vary—brother and sister; husband and wife)

- **USE ILLUSTRATIONS** Ask children whose picture is shown in the thought bubble. (Mom) Talk about why thought balloons are used.

RETURN TO PURPOSES Ask children if they found out more about what they wanted to know from the story. Ask children to recall any words from the story that they know.

LITERARY RESPONSE Ask children to fold a sheet of drawing paper into thirds and to draw a picture in each section to show how the story began, what happened, and how it ended.

Read the Patterned Book

Self-Selected Reading

UNIT SKILLS REVIEW

☑ **Phonics**

☑ **Comprehension**

☑ **High-Frequency Words**

Help children self-select a Patterned Book to read and apply phonics and comprehension skills.

Guided Reading

SET PURPOSES Have children select a patterned book to read. Have them find the pattern in their book.

READ THE BOOK Remind children to run their fingers under each word as they read. You may wish to use these prompts as they read. *Concepts of Print*

- Name the letter that I point to. *(Answers will vary.)*

- Name a word with short *a*. What letters does *a* blend with to make the word? Do the same with short *e, i, o,* and *u*. *(Answers will vary.) Phonics and Decoding*

- Think about what happened on this page. What made it happen? *(Answers will vary.) Cause and Effect*

- How do you think the characters feel? Why? *(Answers will vary.) Make Inferences*

- Tell what is happening on the page using as many of these words as you can: with, was, not, of. *(Answers will vary.) High-Frequency Words*

- Look at the picture. Name the shapes that you see. *(Answers will vary.)*

RETURN TO PURPOSES Have children share the patterns they found in their books. Use these prompts to guide their thoughts.

- How many words were in your pattern? What types of sentences made up your pattern-statements, questions, or both?

- Make a new sentence with your pattern.

LITERARY RESPONSE Have children who read different books work in pairs to compare their stories. Have them consider these questions.

- How did the characters feel in each story?

- Could the story really have happened?

Have children share what they have learned from comparing their stories.

☑ **Phonics and Decoding**

- Initial /h/h, /w/w, /v/v, /kw/qu, /j/j, /y/y, /z/z
- Final /ks/x
- Blending with Short *a, e, i, o, u*

☑ **Comprehension**

- Cause and Effect
- Make Inferences

☑ **Vocabulary**

- High-Frequency Words: *with, was, not, of*

Cross Curricular: Language Arts

EARTH POEMS Discuss with children all the treasures that our planet has for us, such as trees for shade, water for drinking. Then compose a class poem in praise of our planet. Write the poem in a large earth-shaped circle, around which can be displayed children's pictures of favorite things in nature.

▶ **Linguistic/ Intrapersonal**

OBJECTIVES

Children will:

- review high-frequency words *with, was, not, of*

MATERIALS

- word cards from the Word Play Book
- *Zack and Jan*

TEACHING TIP

INSTRUCTIONAL Review the meaning of *not* with children, pointing out that *not* means "no." Have children take turns using *not* in sentences.

Review with, was, not, of

PREPARE

Listen to Words
Say aloud the following sentences emphasizing the underlined high-frequency words. Ask children to listen to the sentences and then repeat each high-frequency word with you after the sentence is finished.

1. Connie <u>was</u> <u>with</u> her brother.

2. They had lots <u>of</u> fun.

3. They did <u>not</u> fight.

TEACH

Model Reading the Word in Context
Read aloud the decodable story "Zack and Jan" in the Pupil Edition. Ask children to listen for and identify the high-frequency words.

Identify the Words
Provide each child with set of the high-frequency words on the cards from the Word Play Book. Identify each of the words and then read aloud sentences from the story that include the words. Ask children to hold up the correct word card as you read. Read the sentences again and have children place a different colored sticky note (blue for *with*, green for *was*, and so on) under the word in their decodable books.

Write the Words
Have children write the words *not* and *of*.

Review the High-Frequency Words
Say each high-frequency word and ask children to hold up the corresponding word card. Include several words form previous lessons.

PRACTICE

Complete the Pupil Edition Page
Read the directions on page 365 to the children, and make sure they clearly understand what they are asked to do. Complete the first item together. Then work through the page with children or have them complete the page independently.

ASSESS/CLOSE

Review the Page
Review children's pages and note any children who need additional support.

Name

1.
was | are I we (was)

2.
of | do he (of) for

3.
with | have said that (with)

4.
not | the (not) and you

Say the first word in the row. • Draw a circle around the word where you see it in the same row.

Unit 6   Review *with, was, not, of*   **365**

Pupil Edition, page 365

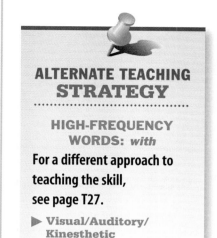

ALTERNATE TEACHING
STRATEGY
....

**HIGH-FREQUENCY
WORDS:** *with*

**For a different approach to
teaching the skill,
see page T27.**

▶ **Visual/Auditory/
Kinesthetic**

Practice **365**

Name _____

1.
Dot, the pup, <u>was</u> <u>not</u> with Mom.

2.
Dot was <u>with</u> Jim and Nan.

3.
Jim, Nan, and Dot had a lot <u>of</u> fun.

Read the sentence. 1. Draw a line under the words *was* and *not*. 2. Draw a line under the word *with*. 3. Draw a line under the word *of*.

Unit 6
Review with, was, not, of

At Home: Play "What Word Am I?" Give each other clues for the words *with, was, not,* and *of*. I begin with *w* and end with *th* or *I rhyme with lot* (*with, not*).

365

PRACTICE BOOK page 365

Meeting Individual Needs for Vocabulary

EASY	ON-LEVEL	CHALLENGE	LANGUAGE SUPPORT
Have children look for signs with the word *not* in them. For example, "Do Not Enter," "Do Not Feed the Animals." Have children report on the signs to the class. Then have them think of signs for the classroom such as "Do Not Run." Help children write and post the signs.	**Have** children work with partners. Explain that one partner should make up a sentence using one of the high-frequency words. The other partner should hold up the correct word card. You may want to have children use words from previous lessons as well.	**Have** children work with a partner to reread the story "Zack and Jan." One partner reads a page aloud and the other partner holds up a word card if there is a high-frequency word in the sentence. Tell partners to take turns so that each child reads and identifies words.	**Ask** children to think of words that rhyme with *not*. Give an example such as *cot*. List children's rhyming words on the chalkboard. Then work with children to make up simple rhymes such as "The pot is not hot."

365

GRAMMAR/SPELLING CONNECTIONS

Model subject-verb agreement, complete sentences, and correct tense so that students may gain increasing control of grammar when speaking and writing.

Interactive Writing

Write a New Version

Prewrite

LOOK AT THE STORY PATTERN Reread *The Big Box*. Then talk about the pattern of the story: Each page has a letter of the alphabet, and includes a word that begins with that letter. Then ask children what things they might make from a blanket, instead of a box. Write their ideas on the chalkboard.

Draft

WRITE A NEW VERSION Explain that children will write a class book, following the pattern of *The Big Box*.

- Begin by having children look at the list on the chalkboard. Ask if there is an idea that begins with the letter *a*. If not, brainstorm to find an idea.

- Continue through the alphabet, writing an idea for each letter of the alphabet, using the Big Book for ideas if necessary.

- Have children write a page for each letter of the alphabet, completing the sentence: *"We can make a ___," said ___.*

Publish

CREATE THE NEW VERSION Have children help you organize the pages alphabetically. Use a three-ring binder to put the pages together. Reread the story to the class and show the illustrations.

"We can make a barn," said Paul.

Presentation Ideas

ORGANIZE THE STORY Take the pages out of the binder, and have partners arrange the pages alphabetically.

▶ **Representing/Viewing**

ACT OUT THE STORY Bring in an old blanket as a prop, and have children act out the story. Children who wrote each page act out the story as you read aloud.

▶ **Representing/Speaking**

COMMUNICATION TIPS

- **Representing** When children role play, remind them to focus on what they are doing, and act in a manner appropriate for the classroom space. Help them to plan ahead and think about how they will use the blanket.

TECHNOLOGY TIP

Use a computer program that alphabetizes. Demonstrate how it works.

LANGUAGE SUPPORT

ESL Use three or four letters at a time to practice alphabetical order. Give children letter cards and have them put them in order. Ask questions such as: *Does (d) come before or after (a)?* Provide an alphabet chart to help.

Meeting Individual Needs for Writing

EASY

Write a New Version Ask children what they could make from a paper bag.

Help them complete the phrase: *I can make a _____.* Children illustrate their ideas.

ON-LEVEL

Write a Description Ask children to describe a blanket that is special to them. Help them write their descriptions. Then invite them to illustrate their ideas.

CHALLENGE

Journal Entry Have children choose a character from the story and write about something that happens to him or her.

Wrap Up
the Theme

> ### Choices
> **We can make good choices and decisions every day.**

REVIEW THE THEME Read the theme statement to children. Engage children in a discussion about individual and group decisions they make during any school day. Ask about some of the things children have to consider before deciding.

READ THE POEM Read the poem "Yesterday's Paper" aloud. Explain to children that the term *yesterday's paper* means the newspaper that was delivered yesterday. Show children how to make a newspaper hat, then set aside some time for them to explore making other things from the poem.

YESTERDAY'S PAPER

Yesterday's paper makes a hat,
  Or a boat,
  Or a plane,
  Or a playhouse mat.
Yesterday's paper makes things
  Like that—
  And a very fine tent
  For a sleeping cat.

Mabel Watts

AUDIO

Student Listening Library

DISCUSS THE POEM Ask children to suggest other things that can be made from a newspaper. Then name another common household item such as a paper bag or an old pillowcase. Have children brainstorm a list of things that could be made from the household item.

LOOKING AT GENRE: FAIRY TALES The Read Aloud selection *The Three Little Pigs* is a fairy tale. Explain how fairy tales often have good and bad characters. Recall the Read Aloud selction *Cinderella* and have children explain whether or not it is a fairy tale. Have children discuss any other fairy tales they may know, such as *Little Red Riding Hood* or *Beauty and the Beast.*

Research *and Inquiry*

Theme Project: Clean-Up!

Give the Presentation Ask children to refer to their before-and-after poster as they tell about the site and the clean-up they propose.

GROUP

Draw Conclusions Children will most likely decide that a cleaner community is a better, more enjoyable place for everyone. Lead them to see that when adults and children work together, they can get a lot accomplished.

Ask More Questions Give children time to think about implementing their proposals. Help them create a list of questions that they would need answers to in order to begin. For example:

• *Who can help us?*

• *Where will we put the garbage we collect?*

• *How can we get people to keep the area clean?*

HIGH-FREQUENCY WORDS

GROUP Play "Who Has it?" Give children in a small group the following word cards: *with, was, not, of, go, the, me, and, I, he, she, is, do, we, that, my,* making sure that each child has two or three cards. Write one of the words on the board and say: *Who has it?* The child holding that card should stand up, say the word, and place the card on the chalkboard ledge.

Unit Review

Hop with a Hog
with

We Win!
was

The Vet Van
not

Jen and Yip
of

Zack and Jan
review: *with, was, not, of*

☑ SKILLS & STRATEGIES

Phonics and Decoding

☑ Initial /h/h, /w/w, /v/v, /kw/qu, /j/j, /y/y, /z/z

☑ Final /ks/x

☑ Blending with Short *a, e, i, o, u*

Comprehension

☑ Cause and Effect

☑ Make Inferences

Vocabulary

☑ High-Frequency Words: *with, was, not, of*

Beginning Reading Concepts

☑ Shapes: Circle, Triangle, Square, Rectangle

☑ Categories

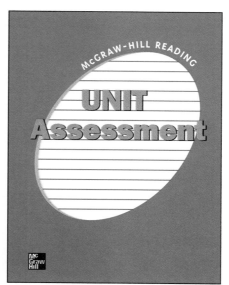

McGRAW-HILL READING

UNIT
Assessment

Mc Graw Hill

UNIT 6 ASSESSMENT

Assessment
Follow-Up

Use the results of the informal and formal assessment opportunities in the unit to help you make decisions about future instruction.

SKILLS AND STRATEGIES	Alternate Teaching Strategies
Phonics and Decoding	
Initial /h/h, /v/v, /kw/qu, /j/j, /y/y, /z/z	T24, T30,T31, T32, T34, T35, T36
Final /b/b, /ks/x	Unit 1 T32, Unit 2 T32, T31
Blending with Short a, e, i, o, u	Unit 1 T32, Unit 2 T32, Unit 3 T30, Unit 4 T32, Unit 5 T30
Comprehension	
Cause and Effect	T26
Make Inferences	T29
Vocabulary	
High-Frequency Words: with, was, not, of, go, the, me, and, I, he, she, is do, we, that, my	T27, Unit 1 T27, Unit 2 T27 Unit 3 T27, Unit 4 T27, Unit 5 T27
Beginning Reading Concepts	
Shapes: Circle, Triangle, Square, Rectangle	T25
Categories	T33
Writing	
Letter Formation	T38

McGraw-Hill School
TECHNOLOGY

 CD-ROM Provides extra phonics support.

 Research & Inquiry Ideas. *Visit www.mhschool.com*

Cover Illustration: Mary Jane Begin

The publisher gratefully acknowledges permission to reprint the following copyrighted material:

"Aekyung's Dream" by Min Paek. Copyright © 1978, 1988 by Children's Book Press.

"Amazing Grace" by Mary Hoffman. Text copyright © 1991 by Mary Hoffman. Illustrations copyright © 1991 by Caroline Binch. Used by permission of Dial Books for Young Readers.

"Annie's Pet" by Barbara Brenner. Text copyright © 1989 by Bank Street College of Education. Used by permission of Bantam Books, a division of Bantam Doubleday Dell Publishing Group, Inc.

ANY KIND OF DOG by Lynn Whisnant Reiser. Copyright © 1992 by Lynn Whisnant Reiser. Reprinted by permission of William Morrow & Company.

THE APPLE PIE TREE by Zoe Hall. Text copyright ©1996 by Zoe Hall. Illustrations copyright ©1996 by Shari Halpern. Reproduced by permission of Scholastic Inc.

"Beehive" from A CHILDREN'S SEASONAL TREASURY compiled by Betty Jones. Copyright © 1971 by Dover Publishing, Inc. Reprinted by permission of Dover Publishing, Inc.

THE CHICK AND THE DUCKLING by Mirra Ginsburg. Text copyright © 1972 by Mirra Ginsburg. Illustration copyright © 1972 by Jose Aruego. Reprinted by permission of Simon & Schuster Children's Publishing Division.

"Cinderella" is primarily based on the version by Charles Perrault, in THE BLUE FAIRY BOOK, edited by A. Lang (1889) and incorporates elements of the Brothers Grimm version, translated by L. Crane (1886), as well as details from the retelling by F. Baker and A. Thorndike in EVERYDAY CLASSICS: THIRD READERS (1920).

"Clay" from A SONG I SANG TO YOU by Myra Cohn Livingston. Copyright © 1958, 1959, 1965, 1967, 1969, 1984 by Myra Cohn Livingston. Used by permission of Marian Reiner for the author.

"The Clever Turtle" retold by Margaret H. Lippert from CHILDREN'S ANTHOLOGY. Copyright © 1988 by Macmillan Publishing Company, a division of Macmillan Inc.

THE EARTH AND I by Frank Asch. Copyright © 1994 by Frank Asch. Reprinted by permission of Harcourt Brace & Company.

THE ENORMOUS CARROT by Vladimir Vagin. Copyright © 1998 by Vladimir Vagin. Reproduced by permission of Scholastic Inc.

"Every Time I Climb a Tree" from FAR AND FEW by David McCord. Copyright © 1929, 1931, 1952 by David McCord. Reprinted by permission of Little, Brown & Company.

"50 Simple Things Kids Can Do to Save the Earth" from 50 SIMPLE THINGS KIDS CAN DO TO SAVE THE EARTH by The EarthWorks Group. Copyright © 1990 by John Javna.

"Five Little Seeds" from THIS LITTLE PUFFIN compiled by Elizabeth Matterson. Copyright © 1969 by Puffin Books. Reproduced by permission of Penguin Books. Reprinted by permission.

FLOWER GARDEN by Eve Bunting. Text copyright ©1994 by Eve Bunting, illustrations copyright ©1994 by Kathryn Hewitt. Reprinted by permission of Harcourt Brace & Company.

"The Hare and the Tortoise" from THE FABLES OF AESOP by Aesop, retold by Joseph Jacobs (c. 1900).

"Helping" from WHERE THE SIDEWALK ENDS by Shel Silverstein. Copyright © 1974 by Evil Eye Music, Inc. Reprinted by permission of HarperCollins Publishers.

"Hill of Fire" from HILL OF FIRE by Thomas P. Lewis. Text copyright © 1971 by Thomas P. Lewis. Used by permission of Harper & Row Publishers, Inc.

"How Many Spots Does a Leopard Have?" from HOW MANY SPOTS DOES A LEOPARD HAVE AND OTHER STORIES by Julius Lester. Copyright © 1989 by Julius Lester. Reprinted by permission of Scholastic Inc.

"It Could Always Be Worse" by Margot Zemach. Copyright © 1976 by Margot Zemach. Reprinted by permission of Farrar, Straus & Giroux, Inc.

"A Kite" from READ-ALOUD RHYMES FOR THE VERY YOUNG. Copyright © 1986 by Alfred A. Knopf, Inc.

"Learning" from POETRY PLACE ANTHOLOGY by M. Lucille Ford. Copyright © 1983 by Instructor Publications, Inc.

"The Legend of the Bluebonnet" by Tomie dePaola. Copyright © 1983 by Tomie dePaola. Used by permission of The Putnam Publishing Group.

"Little Brown Rabbit" from THIS LITTLE PUFFIN compiled by Elizabeth Matterson. Copyright © 1969 by Puffin Books. Reprinted by permission of Penguin Books Ltd.

"The Little Engine That Could" by Watty Piper. Copyright © 1930, 1945, 1954, 1961, 1976 by Platt & Munk, Publishers. Used by permission of Platt & Munk, Publishers, a division of Grosset & Dunlap, Inc., which is a member of the Putnam & Grosset Group, New York.

"The Little Red Hen" from WHAT YOUR KINDERGARTNER NEEDS TO KNOW edited by E. D. Hirsch, Jr., and John Holdren. Copyright © 1996 by The Core Knowledge Foundation. Used by permission of Delta Books, a division of Bantam Doubleday Dell Publishing Group, Inc.

"The Little Turtle" from COLLECTED POEMS by Vachel Lindsay. Copyright © 1920 by Macmillan Publishing Co., Inc., renewed 1948 by Elizabeth C. Lindsay.

"Making Friends" from NATHANIEL TALKING by Eloise Greenfield. Text copyright © 1988 by Eloise Greenfield. Illustrations copyright © by Jan Spivey Gilchrist. Used by permission of Writers and Readers Publishing, Inc., for Black Butterfly Children's Books.

"Mary Had a Little Lamb" from WHAT YOUR KINDERGARTNER NEEDS TO KNOW edited by E. D. Hirsch, Jr., and John Holdren. Copyright © 1996 by The Core Knowledge Foundation. Used by permission of Delta Books, a division of Bantam Doubleday Dell Publishing Group, Inc.

"Morning Verse" from THE KINDERGARTEN SERIES. Copyright ©1983 by Wynstone Press. Reprinted by permission of Wynstone Press.

NATURE SPY by Shelley Rotner and Ken Kreisler. Text copyright © 1992 by Shelley Rotner and Ken Kreisler. Illustrations copyright © 1992 by Shelley Rotner. Reprinted by permission of Simon & Schuster Children's Publishing Division.

PEANUT BUTTER AND JELLY by Nadine Bernard Westcott. Copyright ©1987 by Nadine Bernard Westcott. Reprinted by permission of Dutton Children's Books, a division of Penguin Books USA Inc.

PRETEND YOU'RE A CAT by Jean Marzollo, illustrated by Jerry Pinkney. Text copyright © 1990 by Jean Marzollo. Paintings copyright © 1990 by Jerry Pinkney. Reprinted by permission of Dial Books for Young Readers, a division of Penguin Putnam Inc.

"Shell" from WORLDS I KNOW AND OTHER POEMS by Myra Cohn Livingston. Copyright © 1985 by Myra Cohn Livingston. Reprinted by permission of Margaret K. McElderry Books, an imprint of Simon & Schuster Children's Publishing Division.

Contents

Annie's Pet
by Barbara Brenner

Annie has 5 dollars to buy a pet, but each time she stops, she ends up with 1 dollar less. Can she get a pet for 0 dollars?

On her birthday, Annie went to the zoo with her parents. That's where she got a great idea. "I have five birthday dollars," she said to her family. "I'm going to buy an animal."

Annie didn't know what kind of animal she wanted. But she knew what she didn't want.

"I don't want a bear," she said. "Bears are too hairy. I don't want a snake. You can't take a snake for a walk."

"Try not to buy too big an animal," said her father.

"You don't want too small an animal," said her mother.

"Get a wild animal," said her brother.

"I don't want a wild animal," said Annie. "I want a pet."

So the very next day, Annie and her mom went off to find the perfect pet for Annie.

They walked down the street until they came to a house. There was a girl with a bird in front of the house. The bird gave Annie an idea.

Annie called to the girl, "Will you sell that bird for five dollars?"

"Not for a million dollars. I love this bird."

"But I need a pet to love, too," said Annie.

"Try the pet store," said the little girl. And she went inside with her bird.

Annie and her mom walked a little more. They came to a toy store. The store gave her an idea.

"Do you have toys for pets?" she asked the man inside.

"All kinds," said the man. "Swings, rings, bells, balls."

"I'll take a ball."

"That will be one dollar," said the man. Annie gave the man one dollar. She still had four dollars.

Annie and her mom walked a little more. They came to a gift shop. A pretty tan cat was sitting in the window.

Annie and her mom went into the shop. "How much is that cat in the window?" she asked the woman.

"That cat is not for sale," said the woman. "We do not sell pets. But we do sell pet collars."

"Now that is a great idea," said Annie. "A collar—not too big, not too small."

Annie bought a collar for one dollar. She still had three dollars.

Annie and her mom walked a little more. They went into a shopping mall. Annie saw a nice red pet dish and a nice red pet leash. They each cost one dollar. Annie bought the dish and the leash.

"Now I have all the things I'll need for my pet," she said.

Annie's long walk had made her very hungry. She and her mom stopped to buy a little snack. It only cost one dollar.

At last, Annie and her mom came to the pet store. They looked in the window. There were pets of every size and kind.

"This is it!" cried Annie. "This is where I'll buy my pet." Annie reached into the backpack to get her money. But the money was gone!

She thought about what she had spent–one dollar for a toy . . . one dollar for a collar . . . one dollar for a dish . . . one dollar for a leash . . . and one dollar for a double-dip cone!
Five—Annie had spent all five birthday dollars!

Annie wanted to have a good cry. But then she looked up and saw a sign that read: GIVE A PET A HOME.

That's when Annie got the greatest idea of all! She and her mom went inside.

"I'm looking for a pet," said Annie.

"Can you give a pet a good home?" asked the woman behind the desk.

"Yes," said Annie. "I have a collar, a toy, a dish, and a leash for my pet. But I don't have any money."

"Do you have love?" asked the woman.

"Oh, yes, I have a lot of that," said Annie.

"Then I have just the pet for you," the woman said.

And she did.

Mae Jemison

Do you ever dream of becoming an astronaut? Would you like to look down at Earth from outer space? When Mae Jemison was a young girl, she dreamed about traveling to space. On summer nights, she would gaze up at the stars and wish that she was closer to them. When she grew up, she made her dream come true. In 1992, Mae Jemison became the world's first female African American astronaut.

Mae Jemison grew up in Chicago, Illinois. As a young girl, she was a good student. She loved science. She also was a great dancer.

When it came time for Mae to go to college, she had to make a hard decision. Would she study to become a doctor or a dancer?

After giving it a lot of thought, Mae made up her mind. She chose to become a doctor.

Mae loved working as a doctor. She even worked in Africa for two years, helping sick people to get well. But she never forgot her dream of going to space. So she applied to become an astronaut. Very, very few people are chosen to become astronauts. It is one of the most difficult jobs in the world. But Mae proved she had the ability to learn to become a great astronaut. Mae got the job!

After years of training and waiting, Mae made her first trip to outer space in 1992. The space shuttle she traveled in was called the *Endeavour*. The first thing she saw when she looked out the window of the space shuttle was her hometown of Chicago. In space, Mae performed science experiments. It was a dream come true for the little girl who loved science and loved to look at the stars.

When Mae landed back on Earth, the people of Chicago threw a huge party for her. Everyone was proud of the girl who had followed her dreams.

Mae wants children everywhere to follow their dreams, too. She knows that if you work hard enough, you can become anything you want.

Mae also knows that people can do many different things during their lives. There are lots of interesting jobs to choose from. Maybe you would like to become a teacher, an actor or a taxi driver. Or perhaps you could work for a big company or be a construction worker or a lawyer. And you don't have to choose just one job, either. Mae started out as a doctor and then became an astronaut. Today Mae is in charge of her own company.

What would you like to do when you grow up? What jobs would you like to have? What dreams do you have for your future?

As for Mae, she still has big dreams. She has said, "I'd go to Mars at the drop of a hat." Knowing Mae Jemison, she probably will someday. And maybe, you'll join her.

The Three Little Pigs
by Joseph Jacobs

Long ago there lived a mother pig who had three little pigs. The mother pig was very poor, and at last she had to send her pigs out to seek their fortunes.

The first little pig that went away met a man with a bundle of straw, and he said to him, "Please, man, give me that straw so I can build me a house."

The man gave the straw to the little pig. Then the pig built a house of the straw and lived in the house.

By and by a wolf came along and knocked at the door of thelittle straw house.

"Little pig, little pig, let me come in!" called the wolf.

"No, not by the hair of my chinny, chin chin, I'll not let you in,"answered the pig.

"Then I'll huff and I'll puff and I'll blow your house in," said the wolf.

So he huffed and he puffed and he blew the house in. Then he chased the little pig away.

The second little pig that went away met a man with a bundle of sticks, and he said to the man, "Please, man, give me your bundle of sticks so I can build me a house." The man gave the sticks to the little pig. Then the pig built a house of sticks and lived in the house. By and by the wolf came along and knocked at the door of the little house of sticks.

"Little pig, little pig, let me come in!" called the wolf.

"No, not by the hair of my chinny, chin, chin, I'll not let you in,"answered the pig.

"Then I'll huff and I'll puff and I'll blow your house in," said the wolf.

So he huffed and he puffed and he blew the house in. Then he chased the little pig away.

The third pig that went away met a man with a load of bricks, and he said, "Please, man, give me your load of bricks so I can build me a house." The man gave the bricks to the little pig. Then the pig built a house with the bricks and lived in the house.

At last the wolf came along and knocked at the door of the brick house.

"Little pig, little pig, let me come in!" called the wolf.

"No, not by the hair of my chinny, chin, chin, I'll not let you in," answered the pig.

"Then I'll huff and I'll puff and I'll blow your house in," said the wolf.

So he huffed and he puffed and he puffed and he huffed, but he could not blow the little brick house in.

The wolf rested a few minutes, and then he said, "Little pig, little pig, will you let just the tip of my nose in?"

"No," said the little pig.

"Little pig, little pig, will you let just my paw in?"

"No," said the little pig.

"Little pig, little pig, will you let just the tip of my tail in?"

"No," said the little pig.

"Then I will climb up on the roof and come down through the chimney," said the wolf.

But the little pig made the fire very hot, so the wolf could not come down the chimney. So he went away, and that was the end of him.

The little pig then went and fetched his mother, and they still live happily in their little brick house.

The Little Red Hen

Once a hardworking little red hen lived on a farm with a dog, a cat, and a pig. One day she decided to make bread.

"Who will help me cut the wheat to make my bread?" she asked.

"Not I," said the dog.

"Not I," yawned the cat.

"Not I," grunted the pig.

"Then I will do it myself," said the little red hen.

When she had cut the wheat, the little red hen asked, "Who will help me take the wheat to the miller for grinding?"

"Not I," growled the dog.

"Not I," hissed the cat.

"Not I," snorted the pig.

"Then I will do it myself," said the little red hen.

When the wheat had been ground into flour, the little red hen asked, "Who will help me make the flour into bread dough?"

"Not I," sighed the dog.

"Not I," whined the cat.

"Not I," sniffed the pig.

"Then I will do it myself," said the little red hen.

When she had mixed the dough, the little red hen asked, "Who will help me bake the bread?"

"Not I," muttered the dog.

"Not I," murmured the cat.

"Not I," grumbled the pig.

"Then I will do it myself," said the little red hen.

And so, all by herself, she baked a fine loaf of bread. "Now," said the little red hen, "who will help me eat the bread?"

"I will!" barked the dog.

"I will," purred the cat.

"I will!" grunted the pig.

But the little red hen said, "No you won't. I cut the wheat all by myself. I took it to the miller all by myself. I mixed the dough and baked it all by myself. And now I shall eat the bread—all by myself!"

Write the letters *Hh.* Say the word that names each picture. Color the picture whose name begins with the same sound as *hen.*

At Home: Together, think of words that name things that begin with /h/. Have the child draw a picture of one of these things.

Unit 6
Introduce Initial /h/h 6

306

Find the circles in the picture. Color them orange. Find the triangles in the picture. Color them blue.

26 Unit 6
Review Shapes: Circle, Triangle

At Home: Take turns finding circular shapes in several rooms: door knobs and cup rims. Then find square and rectangular shapes: windows, envelopes and books.

307

Trace the letters *Hh.* Say the word that names each picture. Color each picture whose name begins with the same sound as *hen.* Draw a line from these pictures to the letters *Hh.*

At Home: Play "Hurrah for H." Make picture cards of these and other objects. Take turns picking a card and saying "Hurrah" if the picture name begins with /h/h.

Unit 6
Review Initial /h/h 9

308

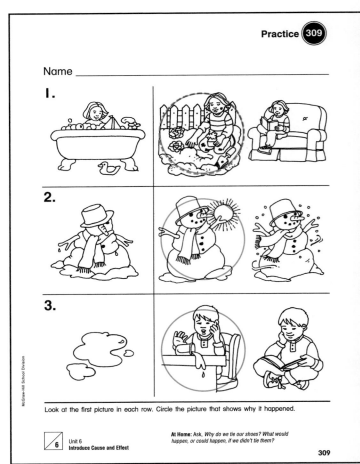

Look at the first picture in each row. Circle the picture that shows why it happened.

6 Unit 6
Introduce Cause and Effect

At Home: Ask, *Why do we tie our shoes? What would happen, or could happen, if we didn't tie them?*

309

Hop with a Hog • PRACTICE

Name _____

1.
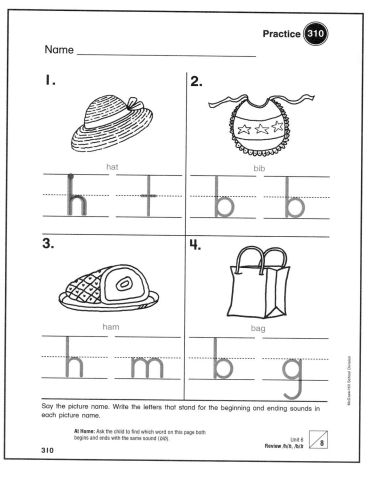

hat

h _ t

2.

bib

b _ b

3.

ham

h _ m

4.

bag

b _ g

Say the picture name. Write the letters that stand for the beginning and ending sounds in each picture name.

At Home: Ask the child to find which word on this page both begins and ends with the same sound (*bib*).

310

Unit 6
Review /h/h, /b/b 8

Name _____

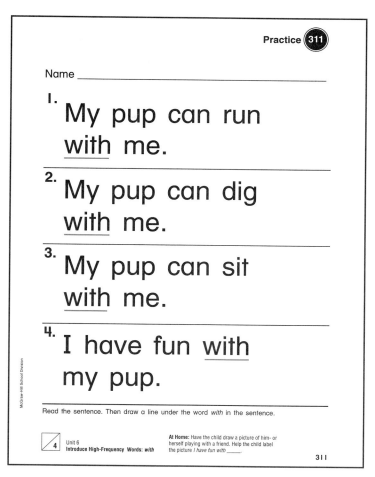

1. My pup can run with me.

2. My pup can dig with me.

3. My pup can sit with me.

4. I have fun with my pup.

Read the sentence. Then draw a line under the word *with* in the sentence.

4 Unit 6
Introduce High-Frequency Words: *with*

At Home: Have the child draw a picture of him- or herself playing with a friend. Help the child label the picture *I have fun with _____*.

311

Name _____

1. h e n

hen

2. h u t

hut

3. h o p

hop

4. h i d

hid

Blend the sounds and say the word. Write the word. Draw a line under the picture that goes with the word.

At Home: Write *hop*. Take turns changing *hop* to *hip*. Change *hip* to *dip*. Change *dip* to *rip*. Together, decide if you made real words.

312

Unit 5
Review Blending with Short *a, e, i, o, u* 8

Hh Name _____

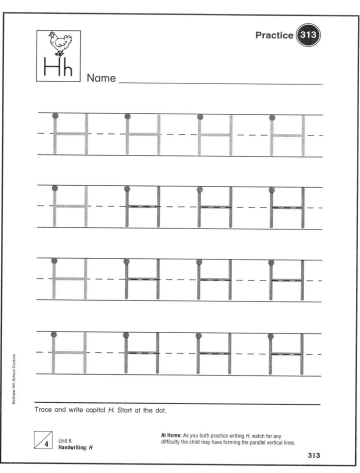

Trace and write capital H. Start at the dot.

4 Unit 6
Handwriting: *H*

At Home: As you both practice writing *H*, watch for any difficulty the child may have forming the parallel vertical lines.

313

Hop with a Hog • PRACTICE

Hh

Name _____

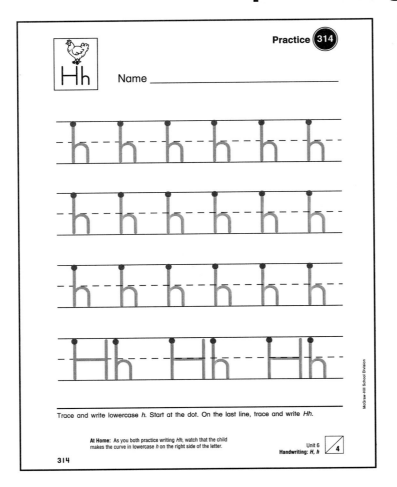

Trace and write lowercase *h*. Start at the dot. On the last line, trace and write *Hh*.

At Home: As you both practice writing *Hh*, watch that the child makes the curve in lowercase *h* on the right side of the letter.

Unit 6
Handwriting: *H, h* | 4

314

Name _____

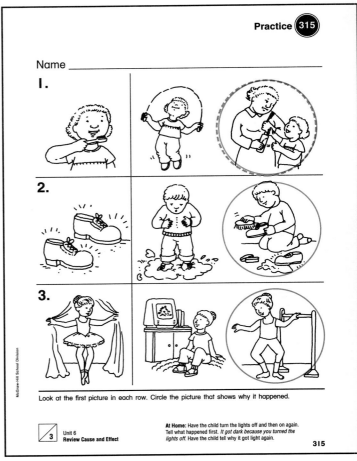

1.

2.

3.

Look at the first picture in each row. Circle the picture that shows why it happened.

3 | Unit 6
Review Cause and Effect

At Home: Have the child turn the lights off and then on again. Tell what happened first. *It got dark because you turned the lights off.* Have the child tell why it got light again.

315

Name _____

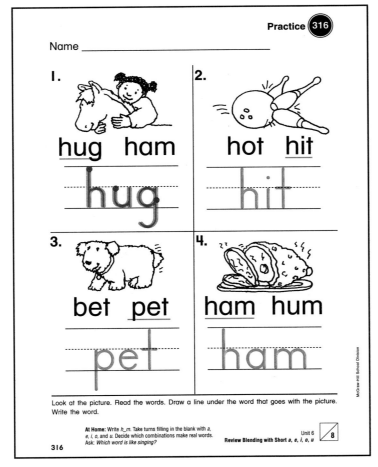

1. hug ham — hug
2. hot hit — hit
3. bet pet — pet
4. ham hum — ham

Look at the picture. Read the words. Draw a line under the word that goes with the picture. Write the word.

At Home: Write *h_m*. Take turns filling in the blank with *a, e, i, o,* and *u.* Decide which combinations make real words. Ask: *Which word is like singing?*

Unit 6
Review Blending with Short *a, e, i, o, u* | 8

316

Name _____

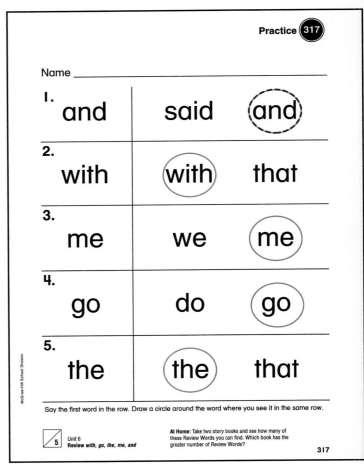

1. and | said | (and)
2. with | (with) | that
3. me | we | (me)
4. go | do | (go)
5. the | (the) | that

Say the first word in the row. Draw a circle around the word where you see it in the same row.

5 | Unit 6
Review *with, go, the, me, and*

At Home: Take two story books and see how many of these Review Words you can find. Which book has the greater number of Review Words?

317

We Win! • PRACTICE

Ww

Name _____

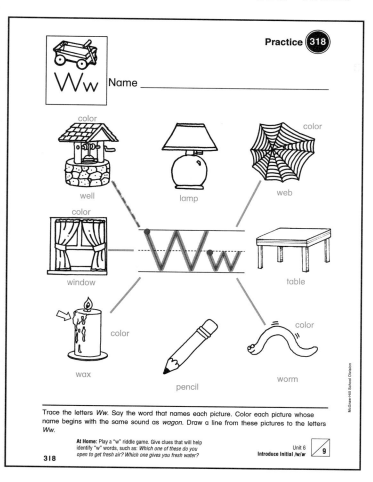

color
well
lamp
color
web
color
window
table
wax
color
pencil
worm
color

Trace the letters *Ww*. Say the word that names each picture. Color each picture whose name begins with the same sound as *wagon*. Draw a line from these pictures to the letters *Ww*.

At Home: Play a "w" riddle game. Give clues that will help identify "w" words, such as: *Which one of these do you open to get fresh air? Which one gives you fresh water?*

318

Unit 6
Introduce Initial /w/w 9

Name _____

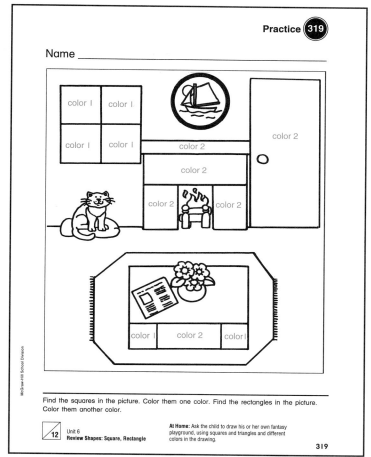

color 1 color 1
color 1 color 1
color 2
color 2
color 2
color 2 color 2
color 1 color 2 color 1

Find the squares in the picture. Color them one color. Find the rectangles in the picture. Color them another color.

12 Unit 6
Review Shapes: Square, Rectangle

At Home: Ask the child to draw his or her own fantasy playground, using squares and triangles and different colors in the drawing.

319

Ww

Name _____

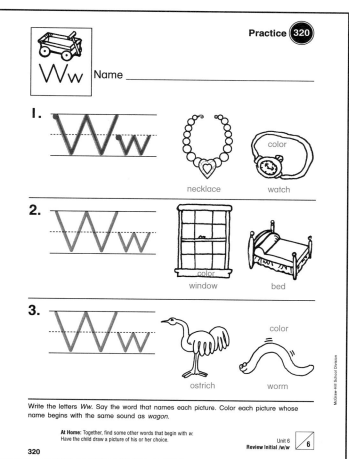

1. Ww
necklace watch
color

2. Ww
window bed
color

3. Ww
ostrich worm
color

Write the letters *Ww*. Say the word that names each picture. Color each picture whose name begins with the same sound as *wagon*.

At Home: Together, find some other words that begin with *w*. Have the child draw a picture of his or her choice.

320

Unit 6
Review Initial /w/w 6

Name _____

1.

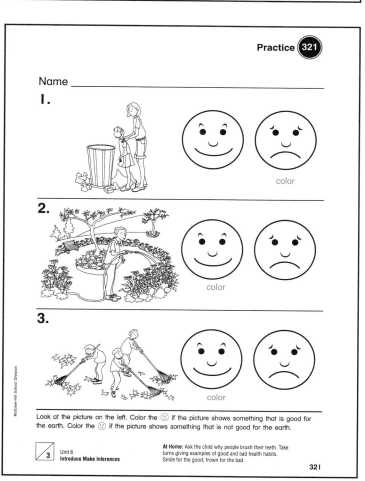

color

2.

color

3.

color

Look at the picture on the left. Color the ☺ if the picture shows something that is good for the earth. Color the ☹ if the picture shows something that is not good for the earth.

3 Unit 6
Introduce Make Inferences

At Home: Ask the child why people brush their teeth. Take turns giving examples of good and bad health habits. Smile for the good; frown for the bad.

321

T11

We Win! • PRACTICE

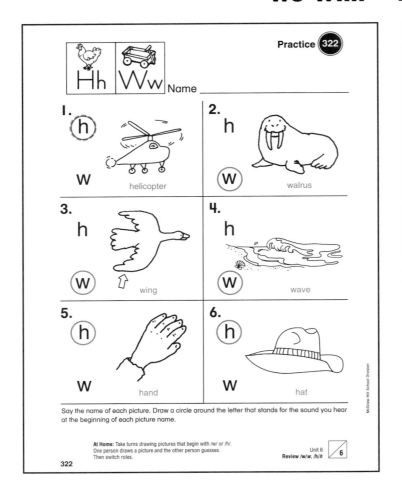

Hh Ww Name _____

1. h / w — helicopter

2. h / w — walrus

3. h / w — wing

4. h / w — wave

5. h / w — hand

6. h / w — hat

Say the name of each picture. Draw a circle around the letter that stands for the sound you hear at the beginning of each picture name.

At Home: Take turns drawing pictures that begin with /w/ or /h/. One person draws a picture and the other person guesses. Then switch roles.

Unit 6
Review /w/w, /h/h 6

322

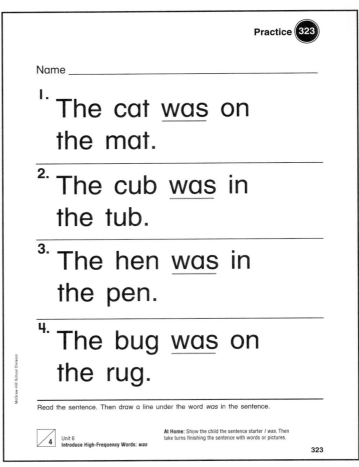

Name _____

1. The cat <u>was</u> on the mat.

2. The cub <u>was</u> in the tub.

3. The hen <u>was</u> in the pen.

4. The bug <u>was</u> on the rug.

Read the sentence. Then draw a line under the word *was* in the sentence.

4 Unit 6
Introduce High-Frequency Words: *was*

At Home: Show the child the sentence starter *I was.* Then take turns finishing the sentence with words or pictures.

323

Name _____

1. w e t — wet

2. w i g — wig

3. h u t — hut

4. w a g — wag

Blend the sounds and say the word. Write the word. Draw a line under the picture that goes with the word.

At Home: Write _ag and _ig on cards. Take turns combining them with initial letters w, r, and t to create words. Is any combination not a word?

Unit 6
Review Blending with Short a, e, i, o, u 8

324

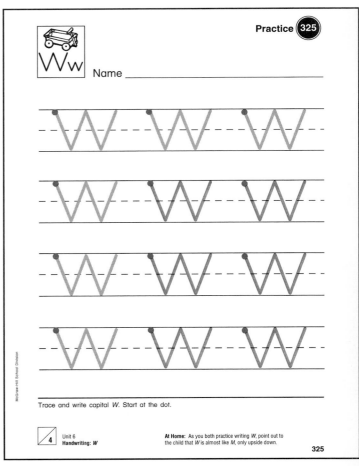

Ww Name _____

W W W

W W W

W W W

W W W

Trace and write capital W. Start at the dot.

4 Unit 6
Handwriting: W

At Home: As you both practice writing W, point out to the child that W is almost like M, only upside down.

325

We Win! • PRACTICE

Ww

Name _____

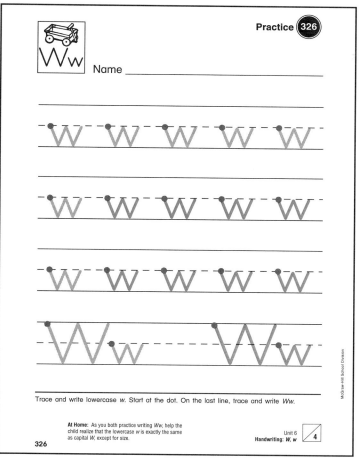

Trace and write lowercase *w*. Start at the dot. On the last line, trace and write *Ww*.

At Home: As you both practice writing *Ww*, help the child realize that the lowercase *w* is exactly the same as capital *W*, except for size.

326

Unit 6
Handwriting: *W, w*   4

Name _____

1.

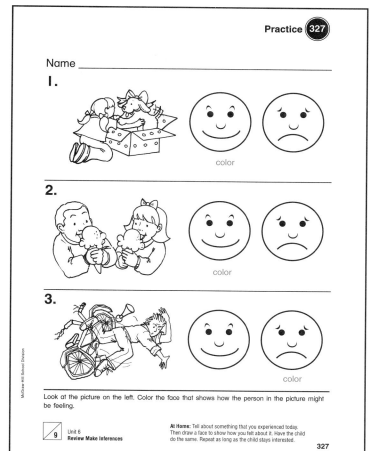

color

2.

color

3.

color

Look at the picture on the left. Color the face that shows how the person in the picture might be feeling.

9   Unit 6
Review Make Inferences

At Home: Tell about something that you experienced today. Then draw a face to show how you felt about it. Have the child do the same. Repeat as long as the child stays interested.

327

Name _____

1.
pin <u>win</u>

win

2.
hum <u>ham</u>

ham

3.
<u>bed</u> wed

bed

4.
lit <u>lock</u>

lock

Look at the picture. Read the words. Draw a line under the word that goes with the picture. Write the word.

At Home: Write *ed*. Take turns writing under it words that end with *ed*. (*bed, red, fed, wed, Ted, led, Ned*)

328

Unit 6
Review Blending with Short *a, e, i, o, u*   8

Name _____

1.

sit   <u>he</u>   (she)

2.

in   (I)   is

3.

<u>was</u>   he   (with)

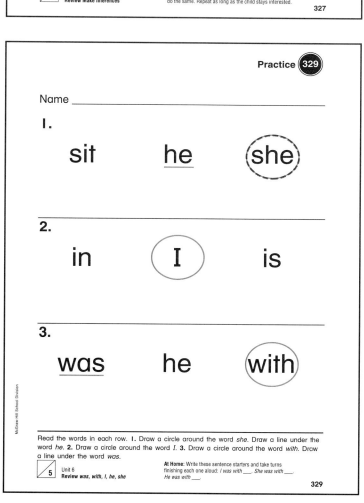

Read the words in each row. **1.** Draw a circle around the word *she*. Draw a line under the word *he*. **2.** Draw a circle around the word *I*. **3.** Draw a circle around the word *with*. Draw a line under the word *was*.

5   Unit 6
Review *was, with, I, he, she*

At Home: Write these sentence starters and take turns finishing each one aloud: *I was with ___. She was with ___. He was with ___.*

329

T13

The Vet Van • PRACTICE

Name _____

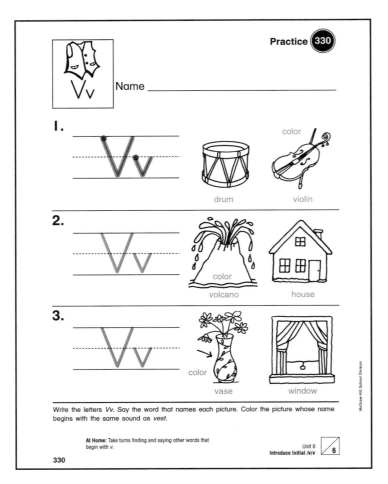

1. drum / violin — color

2. volcano / house — color

3. vase / window — color

Write the letters *Vv*. Say the word that names each picture. Color the picture whose name begins with the same sound as *vest*.

At Home: Take turns finding and saying other words that begin with *v*.

330

Unit 6
Introduce Initial /v/v | 6

Name _____

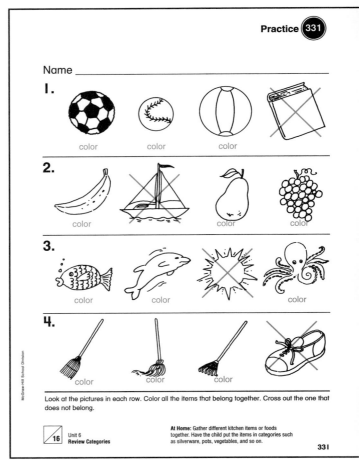

1. color / color / color

2. color / color / color

3. color / color / color

4. color / color / color

Look at the pictures in each row. Color all the items that belong together. Cross out the one that does not belong.

16 | Unit 6
Review Categories

At Home: Gather different kitchen items or foods together. Have the child put the items in categories such as silverware, pots, vegetables, and so on.

331

Name _____

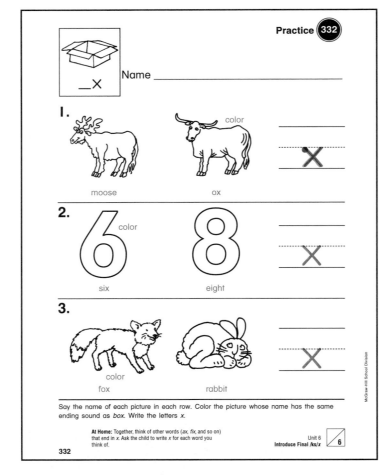

1. moose / ox — color

2. six / eight — color

3. fox / rabbit — color

Say the name of each picture in each row. Color the picture whose name has the same ending sound as *box*. Write the letters *x*.

At Home: Together, think of other words (*ax, fix,* and so on) that end in *x*. Ask the child to write *x* for each word you think of.

332

Unit 6
Introduce Final /ks/x | 6

Name _____

1.

2.

3.

Look at the first picture in each row. Circle the picture that shows why it happened.

3 | Unit 6
Review Cause and Effect

At Home: Reread a favorite story together. Take turns telling why events happened. Explain that sometimes the story leaves *why* to the child's imagination.

333

The Vet Van • PRACTICE

Practice 334

Name _____

1. V (circled) valentine X
2. V six X (circled)
3. V ax X (circled)
4. V (circled) volcano X
5. V wax X (circled)
6. V (circled) vet X

Say the name of each picture. Draw a circle around the *v* if it is the beginning sound (as in *vest*). Draw a circle around the *x* if it is the ending sound (as in *box*).

At Home: Together, make cards of words that begin with *v* and words that end with *x*. Practice reading and saying them.

334

Unit 6
Review Initial /v/v, Final /ks/x 6

Practice 335

Name _____

1. My cat is <u>not</u> on the mat.

2. My cat is <u>not</u> big.

3. My cat is <u>not</u> tan.

4. That is <u>not</u> my cat!

Read the sentence. Then draw a line under the word *not* in the sentence.

4 Unit 6
Introduce High-Frequency Words: *not*

At Home: Play "Not I." Write *Not I* and *I do* on index cards. Take turns asking silly or logical questions, such as "Who has purple fingernails?" Then hold up the appropriate answer card.

335

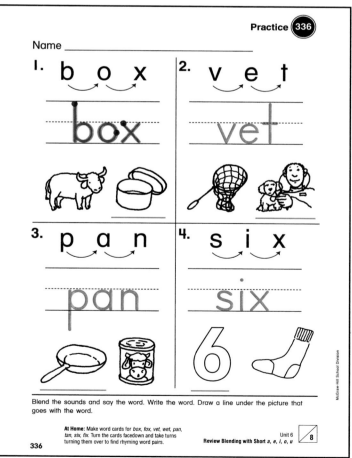

Practice 336

Name _____

1. b o x — box
2. v e t — vet
3. p a n — pan
4. s i x — six

Blend the sounds and say the word. Write the word. Draw a line under the picture that goes with the word.

At Home: Make word cards for *box, fox, vet, wet, pan, tan, six, fix.* Turn the cards facedown and take turns turning them over to find rhyming word pairs.

336

Unit 6
Review Blending with Short *a, e, i, o, u* 8

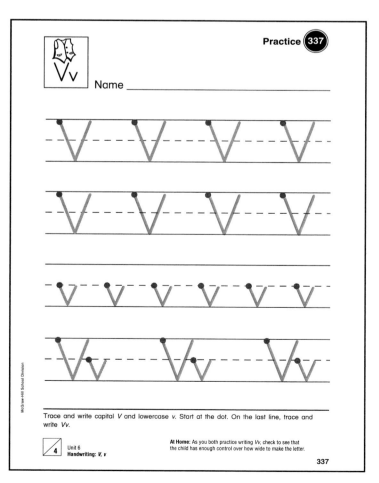

Practice 337

Vv

Name _____

Trace and write capital *V* and lowercase *v*. Start at the dot. On the last line, trace and write *Vv*.

4 Unit 6
Handwriting: *V, v*

At Home: As you both practice writing *Vv*, check to see that the child has enough control over how wide to make the letter.

337

The Vet Van • PRACTICE

Xx Name _____

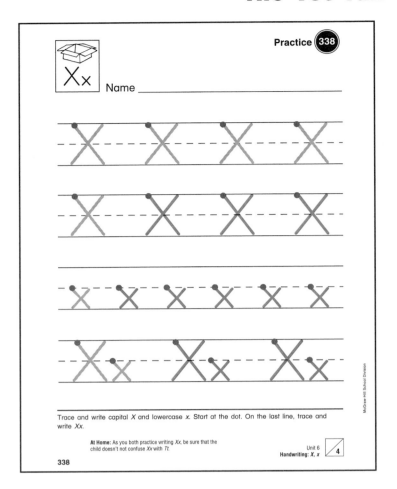

Trace and write capital X and lowercase x. Start at the dot. On the last line, trace and write Xx.

At Home: As you both practice writing Xx, be sure that the child doesn't not confuse Xx with Tt.

Unit 6
Handwriting: X, x   4

338

Name _____

1.

2.

3.

Look at the first picture in each row. Circle the picture that shows why it happened.

Unit 6
Review Cause and Effect   3

At Home: Take turns making up parts of a story. Have the child begin with a character. *One day a big purple dinosaur...* Then you pick it up with a few sentences using the words *why* and *because* when appropriate. Then the child continues and so on.

339

Name _____

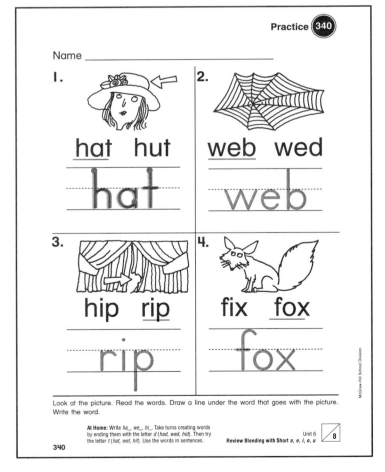

1. hat   hut
    hat

2. web   wed
    web

3. hip   rip
    rip

4. fix   fox
    fox

Look at the picture. Read the words. Draw a line under the word that goes with the picture. Write the word.

At Home: Write ha_, we_, hi_. Take turns creating words by ending them with the letter *d* (*had, wed, hid*). Then try the letter *t* (*hat, wet, hit*). Use the words in sentences.

Unit 6
Review Blending with Short a, e, i, o, u   8

340

Name _____

1. "Is the pup <u>with</u> you?" said Mom.

2. The pup <u>was</u> <u>not</u> with Kim and Tom.

3. "<u>We</u> <u>do</u> not have the pup," said Kim.

4. "Dad and Ben <u>are</u> with the pup," said Tom.

Read each sentence. 1. Draw a line under the words *is* and *with*. 2. Draw a line under the words *was* and *not*. 3. Draw a line under the words *we* and *do*. 4. Draw a line under the word *are*.

Unit 6
Review *not, was, is, do, we, are, with*   7

At Home: Write each of the seven Review Words on two sets of paper strips. Place the strips facedown and take turns finding matching pairs.

341

Jen and Yip • PRACTICE

Name

1. Qu qu — lion — queen

2. Qu qu — bell — quarter

3. Qu qu — question mark — balloon

Write the letters Qu/qu. Say the word that names each picture. Listen for the sound at the beginning of the word. Color the picture whose name begins with the same sound as quilt.

At Home: Together, make a paper "quilt" of letter cards. Ask the child to write Q or q on some of the cards.

Unit 6
Introduce Initial /kw/qu   6

342

Name

1. color — color — color

2. color — color — color

3. color — color — color

4. color — color — color

Look at the pictures in each row. Color all the items that belong together. Cross out the one that does not belong.

16   Unit 6
Review Categories

At Home: Have child sort toys into categories such as puzzles, cars, blocks, art materials, and so on. Label each category with an index card.

343

Name

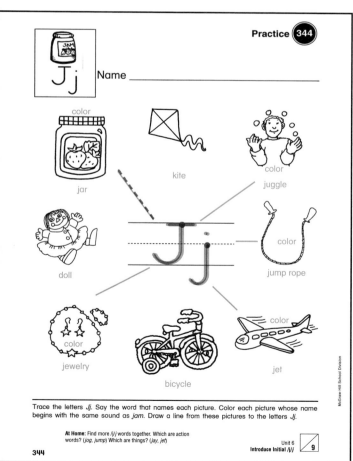

color — jar
kite
color — juggle
doll
color — jump rope
color — jewelry
bicycle
color — jet

Trace the letters Jj. Say the word that names each picture. Color each picture whose name begins with the same sound as jam. Draw a line from these pictures to the letters Jj.

At Home: Find more /j/j words together. Which are action words? (jog, jump) Which are things? (jay, jet)

Unit 6
Introduce Initial /j/j   9

344

Name

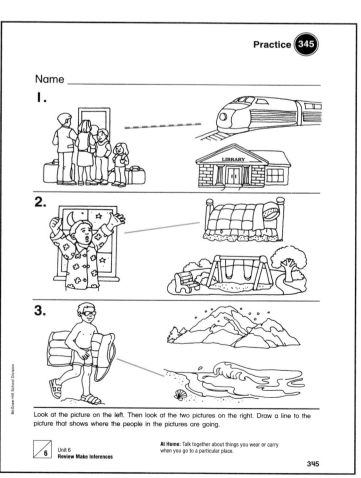

1.

2.

3.

Look at the picture on the left. Then look at the two pictures on the right. Draw a line to the picture that shows where the people in the pictures are going.

6   Unit 6
Review Make Inferences

At Home: Talk together about things you wear or carry when you go to a particular place.

345

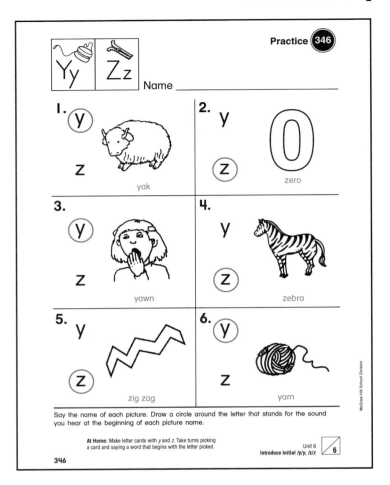

Practice 346

Y y   Z z   Name _____

1. (y) / z — yak

2. y / (z) — zero

3. (y) / z — yawn

4. y / (z) — zebra

5. y / (z) — zig zag

6. (y) / z — yarn

Say the name of each picture. Draw a circle around the letter that stands for the sound you hear at the beginning of each picture name.

At Home: Make letter cards with *y* and *z*. Take turns picking a card and saying a word that begins with the letter picked.

Unit 6
Introduce Initial /y/y, /z/z   6

346

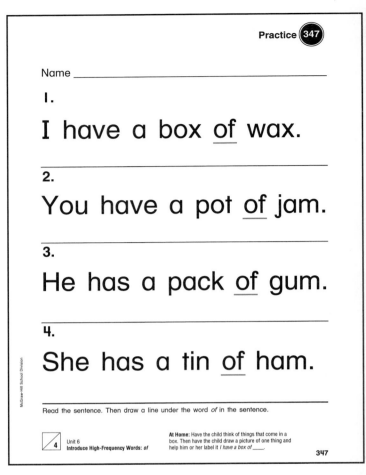

Practice 347

Name _____

1. I have a box <u>of</u> wax.

2. You have a pot <u>of</u> jam.

3. He has a pack <u>of</u> gum.

4. She has a tin <u>of</u> ham.

Read the sentence. Then draw a line under the word *of* in the sentence.

Unit 6
Introduce High-Frequency Words: *of*

At Home: Have the child think of things that come in a box. Then have the child draw a picture of one thing and help him or her label it *I have a box of ____.*

347

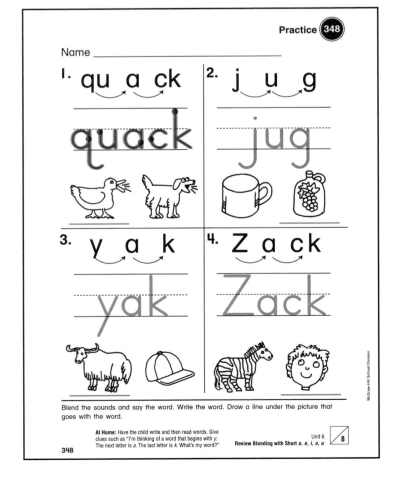

Practice 348

Name _____

1. qu a ck
quack

2. j u g
jug

3. y a k
yak

4. Z a ck
Zack

Blend the sounds and say the word. Write the word. Draw a line under the picture that goes with the word.

At Home: Have the child write and then read words. Give clues such as "I'm thinking of a word that begins with *y*. The next letter is *a*. The last letter is *k*. What's my word?"

Unit 6
Review Blending with Short *a, e, i, o, u*   8

348

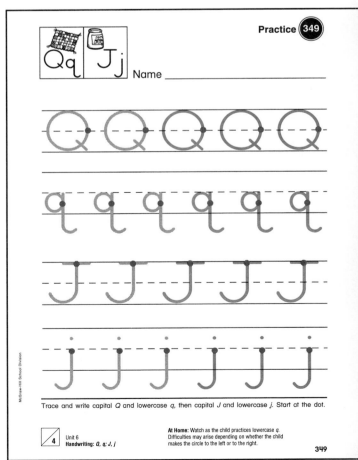

Practice 349

Q q   J j   Name _____

Q Q Q Q Q

q q q q q q

J J J J J

J J J J J J

Trace and write capital *Q* and lowercase *q*, then capital *J* and lowercase *j*. Start at the dot.

Unit 6
Handwriting: *Q, q; J, j*

At Home: Watch as the child practices lowercase *q*. Difficulties may arise depending on whether the child makes the circle to the left or to the right.

349

Jen and Yip • PRACTICE

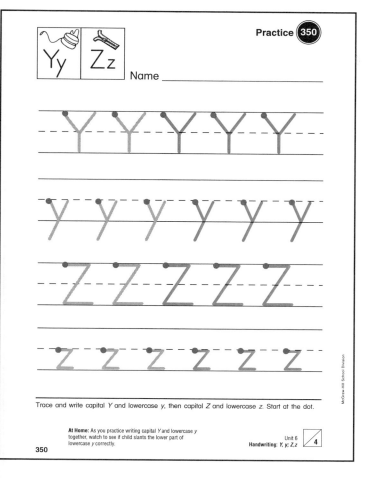

Yy | Zz   Name _____

Trace and write capital Y and lowercase y, then capital Z and lowercase z. Start at the dot.

At Home: As you practice writing capital Y and lowercase y together, watch to see if child slants the lower part of lowercase y correctly.

Unit 6
Handwriting: Y, y; Z, z   4

350

Name _____

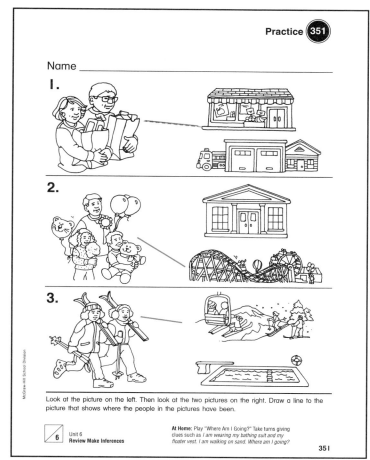

1.

2.

3.

Look at the picture on the left. Then look at the two pictures on the right. Draw a line to the picture that shows where the people in the pictures have been.

Unit 6
Review Make Inferences

At Home: Play "Where Am I Going?" Take turns giving clues such as *I am wearing my bathing suit and my floater vest. I am walking on sand. Where am I going?*

351

Name _____

1.
pen quick

pen

2.
ox wax

ox

3.
yam ham

ham

4.
ax jug

ax

Look at the picture. Read the words. Draw a line under the word that goes with the picture. Write the word.

At Home: Make cards for *a, e, i, o, u* and hide them in a room. Have the child look for them. When one is found, you say a word that uses the selected letter (e.g., *cat, net, pig, pot, sun*). When all five cards are found, switch roles.

Unit 6
Review Blending with Short *a, e, i, o, u*   8

352

Name _____

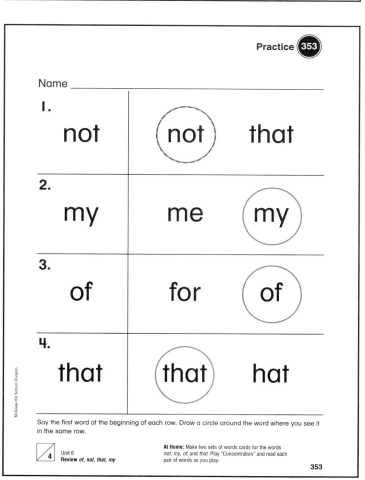

1. not   (not)   that

2. my   me   (my)

3. of   for   (of)

4. that   (that)   hat

Say the first word at the beginning of each row. Draw a circle around the word where you see it in the same row.

Unit 6
Review *of, not, that, my*

At Home: Make two sets of words cards for the words *not, my, of,* and *that.* Play "Concentration" and read each pair of words as you play.

353

Zack and Jan • PRACTICE

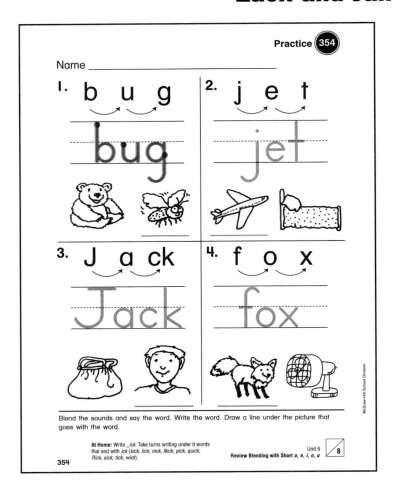

Name _____

1. b u g

bug

2. j e t

jet

3. J a c k

Jack

4. f o x

fox

Blend the sounds and say the word. Write the word. Draw a line under the picture that goes with the word.

At Home: Write _ick. Take turns writing under it words that end with ick (kick, lick, nick, Nick, pick, quick, Rick, sick, tick, wick).

Unit 6
Review Blending with Short a, e, i, o, u 8

354

Name _____

1.

2.

3.

Draw a circle around the *fish*. Draw a triangle around the *toy*. Draw a square around the *child*.

9 Unit 5
Review Shapes and Categories

At Home: Together, find objects that can be grouped into categories (things to read, things to wear, things to eat). Then look for shapes to see if any of the items contain circles, squares, triangles, or rectangles.

355

Name _____

1. m o p

mop

2. z i p

zip

3. j a m

jam

4. s u n

sun

Blend the sounds and say the word. Write the word. Draw a line under the picture that goes with the word.

At Home: Write zip. Ask the child to change zip to zap. Write mop. Ask the child to change mop to map, jam to Jim, and fix to fox. Use each word in a sentence.

Unit 6
Review Blending with Short a, e, i, o, u 8

356

Name _____

1.

2.

3.

Look at the first picture in each row. Circle the picture that shows why it happened.

6 Unit 6
Review Cause and Effect

At Home: Talk about something that happened. Ask the child why it happened. Guide his or her answer where necessary.

357

Zack and Jan • PRACTICE

Name _____

1. pup pad

pup

2. yet jet

jet

3. ox mix

ox

4. pick sick

sick

Look at the picture. Read the words. Draw a line under the word that goes with the picture. Write the word.

At Home: Write words that end with *x*. Say each word before you write it. (*fix, ax, fox, ox, mix, box, six, wax*) Which of them rhyme?

Unit 6
Review Blending with Short *a, e, i, o, u*   8

358

Name _____

1. was (with) of

2. (of) with not

3. with not (was)

4. of (not) with

Read the words in each row. 1. Draw a circle around the word *with*. 2. Draw a circle around the word *of*. 3. Draw a circle around the word *was*. 2. Draw a circle around the word *not*.

4 Unit 6
Review *with, was, not, of*

At Home: Print the Review Words on cards. Take turns removing one card and guessing which word is missing.

359

Name _____

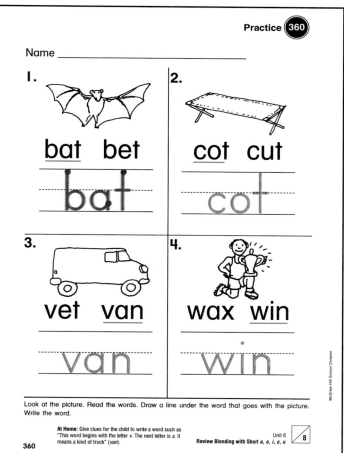

1. bat bet

bat

2. cot cut

cot

3. vet van

van

4. wax win

win

Look at the picture. Read the words. Draw a line under the word that goes with the picture. Write the word.

At Home: Give clues for the child to write a word such as "This word begins with the letter *v*. The next letter is *a*. It means a kind of truck" (*van*).

Unit 6
Review Blending with Short *a, e, i, o, u*   8

360

Name _____

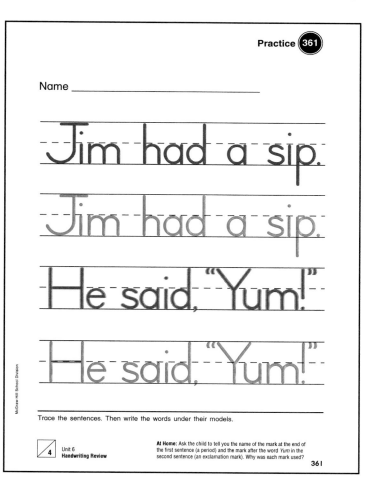

Jim had a sip.

Jim had a sip.

He said, "Yum!"

He said, "Yum!"

Trace the sentences. Then write the words under their models.

4 Unit 6
Handwriting Review

At Home: Ask the child to tell you the name of the mark at the end of the first sentence (a period) and the mark after the word *Yum* in the second sentence (an exclamation mark). Why was each mark used?

361

Practice 362

Name _____

It was hot.

It was hot.

I did not jog.

I did not jog.

Trace the sentences. Then write the words under their models.

At Home: Together, say the alphabet. Ask the child which letters are easy and which are difficult to write. Ask the child to write a letter and tell why it is easy or difficult.

Unit 6
Handwriting Review 4

362

Practice 363

Name _____

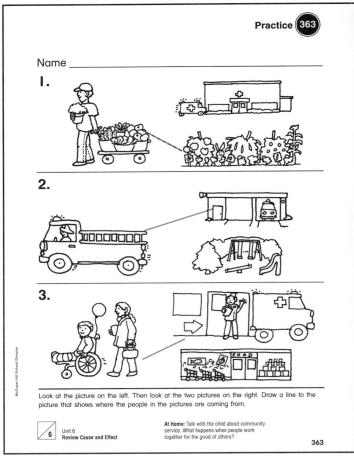

1.

2.

3.

Look at the picture on the left. Then look at the two pictures on the right. Draw a line to the picture that shows where the people in the pictures are coming from.

Unit 6
Review Cause and Effect 6

At Home: Talk with the child about community service. What happens when people work together for the good of others?

363

Practice 364

Name _____

1. bed but
bed

2. hot hop
hop

3. led leg
leg

4. quack ax
quack

Look at the picture. Read the words. Draw a line under the word that goes with the picture. Write the word.

At Home: Change one sound/letter combination at a time as you go from *quack* to *duck*. Write *quack*. Have the child change *quack* to *tack*. Change *tack* to *tuck* and *tuck* to *duck*.

Unit 6
Review Blending with Short *a, e, i, o, u* 8

364

Practice 365

Name _____

1.

Dot, the pup, was not with Mom.

2.

Dot was with Jim and Nan.

3.

Jim, Nan, and Dot had a lot of fun.

Read the sentence. 1. Draw a line under the words *was* and *not*. 2. Draw a line under the word *with*. 3. Draw a line under the word *of*.

Unit 6
Review *with, was, not, of* 4

At Home: Play "What Word Am I?" Give each other clues for the words *with, was, not,* and *of*. *I begin with w and end with th or I rhyme with lot (with, not).*

365

Initial *h*

✓OBJECTIVES Children will apply letter/sound associations for *h.* They will identify words that begin with *h.*

Alternate Activities

Visual

PARTY HATS7

 Materials: construction paper, scissors, tape or glue, crayons or markers

Children will make cone-shaped hats. They will draw and label items whose names begin with *h.*

- For each child, cut a half circle and divide it into thirds. At the bottom of each section (near the curve), write *h.*

- Show children how to bend the half circle to make a party hat. Point out that *hat* begins with *h,* and that the letter *h* stands for that sound.

Ask children to draw on their hats three **WRITING** pictures whose names begin with *h,* one in each section. Help children label their pictures.

- Assist children in bending and taping or gluing their hats to make a cone. Have children model their hats for classmates. ▶**Spatial**

Auditory

FIX IT

 Children will replace a word in a sentence **GROUP** with a word that begins with *h.*

- Tell children that you will say a sentence in which one word needs to be changed to a rhyming word that begins with *h.*

- Provide the following example:

You can catch a fish with a book.

Elicit from children that the sentence should be *You can catch a fish with a hook.*

- If necessary, share other examples, such as:

You can get water from a rose. (hose)

You can wear a ring on your land. (hand)

You can sing a yappy tune. (happy)

- Challenge children to suggest their own sentences to correct. ▶**Logical/Mathematical**

Kinesthetic

HOP TO BLEND

Materials: colored chalk

ONE Children will hop from letter to letter written on a sidewalk to blend sounds to read words.

- Ask children to hop. Point out that *hop* begins with *h,* and that the letter *h* stands for that sound.

- Take children outdoors to a sidewalk or other area. On the sidewalk, write words beginning with *h,* such as *hat, ham, had, hid, hen, hop, hot, hug.* Allow space between each letter so that children can hop from letter to letter.

- Invite children to hop from letter to letter, saying the sound each letter stands for as they blend the sounds to read the words.

- Encourage children to use the words they blend in oral sentences. ▶**Bodily/Kinesthetic**

 **CD-ROM**

Shapes

OBJECTIVES Children will identify the basic shapes: circle, triangle, rectangle.

Alternate

Kinesthetic

SHAPE CHANT

GROUP Children will create a chant describing a basic shape. They will arrange themselves to create the shape.

- Have children identify a circle, a triangle, and a rectangle. Talk about the characteristics of each shape, such as the triangle's three sides.

- Organize children into small groups. Assign each group a basic shape. Have them discuss their shape's characteristics.

- Help the groups create a chant about their shape. For example, *Triangle! Triangle! Has three lines. Each one is side by side. Yay!*

- Have groups practice their chants. Show them how to use their bodies to arrange themselves in their shapes.

- Invite each group to perform its chant and arrangement for the class. ▶**Bodily/Kinesthetic**

Visual

SHAPE HUNT

PARTNERS **Materials:** shape cutouts

Children will find examples of basic shapes in their environment.

- Organize children into pairs. Give each pair a cutout of a circle, a triangle, or a rectangle.

- Have each pair go around the room or other area of the school matching their shape to things they see around them.

- Invite pairs to report on one interesting place they found their shape. ▶**Spatial**

Auditory

SHAPE FINGER PLAY

GROUP Children will participate in a finger play that models drawing basic shapes.

- On the chalkboard, draw a circle, a triangle, and a rectangle. Help children identify each one.

- Share the following finger play with children:

  I can draw a circle. (draw circle in air)

  You can, too. (point to others)

  This is a shape that we can do. (give "thumbs up" signal)

- Repeat the verses, substituting *rectangle* and *triangle* for *circle*. ▶**Bodily/Kinesthetic**

Cause and Effect

 OBJECTIVES Children will recognize examples of cause-and-effect relationships.

Alternate Activities

Auditory

SOUND EFFECTS

 Materials: cassette recorder, cassette tape

GROUP Children will listen to recorded sounds and guess what caused the sound.

- Record a variety of classroom sounds, such as a door closing, chalk being used to write on a chalkboard, a chair tipping over, a window opening, and a pencil being sharpened.

- Play the tape for children. Have them guess what caused each sound to occur.
  ▶**Logical/Mathematical**

Kinesthetic

CAUSING EFFECTS

Children will work in pairs to demonstrate a **PARTNERS** cause-and-effect relationship.

- Demonstrate for children a simple cause-and-effect relationship, such as opening a window and letting fresh air in. Describe the relationship for children with a sentence such as: *Fresh air comes in because I opened the window.*

- Have pairs work together to demonstrate a cause-and-effect relationship. If some children need help, you might suggest pushing over a stack of books, turning off a light switch, or sharpening a pencil. ▶**Interpersonal**

Visual

WHAT'S THE CAUSE?

Materials: baking soda, clear vinegar, water, **GROUP** light corn syrup

Children will explore cause-and-effect relationships by mixing baking soda and different liquids.

- Demonstrate for children what happens when baking soda and vinegar are mixed, but do not tell them what liquid is used to create the reaction.

- Have small groups try to re-create the reaction. Give each group three cups containing baking soda, along with cups containing vinegar, water, and corn syrup. Have the groups experiment to see which liquid causes the reaction.
  ▶**Logical/Mathematical**

High-Frequency Words
with, was, not, of

Alternate Activities

Visual

WORD SEARCH

 Materials: index cards, markers, self-stick notes, pencils
PARTNERS

Children will find high-frequency words in printed material.

- Organize children into pairs. Give each pair a high-frequency word card. Have them search for the word in signs around the room, books, or children's magazines.

 Encourage children to find four examples of their word. For each example, have them WRITING write the word on a self-stick note and attach it to the place where it appears.

- Have pairs share one example of their word. Read aloud the sentence it appears in. ▶**Linguistic**

Kinesthetic

WORDS ON HEAD BANDS

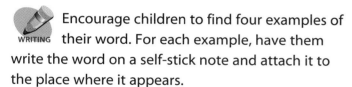 **Materials:** sentence strips, markers, stapler
GROUP Children will read their assigned high-frequency word and find others with the same word.

- Use sentence strips to create a high-frequency word head band for each child.

- Have children read their word. As they wear their head bands, have them walk around the room looking for others who have the same word.

- Encourage children to use their word in an oral sentence. ▶**Bodily/Kinesthetic**

Auditory

SPECIAL WORDS

 Materials: index cards, markers
GROUP Children will identify high-frequency words as they are heard in conversation.

Have each child make a set of individual WRITING word cards for *with, was, not,* and *of.* Help children read the words.

- On the chalkboard, write one of the words and have children read it. Tell children that this word is designated as a special word. They should listen for you to say this word as you give directions or share information. Tell children to hold up their word card when they hear the special word.

- After one of the high-frequency words has been identified, write a new word on the chalkboard and designate it as the special word. ▶**Interpersonal**

Initial w

OBJECTIVES Children will apply letter/sound associations for *w*. They will identify words that begin with *w*.

Alternate Activities

Kinesthetic

PICTURE WHEELS

Materials: two paper plates per child, brads, scissors, crayons or markers, magazine pictures, glue

Children will create *w* wheels with pictures whose names begin with *w*.

- Draw lines to divide paper plates into fourths. Gather enough magazine or catalog pictures of objects whose names begin with *w*, so that each child can have at least two pictures.

- Have children cut a piece from one of their paper plates, creating a window for their picture wheel. Give children two pictures each and have them glue them to sections of the second plate. Lead children to notice that both pictures begin with *w* and the letter *w* stands for this sound.

- On the second plate, ask children to draw two additional pictures whose names begin with *w*.

 Help children attach the two plates with brads. Ask them to label the top plate *w*. Have them turn their wheels and identify the picture names. ▶Spatial

Auditory

W RHYME

Children will identify words that begin with *w* in a rhyme.

- Share the following rhyme with children:

The letter w *begins many words.*

It begins word, *in fact,*

perhaps you heard.

What other words begin that way?

Well, I wonder what we'll say!

- Repeat each line. Have children listen for words that begin the same as *word*. Point out the letter *w* stands for the sound. ▶Linguistic

Visual

WINDOW BLENDING

Children will blend sounds to read *w* words displayed on a window.

- Ask children to identify a window. Point out that *window* begins with *w* and that the letter *w* stands for that sound.

- If possible, display on a window individual letter cards. They should be arranged so they build words that begin with *w* that children can blend to read, such as *wig, wag, web*. (If a window is not available, draw one on butcher paper.)

- Have children blend the sounds to read the words. Encourage children to use the words in an oral sentence. ▶Linguistic

 **CD-ROM**

Make Inferences

OBJECTIVES Children will use clues from spoken words or illustrations to make inferences.

Alternate

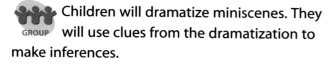

Kinesthetic

WHAT CAN YOU TELL?

GROUP Children will dramatize miniscenes. They will use clues from the dramatization to make inferences.

- Assign small groups a scenario to dramatize, such as winning a soccer game, building a snow person, or riding in a bus.

- After a group completes its brief dramatization, lead children to make inferences. Ask questions, beginning with *What do we know from watching this scene?* Guide children to answer questions about what the characters just did, what they might do next, what time of year it is, and so on. ▶**Bodily/Kinesthetic**

Visual

PICTURE CLUES

PARTNERS **Materials:** magazine photos

Pairs of children will make inferences about the feelings of people depicted in magazine photos.

- Provide pairs of children with a magazine photo of people. Encourage children to make a list of what they can tell by looking at the photo. Ask them how they think the person or people in the photo feel. Encourage children to identify clues that helped them make the inference. ▶**Interpersonal**

Auditory

SOLVING RIDDLES

PARTNERS **Materials:** riddle books (optional)

Partners will pose riddles to one another and make inferences to solve them.

- Model for children posing a riddle, such as *I have an eye, but I cannot see. There is a point to me. What am I?*

- When a volunteer solves the riddle, encourage the child to explain how he or she knew the answer was *needle.* Guide children to realize that thinking about their own experiences is important in making inferences, as well as looking at clues provided.

- Have partners pose riddles to each other. Children may make up the riddles, or choose from riddle books.

- Encourage children to talk about how they solve each riddle. ▶**Logical/Mathematical**

Initial v

OBJECTIVES Children will apply letter/sound associations for *v*. They will identify words that begin with *v*.

Visual

VESTS

Materials: large paper grocery bags, scissors, crayons or markers

Children will create a *v* vest with pictures of objects whose names begin with *v*.

- For each child, make a vest by cutting a slit down the front of a paper bag and arm holes in the sides. Show children the vests. Point out that *vest* begins with *v* and that the letter *v* stands for that sound.

- Help children brainstorm words that begin with *v*. Have them draw pictures of several of these words on their vests. Help children label their drawings.

- Invite children to wear their vests and share them with classmates. ▶**Intrapersonal**

Auditory

V FINGER PLAY

Children will say a finger play and share examples of words that begin with *v*.

- Share the following words and movements with children:

Let's make the letter v (hold up two fingers)

For one and all to see. (point to crowd, then eye)

It's a victory! Victory! V *for victory!* (raise fist twice; hold up two fingers; raise fist)

- Invite children to brainstorm words that begin with the same sound as *victory*. Point out that the letter *v* stands for that sound.
▶**Bodily/Kinesthetic**

Kinesthetic

VELVETY WORDS

Materials: pipe cleaners, sentence strips, glue, scissors

Children will blend sounds to read *v* words formed from pipe cleaners.

- Show children the letter *v* formed from a pipe cleaner. Have children touch the letter. Point out that it feels *velvety*, which begins with *v*. Explain that the letter *v* stands for that sound.

- Use pipe cleaners to form several words that begin with *v*, such as *van, vet,* and *vat*. Cut the pipe cleaners as needed to form the letters. Glue them to a sentence strip.

- Encourage children to touch each letter as they say its sound to blend and read the words. Have children use each word in an oral sentence.
▶**Bodily/Kinesthetic**

 **CD-ROM**

Final /ks/ x

OBJECTIVES Children will apply letter/sound associations for /ks/ *x*. They will identify words that end with /ks/.

Alternate Activities

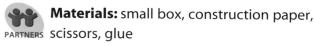

Kinesthetic

X MARKS THE SPOT

Materials: masking tape

GROUP Children will stand in formation of the letter *x* as they name words that end with /ks/.

- On the floor, create a large *X* with masking tape.

- Help children identify the letter. Explain that it stands for the sound heard at the end of many words, such as *six, mix, fox,* and *ax*.

- Organize children into groups of four. Have each child stand in a corner of the letter. Show children how to extend their arms to join hands in the center. Point out that they are forming an *x*.

- Have the groups go around the *x* in turn. As the children extend their arms to meet in the center, have them take turns naming a word that ends with /ks/. ▶**Bodily/Kinesthetic**

Auditory

STORY MIX

Materials: index cards, markers

GROUP Children will collaborate on an oral story, using words that end with /ks/.

- Create word cards for words that end with /ks/.

- Organize children into small groups. Give each group six cards. Have them mix up their cards.

- Give each group a story starter, such as *Max was mixing batter when . . . ; Ms. Fix-it was in her shop when . . . ; Little Fox was in the woods when . . .*

- Help children read their cards. Challenge the group to tell a story that incorporates all the words on the cards. Encourage all group members to participate. ▶**Interpersonal**

Visual

BOX TOSS

Materials: small box, construction paper, **PARTNERS** scissors, glue

Children will toss a cube to blend sounds to read words that end with /ks/.

- Cover a small box with construction paper. On each side, write words with /ks/, such as *fox, fix, six, mix, ox,* and *wax*.

- Have pairs of children take turns tossing the box. Ask them to blend the sounds to read the word on top of the box. Encourage them to use the word in an oral sentence. ▶**Linguistic**

 **Phonics CD-ROM**

Initial /kw/ *qu*

OBJECTIVES Children will apply letter/sound associations for /kw/ *qu*. They will identify words that begin with /kw/.

Alternate

 Activities

Visual

QUILT BOOK

 Materials: fabric squares, fabric markers, glue, quilt or picture of a quilt

Children will create a quilt square with a picture of an object whose name begins with /kw/.

- Show children a quilt or picture of a quilt. Have them identify it. Explain that *quilt* begins with /kw/ and that the letters *qu* stand for that sound.

- Help children brainstorm other words that begin with /kw/, such as *quiet, queen, quack,* and *quick.*

- Invite children to make a quilt book. Give each child a square of fabric. Have children draw an object whose name begins with /kw/. Label children's drawings.

- Bind children's squares together with glue to create a class book. Label squares children can blend to read, such as *quick* and *quack* with the letters *qu.* ▶**Intrapersonal**

Kinesthetic

QUILT TOSS

 Materials: quilt, quarter

Children will name words that begin with /kw/ as they play a parachute-style game in which they will toss a quarter into the air and catch it with a quilt.

- Show children the quilt. Remind them that the word *quilt* begins with /kw/ and that the letters *qu* stand for that sound.

- Have children hold the edges of a quilt. Show them how to raise it parachute-style. Toss a quarter onto the quilt. Point out that *quarter* begins with /kw/. Show children how to toss and catch the quarter with the quilt.

- Each time the quarter is caught, have a volunteer name a word that begins with /kw/. ▶**Bodily/Kinesthetic**

Auditory

QUIET TIME RHYME

Children will participate in reciting a rhyme. They will identify words that begin with /kw/.

- Share the following rhyme with children:

  "Quick! Quick! Get into bed."

  "Quiet! Quiet!" our mother said.

  "The day is done. It is time to quit."

  "Today you did quite a bit."

- Have children repeat the lines after you. Help them identify words in the rhyme that begin with /kw/. ▶**Linguistic**

 **CD-ROM**

Categories

 **OBJECTIVES** Children will categorize words and objects.

Alternate
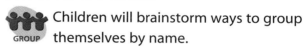

Visual

WHERE DOES IT BELONG?

Materials: construction paper, magazine pictures, scissors, glue, objects to match categories as described below

Children will place objects in a pictorial category.

- Create several category cards by cutting and pasting magazine pictures to a piece of construction paper. For example, you might paste pictures of a knife and a fork, or a ball and a doll.

- For each category card you create, bring in a real object that belongs to the group. For example, for the cards described above, you might bring a spoon or a toy car.

- Invite children to match the objects to the correct cards. ▶**Intrapersonal**

Auditory

NAME THE CATEGORY GAME

One set of partners lists objects in a group. The other set of partners guesses the category.

- Name items in a group, such as *pencils, scissors, crayons, glue*. Have children identify the category to which the items belong. (classroom objects)

- Have pairs of partners play the game. One pair selects a "mystery" category and names objects in the group. The other pair guesses the category. Have pairs switch roles.
  ▶**Logical/Mathematical**

Kinesthetic

GROUPED BY NAME

Children will brainstorm ways to group themselves by name.

- Explain that there are usually many ways to group things together.

- Help children brainstorm ways they can group themselves using their names. For example, you might suggest that they group themselves by the beginning letter of their first name. Challenge children to think of other ways to group themselves according to name. (beginning letter of their last names, boys' names, girls' names, etc.)

- Have children stand in designated areas as they go through several ways to categorize the class by name. ▶**Bodily/Kinesthetic**

Initial *j*

OBJECTIVES Children will apply letter/sound associations for *j*. They will identify words that begin with *j*.

Alternate Activities

Kinesthetic

JUMP ROPE JINGLE

Materials: jump rope

GROUP Children will identify words with *j* in a jump rope jingle. They will supply examples of words that begin with *j* to complete the jingle.

- Share the following jump rope jingle with children:

Jump, Jack! Jump, Jill!

Jump as you go up the hill to fetch a ___.

- Have volunteers turn the rope. Repeat the jingle and have children join in. As children take a turn jumping, have them name something whose name begins with *j* that Jack and Jill could fetch, such as *a jar of jam, a jelly bean,* or *a jug of juice.* ▶**Bodily/Kinesthetic**

Auditory

LITTLE JACK HORNER

Materials: pictures of objects whose names

GROUP begin with *j*, pictures of objects whose names begin with other sounds

Children will participate in reciting a nursery rhyme. They will supply words that begin with *j*.

- Share with children the traditional nursery rhyme "Little Jack Horner." Encourage children to join in.

- Point out that the name *Jack* begins with *j* and that the letter *j* stands for that sound.

- Invite children to create a new version of the rhyme. Tell them that they will replace *plum* with a word that begins with *j*.

- Repeat the rhyme. When it is time to replace *plum,* show two pictures—one that begins with *j,* and one that begins with another sound. Tell children to say the picture name that begins with *j*. ▶**Linguistic**

Visual

WORDS IN A JAR

Materials: plastic jar, word cards

ONE Children will blend sounds to read words that begin with *j*.

- Create word cards with words that begin with *j,* such as *jet, jug, jack, jam,* and *jog.*

- Show children the jar. Explain that *jar* begins with *j* and that the letter *j* stands for that sound.

- Invite children to pull cards from the jar. Ask them to blend the sounds to read the words. Encourage them to use the word in an oral sentence. ▶**Linguistic**

 **CD-ROM**

Initial y

 OBJECTIVES Children will apply letter/sound associations for *y*. They will identify words that begin with *y*.

Alternate

 **Activities**

Visual

YARN NECKLACE

 Materials: yellow yarn, squares of yellow construction paper, hole punch

Children will create a yarn necklace with pictures whose names begin with y.

- Show children the yellow yarn. Point out that *yellow* and *yarn* begin with y and that the letter *y* stands for that sound.

- Help children brainstorm other words that begin with y, such as *yolk, yo-yo, yard, yawn,* and *yes.*

 Give each child three squares of yellow **WRITING** paper. Ask them to draw pictures whose names begin with y. Have children label each picture *y.*

- Punch holes in each child's picture. Help children thread the yarn through the pictures to create a necklace. ▶**Intrapersonal**

Auditory

CHANGE TO Y

Children will change the beginning sound in words they hear to say a word that begins with y.

- Read aloud the following list of words. Have a volunteer repeat the word with one change— make the beginning sound y.

jam	*met*	*lawn*	*folk*
barn	*mellow*	*well*	*hear*

- Invite children to use each y word in an oral sentence. ▶**Musical**

Kinesthetic

YARN WORDS

Materials: yarn, sentence strips, glue

Children will blend sounds to read words that begin with y.

- On sentence strips, use glue and yarn to create words that begin with *y* that children can blend to read. For example, write *yes, yam, yet,* and *yo-yo.*

- Have children touch each letter with their finger and say the letter's sound to blend and read the words. Encourage children to use the word in an oral sentence. ▶**Bodily/Kinesthetic**

 **CD-ROM**

Initial z

OBJECTIVES Children will apply letter/sound associations for z. They will identify words that begin with z.

Alternate Activities

Kinesthetic

ZIGZAG PATH

 Materials: masking tape

GROUP Children will name words that begin with z as they walk along a zigzag path.

- Create a zigzag path on the floor with masking tape.

- Ask children who are wearing zippers to stand up. Point out that *zipper* begins with z and that the letter z stands for that sound.

- Help children brainstorm other words that begin with z.

- Have children take turns walking down the zigzag path. Before children can start on the path, they must supply a word that begins with z. ▶**Bodily/Kinesthetic**

Auditory

RIDDLES

 Children will solve riddles whose answers

PARTNERS begin with z.

- Share the following riddles with children. Tell them that the answers all begin with z.

  I am a place where animals live. (zoo)

  I am a number that stands for nothing. (zero)

  I close up your clothes. (zipper)

- Suggest that partners take turns giving clues and answering riddles. ▶**Logical/Mathematical**

Visual

ZUCCHINI PRINTS

 Materials: zucchini, tempera paint, paper,

ONE marker

Children will stamp the letter z at the beginning of words to blend and read.

- Cut off the top of a zucchini, and carve a z for children to use as a stamp.

- Show children the zucchini, and help them identify it. Point out that *zucchini* begins with z and that the letter z stands for that sound.

- Give each child a paper that has the partial words *_ip, _ap,* and *_igzag* printed on it. Have children stamp z at the beginning to complete the word.

- Ask children to say each letter's sound to blend and read the words. Encourage children to use each word in an oral sentence. ▶**Spatial**

 **CD-ROM**

Writing Readiness

Before children begin to write, fine motor skills need to be developed. Here are examples of activities that can be used:

- **Simon Says** Play Simon Says using just finger positions.
- **Finger Plays and Songs** Sing songs such as "Where Is Thumbkin" or "The Eensie, Weensie, Spider" or songs that use Signed English or American Sign Language.
- **Mazes** Use or create mazes, especially ones that require moving the writing instruments from left to right.

The Mechanics of Writing

POSTURE

- Chair height should allow for the feet to rest flat on the floor.
- Desk height should be two inches above the elbows.
- There should be an inch between the child and the desk.
- Children sit erect with the elbows resting on the desk.
- Letter models should be on the desk or at eye level.

PAPER POSITION

- **Right-handed children** should turn the paper so that the lower left-hand corner of the paper points to the abdomen.
- **Left-handed children** should turn the paper so that the lower right-hand corner of the paper points to the abdomen.
- The nondominant hand should anchor the paper near the top so that the paper doesn't slide.
- The paper should be moved up as the child nears the bottom of the paper. Many children won't think of this.

The Writing Instrument Grasp

For handwriting to be functional, the writing instrument must be held in a way that allows for fluid dynamic movement.

FUNCTIONAL GRASP PATTERNS

- **Tripod Grasp** The writing instrument is held with the tip of the thumb and the index finger and rests against the side of the third finger. The thumb and index finger form a circle.
- **Quadrupod Grasp** The writing instrument is held with the tip of the thumb and index finger and rests against the fourth finger. The thumb and index finger form a circle.

INCORRECT GRASP PATTERNS

- **Fisted Grasp** The writing instrument is held in a fisted hand.
- **Pronated Grasp** The instrument is held diagonally within the hand with the tips of the thumb and index finger but with no support from other fingers.
- **Five-Finger Grasp** The writing instrument is held with the tips of all five fingers.
- **Flexed or Hooked Wrist** Flexed or bent wrist is typically seen with left-handed writers but is also present in some right-handed writers.
- To correct wrist position, have children check their writing posture and paper placement.

TO CORRECT GRASPS

- Have children play counting games with an eye dropper and water.
- Have children pick up small objects with a tweezer.
- Do counting games with children picking up small coins using just the thumb and index finger.

Evaluation Checklist

Formation and Strokes

- ☑ Does the child begin letters at the top?
- ☑ Do circles close?
- ☑ Are the horizontal lines straight?
- ☑ Do circular shapes and extender and descender lines touch?
- ☑ Are the heights of all upper-case letters equal?
- ☑ Are the heights of all lower-case letters equal?
- ☑ Are the lengths of the extenders and descenders the same for all letters?

Directionality

- ☑ Do the children form letters starting at the top and moving to the bottom?
- ☑ Are letters formed from left to right?

Spacing

- ☑ Are the spaces between letters equidistant?
- ☑ Are the spaces between words equidistant?
- ☑ Do the letters rest on the line?
- ☑ Are the top, bottom and side margins on the paper even?

Write the Alphabet

Trace and write the letters.

Trace and write the letters.

C C C

c c c

D D D

d d d

Trace and write the letters.

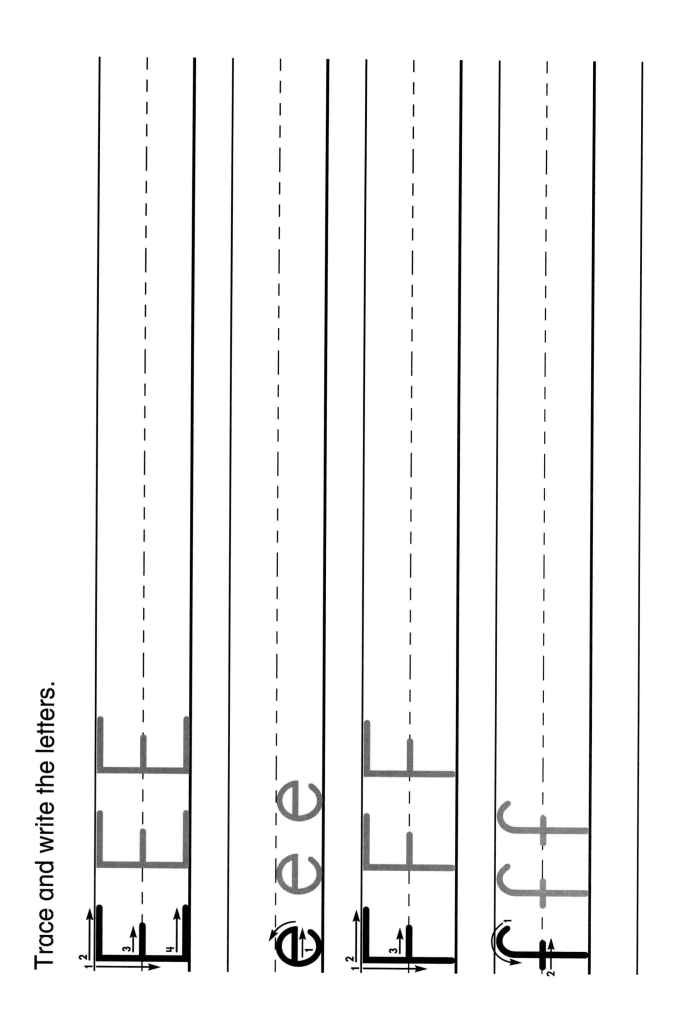

Trace and write the letters.

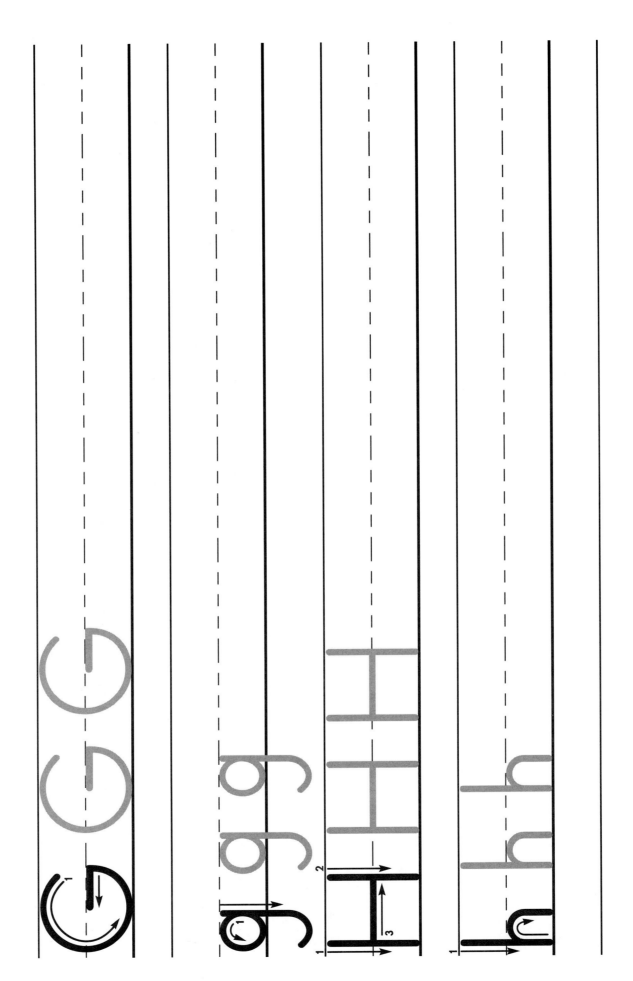

Trace and write the letters.

Trace and write the letters.

Trace and write the letters.

Trace and write the letters.

O O O

o o o

P P P

p p p

Trace and write the letters.

Q Q Q

q q q

R R R

r r r

Trace and write the letters.

Ss Ss Ss

Tt Tt

Trace and write the letters.

U U U

u u u

V V V

v v v

Trace and write the letters.

Trace and write the letters.

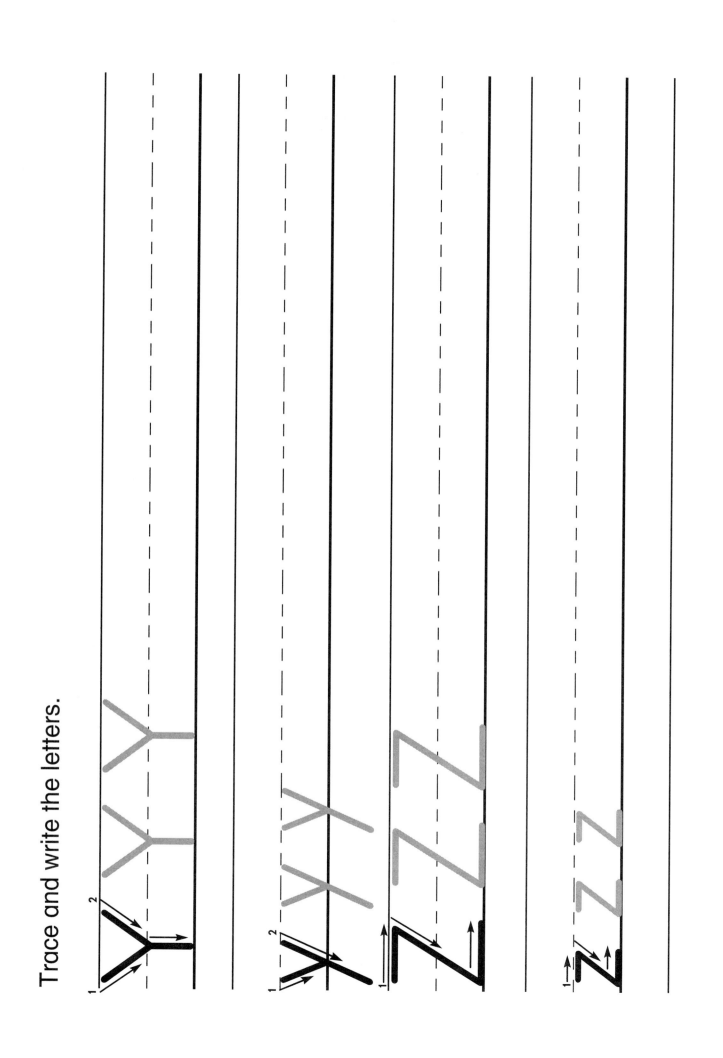

The Earth and I

FRANK ASCH

McGraw Hill

FRANK ASCH

The Earth and I

McGraw-Hill
School Division
New York   Farmington

The Earth and I are friends.

1

Sometimes we go for long walks together.

I tell her what's on my mind.

She listens to every word.

Then I listen to her.

2

3

4

5

6

7

8

9

10

The Earth and I are friends.

11

We play together in my backyard.

12

13

I help her to grow.

14

She helps me to grow.

15

I sing for her.

16

She sings for me.

17

I dance for her.

18

19

She dances for me.

20   21

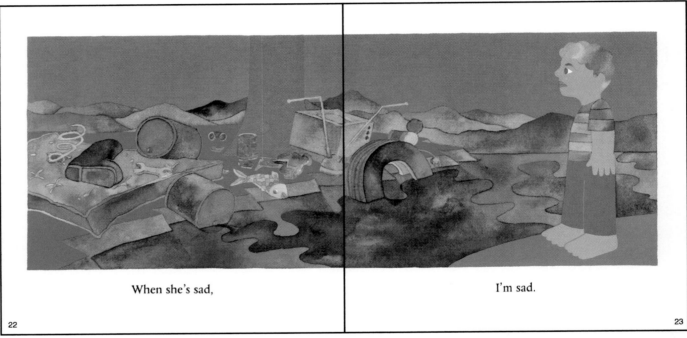

When she's sad,   I'm sad.

22   23

24   25

When she's happy,

I'm happy.

The Earth and I are friends.

One day, White Rabbit found
three big tubs of paint,
red, yellow, and blue.

3

Sunshine yellow,
she thought.
Lovely.

4

A quick dip
and ...

5

... yellow rabbit,
bright as the Sun.

6

Now what about red,
thought Rabbit.

7

What's this?
Orange Rabbit?
Look. Red and yellow
together make
orange!

8

Time for
a wash,
thought
Rabbit.

9

Red on its own this time.

10

Splash!

11

Red Rabbit,
sizzling hot red.

12

How cool blue looks, thought Rabbit.

13

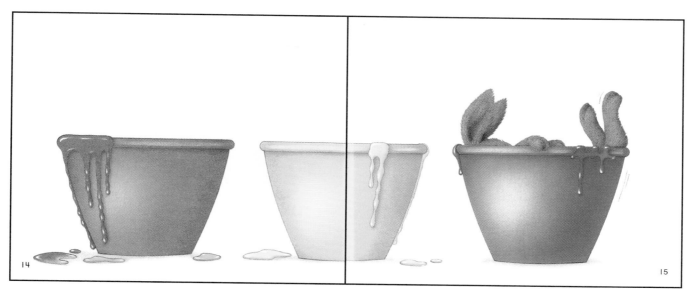

14

15

What's this? Purple Rabbit?
Look. Red and blue
together make purple.
I'm a very important
Royal Purple
Rabbit.

16

Princess
Purple
Rabbit
in the shower.

Blue will do,
thought Rabbit.

17

Blue Rabbit,
icy cold blue.
Brrr.

18

How warm
yellow looks,
thought Rabbit.

19

What's this? Green Rabbit. Look. Blue and yellow together make green!

20

Oh dear, no more water.

21

All that's left is a little red paint.

22

Now what would happen? thought Rabbit.

23

Hooray! Brown Rabbit. Lovely warm brown. Blue, yellow, and red together make brown. And brown's just right for me.

24

THE BIG BOX

An ABC Book

WRITTEN BY JUDY NAYER
ILLUSTRATED BY SUSAN SWAN

McGraw Hill

THE BIG BOX

WRITTEN BY JUDY NAYER
ART BY SUSAN SWAN

AN ABC BOOK

McGraw-Hill School Division
New York   Farmington

1

"What can we do with it?" asked Miya.

3

"We can make an **alphabet** box," said Gina.

4

"We can make a **boat**," said Rob.

5

"We can make a **castle**," said Matt.

6

"We can make a **dinosaur**," said Miya.

7

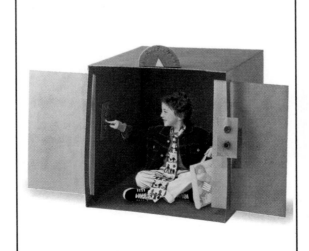

"We can make an **elevator**," said Sam.

8

"We can make a **fire** truck," said Ann.

9

"We can make a **game**," said Rob.

10

"We can make a **house**," said Gina.

11

"We can make an **igloo**," said Matt.

12

"We can make a **jungle**," said Miya.

13

"We can make a **kitchen**," said Rob.

14

"We can make a **lake** and go swimming," said Gina.

15

"We can make a **mailbox**," said Miya.

16

"We can make a **nest**," said Sam.

17

"We can make an **octopus** with 8 arms," said Ann.

18

"We can make a **puppet** stage," said Rob.

19

"We can make a **quilt** for a bed," said Gina.

20

"We can make a **robot**," said Matt.

21

"We can make a **sandbox**,"
said Sam.

22

"We can make a **tunnel** and
crawl through," said Miya.

23

"We can make a giant **umbrella**,"
said Rob.

24

"We can make a **van**,"
said Ann.

25

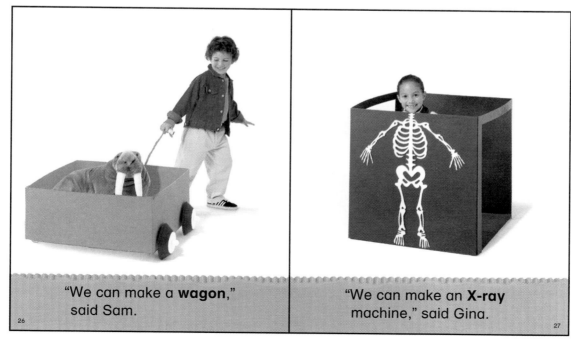

"We can make a **wagon**,"
said Sam.

26

"We can make an **X-ray**
machine," said Gina.

27

"We can paint **yellow** things on the box," said Matt.

28

"We can make a **zebra** with black and white stripes," said Ann.

29

"So what will you make with the box?" asked Mom.

30

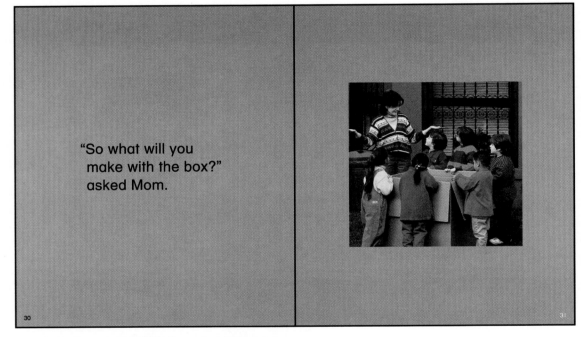

31

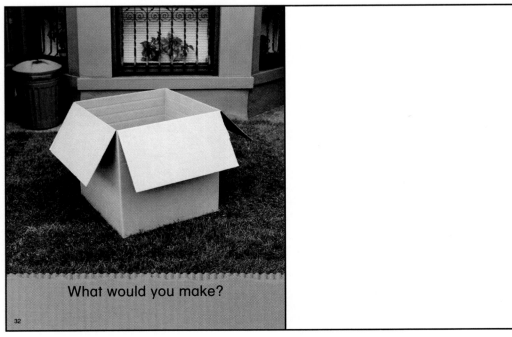

What would you make?

32

Selection Titles	Honors, Prizes, and Awards
SHOW AND TELL DAY by **Anne Rockwell**	**Author/Ilustrator** *Anne Rockwell,* winner of American Booksellers' Award Pick of the List for *Boats* (1985) and *Cars* (1986); National Science Teachers Association Award for Outstanding Science Trade Book for Children (1988) for *Trains*
CHICK AND THE DUCKLING by **Mirra Ginsburg** Illustrated by **Jose Aruego and Ariane Dewey**	**Illustrators: *Jose Aruego and Ariane Dewey,*** winners of Boston Globe-Horn Book Honor (1974) for *Herman the Helper*
FLOWER GARDEN by **Eve Bunting** Illustrated by **Kathryn Hewitt**	**Author: *Eve Bunting,*** winner of ALA Notable Book (1990), IRA-CBC Children's Choice, IRA-Teachers' Choice, School Library Journal Best Book (1989) for *The Wednesday Surprise;* Mark Twain Award (1989) for *Sixth Grade Sleepover;* ALA Notable (1990) for *Wall;* ALA Notable (1992) for *Fly Away Home;* Edgar Allen Poe Juvenile Award (1993) for *Coffin on a Case;* ALA Notable, Caldecott Medal (1995) for *Smoky Night;* Booklist Editors' Choice (1995) for *Spying on Miss Müller;* ALA Notable, Booklist Editors' Choice (1997) for *Train to Somewhere;* National Council for Social Studies Notable Children's Book Award (1998) for *Moonstick,* and *I Am the Mummy Heb-Nefert,* and *On Call Back Mountain;* Young Reader's Choice Award (1997) for *Nasty Stinky Sneakers* **Illustrator: *Kathryn Hewitt,*** winner of Association of Booksellers for Children, Children's Choice Award (1998) for *Lives of the Athletes: Thrills, Spills (And What the Neighbors Thought);* ALA Notable (1994) Boston Globe-Horn Book Honor (1993) for *Lives of the Musicians: Good Times, Bad Times (and What the Neighbors Thought)*
PRETEND YOU'RE A CAT by **Jean Marzolla** Illustrated by **Jerry Pinkney**	**Author: *Jean Marzolla,*** winner of 1998 Association of Booksellers for Children, Children's Choice Award for *I Spy Little Book* **Illustrator: *Jerry Pinkney,*** winner of Coretta Scott King Award, ALA Notable, Christopher Award (1986) for *Patchwork Quilt;* Newbery Medal, Boston Globe-Horn Book Honor (1977) for *Roll of Thunder, Hear My Cry;* Boston Globe-Horn Book Honor (1980) *Childtimes: A Three Generation Memoir;* Coretta Scott King Award (1987) for *Half a Moon and One Whole Star;* ALA Notable (1988) for

Selection Titles	Honors, Prizes, and Awards
PRETEND YOU'RE A CAT (CONTINUED) by *Jean Marzolla* Illustrated by *Jerry Pinkney*	*Tales of Uncle Remus: The Adventures of Brer Rabbit;* ALA Notable, Caldecott Honor, Coretta Scott King Award (1989) for *Mirandy and Brother Wind;* ALA Notable, Caldecott Honor, Coretta Scott King Honor (1990) for *Talking Eggs: A Folktale for the American South;* Golden Kite Award Book (1990) for *Home Place;* ALA Notable (1991) for *Further Tales of Uncle Remus: The Misadventures of Brer Rabbit, Brer Fox . . .;* ALA Notable (1993) for *Back Home;* ALA Notable, Boston Globe-Horn Book Award, Caldecott Honor (1995) for *John Henry;* ALA Notable, Blue Ribbon, Booklist Editors' Choice (1997) for *Sam and the Tigers;* ALA Notable, Christopher Award, Coretta Scott King Award, Golden Kite Honor Book (1997) for *Minty: A Story of Young Harriet Tubman;* Aesop Prize (1997) for *The Hired Hand;* National Council for Social Studies Notable Children's Book Award (1998) for *The Hired Hand* and *Rikki-Tikki-Tavi* (also Children's Choice Award, Association of Booksellers for Children, and Booklist Editors' Choice, 1998); Rip Van Winkle Award (1998); 1998 Hans Christian Andersen nominee
ANY KIND OF DOG by *Lynn Reiser*	**Author/Illustrator:** *Lynn Reiser,* winner of ALA Notable (1995) for *The Surprise Family*
THE EARTH AND I by *Frank Asch*	**Author/Illustrator:** *Frank Asch,* winner of American Book Award Pick of the List Award (1997) for *Barnyard Animals*

Trade Books

Additional fiction and nonfiction trade books related to each selection can be shared with children throughout the unit.

Max
Rachel Isadora (Macmillan, 1976)

Baseball-loving Max finds a new interest when he peeks into his sister's ballet class.

My Grandfather and the Sea
Katherine Orr (Carolrhoda Books, 1998)

When Grandfather is forced from his livelihood as a fisherman due to the depletion of fish, he creates an ecologically sound sea moss farm.

Would You Rather?
John Burningham (Crowell, 1978)

Readers are presented with making choices, such as living with a gerbil in a cage or a rabbit in a hutch.

Amazon Boy
Ted Lewin (Macmillan, 1993)

A Brazilian boy makes his first trip up the Amazon River and learns of the river's many treasures.

Dinosaurs to the Rescue
Laurie Krasny Brown and Marc Brown (Joy Street Books, 1992)

Dinosaur characters introduce Earth's environmental problems and ways to solve them.

My First Green Book
Angela Wilkes (Knopf, 1991)

Young readers are presented with environmental activities on water pollution, recycling, and wildlife gardening.

Technology

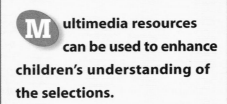

Multimedia resources can be used to enhance children's understanding of the selections.

 I Can Do It! (Coronet/MTI) Video, 10 min. A young girl is determined to try something new, no matter what it takes.

 Swiss Family Robinson (Troll) CD-ROM, Macintosh and Windows. Using animation and sound, children participate in the Swiss Family Robinson's adventures and help the family solve the problems they face daily.

 The Ant and the Grasshopper (BFA Educational Media) Video, 10 min. The grasshoppers enjoy themselves all through the summer as they watch the ant prepare for winter. Then they learn a lesson from the choices they have made.

 Kids and the Environment (Tom Snyder Productions) CD-ROM, Macintosh and Windows. The school playing field is littered with trash, and children must weigh cleaning it up or ignoring it. The program addresses environmental concerns and how choices affect the world around us.

Hunches in Bunches
Dr. Seuss (Random House, 1982)

A boy has a hard time making decisions even though a bunch of hunches help him.

The Salamander Room
Anne Mazer, illustrated by Steve Johnson (Knopf, 1991)

A young boy finds a salamander and thinks of the many things he can do to make a perfect home for it.

The Giant Jam Sandwich
John Vernon Lord, with verses by Janet Burroway (Houghton Mifflin, 1972)

This tall tale told in rhyme describes how a town, plagued by an invasion of wasps, comes up with a solution to the problem.

On the Playground (Tom Snyder Productions) CD-ROM, Macintosh and Windows. In this interactive program, children make choices about how they will play together and how they will treat the new kid at school.

Taking Responsibility (Tom Snyder Productions) CD-ROM, Macintosh and Windows. The issues of honesty and responsibility are addressed in this interactive program, where children must decide what to do when they see someone break the rules.

Publishers Directory

Abdo & Daughters
4940 Viking Drive, Suite 622
Edina, MN 55435
(800) 458-8399 • www.abdopub.com

Aladdin Paperbacks
(Imprint of Simon & Schuster Children's
Publishing)

Atheneum
(Imprint of Simon & Schuster Children's
Publishing)

**Bantam Doubleday Dell Books for
Young Readers**
(Imprint of Random House)

Blackbirch Press
1 Bradley Road, Suite 205
Woodbridge, CT 06525
(203) 387-7525 • (800) 831-9183

Blue Sky Press
(Imprint of Scholastic)

Boyds Mills Press
815 Church Street
Honesdale, PA 18431
(570) 253-1164 • Fax (570) 251-0179 •
(800) 949-7777

Bradbury Press
(Imprint of Simon & Schuster Children's
Publishing)

BridgeWater Books
(Distributed by Penguin Putnam)

Candlewick Press
2067 Masssachusetts Avenue
Cambridge, MA 02140
(617) 661-3330 • Fax (617) 661-0565

Carolrhoda Books
(Division of Lerner Publications Co.)

Charles Scribners's Sons
(Imprint of Simon & Schuster Children's
Publishing)

Children's Press (Division of Grolier, Inc.)
P.O. Box 1796
Danbury, CT 06813-1333
(800) 621-1115 • www.grolier.com

Child's World
P.O. Box 326
Chanhassen, MN 55317-0326
(612) 906-3939 • (800) 599-READ •
www.childsworld.com

Chronicle Books
85 Second Street, Sixth Floor
San Francisco, CA 94105
(415) 537-3730 • (415) 537-4460 • (800)
722-6657 • www.chroniclebooks.com

Clarion Books
(Imprint of Houghton Mifflin, Inc.)
215 Park Avenue South
New York, NY 10003
(212) 420-5800 • (800) 726-0600 •
www.hmco.com/trade/childrens/
shelves.html

Crowell (Imprint of HarperCollins)

Crown Publishing Group
(Imprint of Random House)

Dial Books
(Imprint of Penguin Putnam Inc.)

Dorling Kindersley (DK Publishing)
95 Madison Avenue
New York, NY 10016
(212) 213-4800 • Fax (800) 774-6733 •
(888) 342-5357 • www.dk.com

Doubleday (Imprint of Random House)

E. P. Dutton Children's Books
(Imprint of Penguin Putnam Inc.)

Farrar Straus & Giroux
19 Union Square West
New York, NY 10003
(212) 741-6900 • Fax (212) 633-2427 •
(888) 330-8477

Four Winds Press
(Imprint of Macmillan, see Simon &
Schuster Children's Publishing)

Greenwillow Books
(Imprint of William Morrow & Co, Inc.)

Grosset & Dunlap
(Imprint of Penguin Putnam, Inc.)

Harcourt Brace & Co.
525 "B" Street
San Diego, CA 92101
(619) 231-6616 • (800) 543-1918 •
www.harcourtbooks.com

Harper & Row (Imprint of HarperCollins)

HarperCollins Children's Books
10 East 53rd Street
New York, NY 10022
(212) 207-7000 • Fax (212) 202-7044 •
(800) 242-7737 •
www.harperchildrens.com

Henry Holt and Company
115 West 18th Street
New York, NY 10011
(212) 886-9200 • (212) 633-0748 • (888)
330-8477 • www.henryholt.com/byr/

Holiday House
425 Madison Avenue
New York, NY 10017
(212) 688-0085 • Fax (212) 421-6134

Houghton Mifflin
222 Berkeley Street
Boston, MA 02116
(617) 351-5000 • Fax (617) 351-1125 •
(800) 225-3362 • www.hmco.com/trade

Hyperion Books
(Imprint of Buena Vista Publishing Co.)
114 Fifth Avenue
New York, NY 10011
(212) 633-4400 • (800) 759-0190 •
www.disney.com

Ideals Children's Books
(Imprint of Hambleton-Hill Publishing, Inc.)
1501 County Hospital Road
Nashville, TN 37218
(615) 254-2480 • (800) 336-6438

Joy Street Books
(Imprint of Little, Brown & Co.)

Just Us Books
356 Glenwood Avenue
E. Orange, NJ 07017
(973) 672-0304 • Fax (973) 677-7570

Alfred A. Knopf
(Imprint of Random House)

Lee & Low Books
95 Madison Avenue
New York, NY 10016
(212) 779-4400 • Fax (212) 683-1894

Lerner Publications Co.
241 First Avenue North
Minneapolis, MN 55401
(612) 332-3344 • Fax (612) 332-7615 •
(800) 328-4929 • www.lernerbooks.com

Little, Brown & Co.
3 Center Plaza
Boston, MA 02108
(617) 227-0730 • Fax (617) 263-2864 •
(800) 343-9204 • www.littlebrown.com

Lothrop Lee & Shepard
(Imprint of William Morrow & Co.)

Macmillan
(Imprint of Simon & Schuster
Children's Publishing)

Marshall Cavendish
99 White Plains Road
Tarrytown, NY 10591
(914) 332-8888 • Fax (914) 332-1082 •
(800) 821-9881 •
www.marshallcavendish.com

William Morrow & Co.
1350 Avenue of the Americas
New York, NY 10019
(212) 261-6500 • Fax (212) 261-6619 •
(800) 843-9389 •
www.williammorrow.com

Morrow Junior Books
(Imprint of William Morrow & Co.)

Mulberry Books
(Imprint of William Morrow & Co.)

National Geographic Society
1145 17th Street, NW
Washington, DC 20036
(202) 828-5667 • (800) 368-2728 •
www.nationalgeographic.com

Northland Publishing
(Division of Justin Industries)
P.O. Box 62
Flagstaff, AZ 86002
(520) 774-5251 • Fax (800) 257-9082 •
(800) 346-3257 • www.northlandpub.com

North-South Books
1123 Broadway, Suite 800
New York, NY 10010
(212) 463-9736 • Fax (212) 633-1004 •
(800) 722-6657 • www.northsouth.com

Orchard Books (A Grolier Company)
95 Madison Avenue
New York, NY 10016
(212) 951-2600 • Fax (212) 213-6435 •
(800) 621-1115 • www.grolier.com

Owlet (Imprint of Henry Holt & Co.)

Willa Perlman Books
(Imprint of Simon & Schuster
Children's Publishing)

Philomel Books
(Imprint of Putnam Penguin, Inc.)

Puffin Books
(Imprint of Penguin Putnam, Inc.)

G.P. Putnam's Sons Publishing
(Imprint of Penguin Putnam, Inc.)

Penguin Putnam, Inc.
345 Hudson Street
New York, NY 10014
(212) 366-2000 • Fax (212) 366-2666 •
(800) 631-8571 •
www.penguinputnam.com

Random House
201 East 50th Street
New York, NY 10022
(212) 751-2600 • Fax (212) 572-2593 •
(800) 726-0600 • www.randomhouse/kids

Rourke Corporation
P.O. Box 3328
Vero Beach, FL 32964
(561) 234-6001 • (800) 394-7055 •
www.rourkepublishing.com

Scholastic
555 Broadway
New York, NY 10012
(212) 343-6100 • Fax (212) 343-6930 •
(800) SCHOLASTIC • www.scholastic.com

Sierra Junior Club
85 Second Street, Second Floor
San Francisco, CA 94105-3441
(415) 977-5500 • Fax (415) 977-5799 •
(800) 935-1056 • www.sierraclub.org

Simon & Schuster Children's Books
1230 Avenue of the Americas
New York, NY 10020
(212) 698-7200 • (800) 223-2336 •
www.simonsays.com/kidzone

Smith & Kraus
4 Lower Mill Road
N. Stratford, NH 03590
(603) 643-6431 • Fax (603) 643-1831 •
(800) 895-4331 • www.smithkraus.com

Teacher Ideas Press
(Division of Libraries Unlimited)
P.O. Box 6633
Englewood, CO 80155-6633
(303) 770-1220 • Fax (303) 220-8843 •
(800) 237-6124 • www.lu.com

Ticknor & Fields
(Imprint of Houghton Mifflin, Inc.)

Usborne (Imprint of EDC Publishing)
10302 E. 55th Place, Suite B
Tulsa, OK 74146-6515
(918) 622-4522 • (800) 475-4522 •
www.edcpub.com

Viking Children's Books
(Imprint of Penguin Putnam Inc.)

Watts Publishing
(Imprint of Grolier Publishing;
see Children's Press)

Walker & Co.
435 Hudson Street
New York, NY 10014
(212) 727-8300 • (212) 727-0984 • (800)
AT-WALKER

Whispering Coyote Press
300 Crescent Court, Suite 860
Dallas, TX 75201
(800) 929-6104 • Fax (214) 319-7298

Albert Whitman
6340 Oakton Street
Morton Grove, IL 60053-2723
(847) 581-0033 • Fax (847) 581-0039 •
(800) 255-7675 • www.awhitmanco.com

Workman Publishing Co., Inc.
708 Broadway
New York, NY 10003
(212) 254-5900 • Fax (800) 521-1832 •
(800) 722-7202 • www.workman.com

Multimedia Resources

AGC/United Learning
6633 West Howard Street
Niles, IL 60714-3389
(800) 424-0362 • www.unitedlearning.com

AIMS Multimedia
9710 DeSoto Avenue
Chatsworth, CA 91311-4409
(800) 367-2467 •
www.AIMS-multimedia.com

BFA Educational Media
(see Phoenix Learning Group)

Broderbund
(Parsons Technology;
also see The Learning Company)
500 Redwood Blvd
Novato, CA 94997
(800) 521-6263 • Fax (800) 474-8840 •
www.broderbund.com

Carousel Film and Video
260 Fifth Avenue, Suite 705
New York, NY 10001
(212) 683-1660 • e-mail:
carousel@pipeline.com

Cloud 9 Interactive
(888) 662-5683 • www.cloud9int.com

Computer Plus (see ESI)

Coronet/MTI
(see Phoenix Learning Group)

Davidson (see Knowledge Adventure)

Direct Cinema, Ltd.
P.O. Box 10003
Santa Monica, CA 90410-1003
(800) 525-0000

Disney Interactive
(800) 900-9234 •
www.disneyinteractive.com

DK Multimedia (Dorling Kindersley)
95 Madison Avenue
New York, NY 10016
(212) 213-4800 • Fax: (800) 774-6733 •
(888) 342-5357 • www.dk.com

Edmark Corp.
P.O. Box 97021
Redmond, CA 98073-9721
(800) 362-2890 • www.edmark.com

Encyclopaedia Britannica Educational Corp.
310 South Michigan Avenue
Chicago, IL 60604
(800) 554-9862 • www.eb.com

ESI/Educational Software
4213 S. 94th Street
Omaha, NE 68127
(800) 955-5570 • www.edsoft.com

GPN/Reading Rainbow
University of Nebraska-Lincoln
P.O. Box 80669
Lincoln, NE 68501-0669
(800) 228-4630 • www.gpn.unl.edu

Hasbro Interactive
(800) 683-5847 • www.hasbro.com

Humongous
13110 NE 177th Pl., Suite B101, Box 180
Woodenville, WA 98072
(800) 499-8386 • www.humongous.com

IBM Corp.
1133 Westchester Ave.
White Plains, NY 10604
(770) 863-1234 • Fax (770) 863-3030 •
(888) 411-1932 •
www.pc.ibm.com/multimedia/crayola

ICE, Inc.
(Distributed by Arch Publishing)
12B W. Main St.
Elmsford, NY 10523
(914) 347-2464 • (800) 843-9497 •
www.educorp.com

Knowledge Adventure
19840 Pioneer Avenue
Torrence, CA 90503
(800) 542-4240 • (800) 545-7677 •
www.knowledgeadventure.com

The Learning Company
6160 Summit Drive North
Minneapolis, MN 55430
(800) 685-6322 • www.learningco.com

Listening Library
One Park Avenue
Greenwich, CT 06870-1727
(800) 243-4504 • www.listeninglib.com

Macmillan/McGraw-Hill
(see SRA/McGraw-Hill)

Maxis
2121 N. California Blvd
Walnut Creek, CA 94596-3572
(925) 933-5630 • Fax (925) 927-3736 •
(800) 245-4525 • www.maxis.com

MECC
(see the Learning Company)

Microsoft
One Microsoft Way
Redmond, WA 98052-6399
(800) 426-9400 • www.microsoft.com/kids

National Geographic Society Educational Services
P.O. Box 10597
Des Moines, IA 50340-0597
(800) 368-2728 •
www.nationalgeographic.com

National School Products
101 East Broadway
Maryville, TN 37804
(800) 251-9124 • www.ierc.com

PBS Video
1320 Braddock Place
Alexandria, VA 22314
(800) 344-3337 • www.pbs.org

Phoenix Films
(see Phoenix Learning Group)

The Phoenix Learning Group
2348 Chaffee Drive
St. Louis, MO 63146
(800) 221-1274 • e-mail:
phoenixfilms@worldnet.att.net

Pied Piper (see AIMS Multimedia)

Scholastic New Media
555 Broadway
New York, NY 10003
(800) 724-6527 • www.scholastic.com

Simon & Schuster Interactive
(see Knowledge Adventure)

SRA/McGraw-Hill
220 Daniel Dale Road
De Soto, TX 75115
(800) 843-8855 • www.sra4kids.com

SVE/Churchill Media
6677 North Northwest Highway
Chicago, IL 60631
(800) 829-1900 •www.svemedia.com

Tom Snyder Productions (also see ESI)
80 Coolidge Hill Rd.
Watertown, MA 02472
(800) 342-0236 • www.teachtsp.com

Troll Associates
100 Corporate Drive
Mahwah, NJ 07430
(800) 929-8765 • Fax (800) 979-8765 •
www.troll.com

Voyager (see ESI)

Weston Woods
12 Oakwood Avenue
Norwalk, CT 06850
(800) 243-5020 • Fax (203) 845-0498

Zenger Media
10200 Jefferson Blvd., Room 94,
P.O. Box 802
Culver City, CA 90232-0802
(800) 421-4246 • (800) 944-5432 •
www.Zengermedia.com

UNIT 1
Decodable Words

Vocabulary

	Decodable Words				Vocabulary
THE HOUSE					**High-Frequency Words** the
A PRESENT					**High-Frequency Words** a
MY SCHOOL					**High-Frequency Words** my
NAN	an	**Nan**			**High-Frequency Words** that
THAT NAN!	Review				**High-Frequency Words** Review

UNIT 2

	Decodable Words				Vocabulary
DAN AND DAD	**Dad**	**Dan**			**High-Frequency Words** and
DAD, DAN, AND I	sad				**High-Frequency Words** I
I AM SAM!	**am** dam	mad	man	**Sam**	**High-Frequency Words** is
SID SAID	did dim	in	**Min**	**Sid**	**High-Frequency Words** said
IS SAM MAD?	Review				**High-Frequency Words** Review

Boldfaced words appear in the selection.

UNIT 3

	Decodable Words				Vocabulary
THAT TAM!					**High-Frequency Words**
	at	Nat	**Tam**	**Tim**	we
	it	**sat**	tan	tin	
	mat	**sit**			
NAT IS MY CAT					**High-Frequency Words**
	can	**cat**			are
ON THE DOT					**High-Frequency Words**
	cot	**dot**	**not**	**Tom**	you
	Dom	**Mom**	**on**	tot	
	Don				
WE FIT!					**High-Frequency Words**
	fan	fat	fin	**fit**	have
THE TAN CAT					**High-Frequency Words**
	Review				Review

UNIT 4

	Decodable Words				Vocabulary
YOU ARE IT!					**High-Frequency Words**
	ran	rod	**Ron**	rot	to
	rat				
TAP THE SAP					**High-Frequency Words**
	cap	pad	pod	**sip**	me
	dip	**Pam**	**pot**	tap	
	map	**pan**	rip	tip	
	mop	pat	**sap**	**top**	
	nap				
NAP IN A LAP					**High-Frequency Words**
	lad	lid	lit	lot	go
	lap	lip			
MUD FUN					**High-Frequency Words**
	cup	**mud**	run	sun	do
	cut	nut	rut	up	
	fun	pup			
FUN IN THE SUN					**High-Frequency Words**
	Review				Review

UNIT 5

	Decodable Words				Vocabulary
TOM IS SICK					**High-Frequency Words**
	dock	lock	**pick**	**sock**	**for**
	duck	luck	rack	tack	
	kid	Mack	rock	tick	
	Kim	Mick	sack	tock	
	kit	muck	**sick**	tuck	
	lick	pack			
PUG					**High-Frequency Words**
	dug	gum	**Pug**	tag	**he**
	fog	log	rag	tug	
	got	**mug**	rug		
A PET FOR KEN					**High-Frequency Words**
	den	leg	Ned	**red**	**she**
	fed	**let**	net	set	
	get	Meg	pen	Ted	
	Ken	men	**pet**	ten	
	led	met			
A BIG BUG					**High-Frequency Words**
	bad	bet	bog	cub	**has**
	bag	**big**	bud	Rob	
	bat	bin	**bug**	rub	
	bed	bit	but	tub	
	Ben				
A PUP AND A CAT					**High-Frequency Words**
	Review				Review

UNIT 6

	Decodable Words				Vocabulary
HOP WITH A HOG	had ham **hat** hen	him hip **hit**	**hog** **hop** hot	**hug** **hum** hut	**High-Frequency Words** **with**
WE WIN!	wag web	wed wet	wig	**win**	**High-Frequency Words** **was**
THE VET VAN	ax box **fix**	fox **Max** mix	ox **Rex** six	**van** **vet** wax	**High-Frequency Words** **not**
JEN AND YIP	jam Jan **Jen** jet jig Jim	job **jog** jot jug **quack** **quick**	quit yam yet **Yip** yuck	yum Zack Zeb **zigzag** zip	**High-Frequency Words** **of**
ZACK AND JAN	Review				**High-Frequency Words** Review

Listening, Speaking, Viewing, Representing

☑ Tested Skill

Tinted panels show skills, strategies, and other teaching opportunities

LISTENING

	K	1	2	3	4	5	6
Learn the vocabulary of school (numbers, shapes, colors, directions, and categories)							
Identify the musical elements of literary language, such as rhymes, repeated sounds, onomatopoeia							
Determine purposes for listening (get information, solve problems, enjoy and appreciate)							
Listen critically and responsively							
Ask and answer relevant questions							
Listen critically to interpret and evaluate							
Listen responsively to stories and other texts read aloud, including selections from classic and contemporary works							
Connect own experiences, ideas, and traditions with those of others							
Apply comprehension strategies in listening activities							
Understand the major ideas and supporting evidence in spoken messages							
Participate in listening activities related to reading and writing (such as discussions, group activities, conferences)							
Listen to learn by taking notes, organizing, and summarizing spoken ideas							

SPEAKING

	K	1	2	3	4	5	6
Learn the vocabulary of school (numbers, shapes, colors, directions, and categories)							
Use appropriate language and vocabulary learned to describe ideas, feelings, and experiences							
Ask and answer relevant questions							
Communicate effectively in everyday situations (such as discussions, group activities, conferences)							
Demonstrate speaking skills (audience, purpose, occasion, volume, pitch, tone, rate, fluency)							
Clarify and support spoken messages and ideas with objects, charts, evidence, elaboration, examples							
Use verbal and nonverbal communication in effective ways when, for example, making announcements, giving directions, or making introductions							
Retell a spoken message by summarizing or clarifying							
Connect own experiences, ideas, and traditions with those of others							
Determine purposes for speaking (inform, entertain, give directions, persuade, express personal feelings and opinions)							
Demonstrate skills of reporting and providing information							
Demonstrate skills of interviewing, requesting and providing information							
Apply composition strategies in speaking activities							
Monitor own understanding of spoken message and seek clarification as needed							

VIEWING

	K	1	2	3	4	5	6
Demonstrate viewing skills (focus attention, organize information)							
Respond to audiovisual media in a variety of ways							
Participate in viewing activities related to reading and writing							
Apply comprehension strategies in viewing activities							
Recognize artists' craft and techniques for conveying meaning							
Interpret information from various formats such as maps, charts, graphics, video segments, technology							
Evaluate purposes of various media (information, appreciation, entertainment, directions, persuasion)							
Use media to compare ideas and points of view							

REPRESENTING

	K	1	2	3	4	5	6
Select, organize, or produce visuals to complement or extend meanings							
Produce communication using appropriate media to develop a class paper, multimedia or video reports							
Show how language, medium, and presentation contribute to the message							

Reading: Alphabetic Principle, Sounds/Symbols

☑ Tested Skill

Tinted panels show skills, strategies, and other teaching opportunities

PRINT AWARENESS

	K	1	2	3	4	5	6
Know the order of the alphabet							
Recognize that print represents spoken language and conveys meaning							
Understand directionality (tracking print from left to right; return sweep)							
Understand that written words are separated by spaces							
Know the difference between individual letters and printed words							
Understand that spoken words are represented in written language by specific sequence of letters							
Recognize that there are correct spellings for words							
Know the difference between capital and lowercase letters							
Recognize how readers use capitalization and punctuation to comprehend							
Recognize the distinguishing features of a paragraph							
Recognize that parts of a book (such as cover/title page and table of contents) offer information							

PHONOLOGICAL AWARENESS

	K	1	2	3	4	5	6
Identify letters, words, sentences							
Divide spoken sentence into individual words							
Produce rhyming words and distinguish rhyming words from nonrhyming words							
Identify, segment, and combine syllables within spoken words							
Identify and isolate the initial and final sound of a spoken word							
Add, delete, or change sounds to change words (such as *cow* to *how*, *pan* to *fan*)							
Blend sounds to make spoken words							
Segment one-syllable spoken words into individual phonemes							

PHONICS AND DECODING

	K	1	2	3	4	5	6
Alphabetic principle: Letter/sound correspondence	☑	☑	☑				
Blending CVC words	☑						
Segmenting CVC words	☑						
Blending CVC, CVCe, CCVC, CVCC, CVVC words	☑	☑	☑				
Segmenting CVC, CVCe, CCVC, CVCC, CVVC words	☑	☑	☑				
Initial and final consonants: /n/n, /d/d, /s/s, /m/m, /t/t, /k/c, /f/f, /r/r, /p/p, /l/l, /k/k, /g/g, /b/b, /h/h, /w/w, /v/v, /ks/x, /kw/qu, /j/j, /y/y, /z/z	☑	☑					
Initial and medial short vowels: *a, i, u, o, e*	☑	☑	☑				
Long vowels: *a-e, i-e, o-e, u-e* (vowel-consonant-e)		☑	☑				
Long vowels, including *ay, ai; e, ee, ie, ea, o, oa, oe, ow; i, y, igh*		☑	☑				
Consonant Digraphs: *sh, th, ch, wh*		☑					
Consonant Blends: continuant/continuant, including *sl, sm, sn, fl, fr, ll, ss, ff*		☑					
Consonant Blends: continuant/stop, including *st, sk, sp, ng, nt, nd, mp, ft*		☑					
Consonant Blends: stop/continuant, including *tr, pr, pl, cr, tw*		☑					
Variant vowels: including /u/oo; /ô/a, aw, au; /ü/ue, ew		☑	☑				
Diphthongs, including /ou/ou, ow; /oi/oi, oy		☑	☑				
r-controlled vowels, including /âr/are; /ôr/or, ore; /îr/ear			☑				
Soft *c* and soft *g*			☑				
nk		☑	☑				
Consonant Digraphs: *ck*	☑	☑					
Consonant Digraphs: *ph, tch, ch*			☑				
Short *e: ea*			☑				
Long *e: y, ey*			☑				
/ü/oo		☑	☑				
/är/ar; /ûr/ir, ur, er		☑	☑				
Silent letters: including *l, b, k, w, g, h, gh*			☑				
Schwa: /ər/er; /ən/en; /əl/le;			☑				
Reading/identifying multisyllabic words		☑	☑				

Reading: Vocabulary/Word Identification

WORD STRUCTURE	K	1	2	3	4	5	6
Common spelling patterns							
Syllable patterns							
Plurals							
Possessives							
Contractions							
Root, or base, words and inflectional endings (-s, -es, -ed, -ing)							
Compound Words							
Prefixes and suffixes (such as un-, re-, dis-, non-; -ly, -y, -ful, -able, -tion)							
Root words and derivational endings							

WORD MEANING	K	1	2	3	4	5	6
Develop vocabulary through concrete experiences							
Develop vocabulary through selections read aloud							
Develop vocabulary through reading							
Cueing systems: syntactic, semantic, phonetic							
Context clues, including semantic clues (word meaning), syntactical clues (word order), and phonetic clues	☑	☑	☑	☑	☑	☑	☑
High-frequency words (such as the, a, an, and, said, was, where, is)							
Identify words that name persons, places, things, and actions							
Automatic reading of regular and irregular words							
Use resources and references dictionary, glossary, thesaurus, synonym finder, technology and software, and context)							
Synonyms and antonyms							
Multiple-meaning words							
Figurative language							
Decode derivatives (root words, such as like, pay, happy with affixes, such as dis-, pre-, -un)							
Systematic study of words across content areas and in current events							
Locate meanings, pronunciations, and derivations (including dictionaries, glossaries, and other sources)							
Denotation and connotation							
Word origins as aid to understanding historical influences on English word meanings							
Homophones, homographs							
Analogies							
Idioms							

Reading: Comprehension

PREREADING STRATEGIES	K	1	2	3	4	5	6
Preview and Predict							
Use prior knowledge							
Establish and adjust purposes for reading							
Build background							

MONITORING STRATEGIES	K	1	2	3	4	5	6
Adjust reading rate							
Reread, search for clues, ask questions, ask for help							
Visualize							
Read a portion aloud, use reference aids							
Use decoding and vocabulary strategies							
Paraphrase							
Create story maps, diagrams, charts, story props to help comprehend, analyze, synthesize and evaluate texts							

(continued on next page

☑ Tested Skill

Tinted panels show skills, strategies, and other teaching opportunities

SKILLS AND STRATEGIES	K	1	2	3	4	5	6
Story details	☑						
Use illustrations	☑	☑					
Reality and fantasy	☑	☑	☑	☑			
Classify and categorize	☑						
Make predictions	☑	☑	☑	☑	☑	☑	☑
Sequence of events (tell or act out)	☑	☑	☑	☑	☑	☑	☑
Cause and effect			☑	☑	☑	☑	☑
Compare and contrast	☑	☑	☑	☑	☑	☑	☑
Summarize	☑	☑	☑	☑	☑	☑	☑
Make and explain inferences			☑	☑	☑	☑	☑
Draw conclusions			☑	☑	☑	☑	☑
Important and unimportant information				☑	☑	☑	☑
Main idea and supporting details					☑	☑	☑
Form conclusions or generalizations and support with evidence from text	☑	☑	☑	☑	☑	☑	☑
Fact and opinion (including news stories and advertisements)			☑	☑	☑	☑	☑
Problem and solution				☑	☑	☑	☑
Steps in a process				☑	☑	☑	☑
Make judgments and decisions		☑	☑	☑	☑	☑	☑
Fact and nonfact					☑	☑	☑
Recognize techniques of persuasion and propaganda					☑	☑	☑
Evaluate evidence and sources of information					☑	☑	☑
Identify similarities and differences across texts (including topics, characters, problems, themes, treatment, scope, or organization)							
Practice various questions and tasks (test-like comprehension questions)							
Paraphrase and summarize to recall, inform, and organize							
Answer various types of questions (open-ended, literal, interpretative, test-like such as true-false, multiple choice, short-answer)							
Use study strategies to learn and recall (preview, question, reread, and record)							

LITERARY RESPONSE	K	1	2	3	4	5	6
Listen to stories being read aloud							
React, speculate, join in, read along when predictable and patterned selections are read aloud							
Respond through talk, movement, music, art, drama, and writing to a variety of stories and poems							
Show understanding through writing, illustrating, developing demonstrations, and using technology							
Connect ideas and themes across texts							
Support responses by referring to relevant aspects of text and own experiences							
Offer observations, make connections, speculate, interpret, and raise questions in response to texts							
Interpret text ideas through journal writing, discussion, enactment, and media							

TEXT STRUCTURE/LITERARY CONCEPTS	K	1	2	3	4	5	6
Distinguish forms of texts and the functions they serve (lists, newsletters, signs)							
Understand story structure							
Identify narrative (for entertainment) and expository (for information)							
Distinguish fiction from nonfiction, including fact and fantasy							
Understand literary forms (stories, poems, plays, and informational books)							
Understand literary terms by distinguishing between roles of author and illustrator							
Understand title, author, and illustrator across a variety of texts							
Analyze character, character's point of view, plot, setting, style, tone, mood		☑	☑	☑	☑	☑	☑
Compare communication in different forms							
Understand terms such as title, author, illustrator, playwright, theater, stage, act, dialogue, and scene							
Recognize stories, poems, myths, folktales, fables, tall tales, limericks, plays, biographies, and autobiographies							
Judge internal logic of story text							
Recognize that authors organize information in specific ways							
Identify texts to inform, influence, express, or entertain							
Describe how author's point of view affects text							
Recognize biography, historical fiction, realistic fiction, modern fantasy, informational texts, and poetry							
Analyze ways authors present ideas (cause/effect, compare/contrast, inductively, deductively, chronologically)							
Recognize flashback, foreshadowing, symbolism							

(continued on next page)

(Reading: Comprehension continued)

	K	1	2	3	4	5	6
VARIETY OF TEXT							
Read a variety of genres							
Use informational texts to acquire information							
Read for a variety of purposes							
Select varied sources when reading for information or pleasure							
FLUENCY							
Read regularly in independent-level and instructional-level materials							
Read orally with fluency from familiar texts							
Self-select independent-level reading							
Read silently for increasing periods of time							
Demonstrate characteristics of fluent and effective reading							
Adjust reading rate to purpose							
Read aloud in selected texts, showing understanding of text and engaging the listener							
CULTURES							
Connect own experience with culture of others							
Compare experiences of characters across cultures							
Articulate and discuss themes and connections that cross cultures							
CRITICAL THINKING							
Experiences (comprehend, apply, analyze, synthesize, evaluate)							
Make connections (comprehend, apply, analyze, synthesize, evaluate)							
Expression (comprehend, apply, analyze, synthesize, evaluate)							
Inquiry (comprehend, apply, analyze, synthesize, evaluate)							
Problem solving (comprehend, apply, analyze, synthesize, evaluate)							
Making decisions (comprehend, apply, analyze, synthesize, evaluate)							

Study Skills

	K	1	2	3	4	5	6
INQUIRY/RESEARCH							
Follow directions							
Use alphabetical order							
Identify/frame questions for research							
Obtain, organize, and summarize information: classify, take notes, outline							
Evaluate research and raise new questions							
Use technology to present information in various formats							
Follow accepted formats for writing research, including documenting sources							
Use test-taking strategies							
Use text organizers (book cover; title page—title, author, illustrator; contents; headings; glossary; index)		☑	☑	☑	☑	☑	☑
Use graphic aids, including maps, diagrams, charts, graphs		☑	☑	☑	☑	☑	☑
Read and interpret varied texts including environmental print, signs, lists, encyclopedia, dictionary, glossary, newspaper, advertisement, magazine, calendar, directions, floor plans		☑	☑	☑	☑	☑	☑
Use reference sources, such as glossary, dictionary, encyclopedia, telephone directory, technology resources		☑	☑	☑	☑	☑	☑
Recognize Library/Media center resources, such as computerized references; catalog search—subject, author, title; encyclopedia index		☑	☑	☑	☑	☑	☑

Writing

MODES AND FORMS	K	1	2	3	4	5	6
Interactive writing							
Personal narrative (Expressive narrative)			☑	☑	☑	☑	☑
Writing that compares (Informative classificatory)			☑	☑	☑	☑	☑
Explanatory writing (Informative narrative)		☑	☑	☑	☑	☑	☑
Persuasive writing (Persuasive descriptive)			☑	☑	☑	☑	☑
Writing a story		☑	☑	☑	☑	☑	☑
Expository writing	☑	☑	☑	☑	☑	☑	☑
Write using a variety of formats, such as advertisement, autobiography, biography, book report/report, comparison-contrast, critique/review/editorial, description, essay, how-to, interview, invitation, journal/log/notes, message/list, paragraph/multi-paragraph composition, picture book, play (scene), poem/rhyme, story, summary, note, letter							

PURPOSES/AUDIENCES							
Dictate messages such as news and stories for others to write							
Write labels, notes, and captions for illustrations, possessions, charts, and centers							
Write to record, to discover and develop ideas, to inform, to influence, to entertain							
Exhibit an identifiable voice in personal narratives and stories							
Use literary devices (suspense, dialogue, and figurative language)							
Produce written texts by organizing ideas, using effective transitions, and choosing precise wording							

PROCESSES							
Generate ideas for self-selected and assigned topics using prewriting strategies							
Develop drafts							
Revise drafts for varied purposes							
Edit for appropriate grammar, spelling, punctuation, and features of polished writings							
Proofread own writing and that of others							
Bring pieces to final form and "publish" them for audiences							
Use technology to compose text							
Select and use reference materials and resources for writing, revising, and editing final drafts							

SPELLING							
Spell own name and write high-frequency words							
Words with short vowels (including CVC and one-syllable words with blends CCVC, CVCC, CCVCC)							
Words with long vowels (including CVCe)							
Words with digraphs, blends, consonant clusters, double consonants							
Words with diphthongs							
Words with variant vowels							
Words with r-controlled vowels							
Words with /ər/, /əl/, and /ən/							
Words with silent letters							
Words with soft c and soft g							
Inflectional endings (including plurals and past tense and words that drop the final e when adding -ing, -ed)							
Compound words							
Contractions							
Homonyms							
Suffixes including -able, -ly, or -less, and prefixes including dis-, re-, pre-, or un-							
Spell words ending in -tion and -sion, such as station and procession							
Accurate spelling of root or base words							
Orthographic patterns and rules such as keep/can; sack/book; out/now; oil/toy; match/speech; ledge/cage; consonant doubling, dropping e, changing y to i							
Multisyllabic words using regularly spelled phonogram patterns							
Syllable patterns (including closed, open, syllable boundary patterns)							
Synonyms and antonyms							
Words from Social Studies, Science, Math, and Physical Education							
Words derived from other languages and cultures							
Use resources to find correct spellings, synonyms, and replacement words							
Use conventional spelling of familiar words in writing assignments							
Spell accurately in final drafts							

(continued on next page)

☑ Tested Skill

☐ Tinted panels show skills, strategies, and other teaching opportunities

GRAMMAR AND USAGE

	K	1	2	3	4	5	6
Understand sentence concepts (word order, statements, questions, exclamations, commands)							
Recognize complete and incomplete sentences							
Nouns (common; proper; singular; plural; irregular plural; possessives)							
Verbs (action; helping; linking; irregular)							
Verb tense (present, past, future, perfect, and progressive)							
Pronouns (possessive, subject and object, pronoun-verb agreement)							
Use objective case pronouns accurately							
Adjectives							
Adverbs that tell how, when, where							
Subjects, predicates							
Subject-verb agreement							
Sentence combining							
Recognize sentence structure (simple, compound, complex)							
Synonyms and antonyms							
Contractions							
Conjunctions							
Prepositions and prepositional phrases							

PENMANSHIP

	K	1	2	3	4	5	6
Write each letter of alphabet (capital and lowercase) using correct formation, appropriate size and spacing							
Write own name and other important words							
Use phonological knowledge to map sounds to letters to write messages							
Write messages that move left to right, top to bottom							
Gain increasing control of penmanship, pencil grip, paper position, beginning stroke							
Use word and letter spacing and margins to make messages readable							
Write legibly by selecting cursive or manuscript as appropriate							

MECHANICS

	K	1	2	3	4	5	6
Use capitalization in sentences, proper nouns, titles, abbreviations and the pronoun *I*							
Use end marks correctly (period, question mark, exclamation point)							
Use commas (in dates, in addresses, in a series, in letters, in direct address)							
Use apostrophes in contractions and possessives							
Use quotation marks							
Use hyphens, semicolons, colons							

EVALUATION

	K	1	2	3	4	5	6
Identify the most effective features of a piece of writing using class/teacher generated criteria							
Respond constructively to others' writing							
Determine how his/her own writing achieves its purpose							
Use published pieces as models for writing							
Review own written work to monitor growth as writer							

For more detailed scope and sequence including page numbers and additional phonics information, see McGraw-Hill Reading Program scope and sequence (K-6)

Scoring Chart

The Scoring Chart is provided for your convenience in grading your students' work.

- Find the column that shows the total number of items.
- Find the row that matches the number of items answered correctly.
- The intersection of the two rows provides the percentage score.

TOTAL NUMBER OF ITEMS

NUMBER CORRECT	1	2	3	4	5	6	7	8	9	10	11	12	13	14	15	16	17	18	19	20	21	22	23	24	25	26	27	28	29	30
1	100	50	33	25	20	17	14	13	11	10	9	8	8	7	7	6	6	6	5	5	5	5	4	4	4	4	4	4	3	3
2		100	66	50	40	33	29	25	22	20	18	17	15	14	13	13	12	11	11	10	10	9	9	8	8	8	7	7	7	7
3			100	75	60	50	43	38	33	30	27	25	23	21	20	19	18	17	16	15	14	14	13	13	12	12	11	11	10	10
4				100	80	67	57	50	44	40	36	33	31	29	27	25	24	22	21	20	19	18	17	17	16	15	15	14	14	13
5					100	83	71	63	56	50	45	42	38	36	33	31	29	28	26	25	24	23	22	21	20	19	19	18	17	17
6						100	86	75	67	60	55	50	46	43	40	38	35	33	32	30	29	27	26	25	24	23	22	21	21	20
7							100	88	78	70	64	58	54	50	47	44	41	39	37	35	33	32	30	29	28	27	26	25	24	23
8								100	89	80	73	67	62	57	53	50	47	44	42	40	38	36	35	33	32	31	30	29	28	27
9									100	90	82	75	69	64	60	56	53	50	47	45	43	41	39	38	36	35	33	32	31	30
10										100	91	83	77	71	67	63	59	56	53	50	48	45	43	42	40	38	37	36	34	33
11											100	92	85	79	73	69	65	61	58	55	52	50	48	46	44	42	41	39	38	37
12												100	92	86	80	75	71	67	63	60	57	55	52	50	48	46	44	43	41	40
13													100	93	87	81	76	72	68	65	62	59	57	54	52	50	48	46	45	43
14														100	93	88	82	78	74	70	67	64	61	58	56	54	52	50	48	47
15															100	94	88	83	79	75	71	68	65	63	60	58	56	54	52	50
16																100	94	89	84	80	76	73	70	67	64	62	59	57	55	53
17																	100	94	89	85	81	77	74	71	68	65	63	61	59	57
18																		100	95	90	86	82	78	75	72	69	67	64	62	60
19																			100	95	90	86	83	79	76	73	70	68	66	63
20																				100	95	91	87	83	80	77	74	71	69	67
21																					100	95	91	88	84	81	78	75	72	70
22																						100	96	92	88	85	81	79	76	73
23																							100	96	92	88	85	82	79	77
24																								100	96	92	89	86	83	80
25																									100	96	93	89	86	83
26																										100	96	93	90	87
27																											100	96	93	90
28																												100	97	93
29																													100	97
30																														100